Hedge Fund Regulation by Banking Supervision

European University Studies

Europäische Hochschulschriften

Publications Universitaires Européennes

Series V

Economics and Management

Reihe V Série V

Volks- und Betriebswirtschaft

Sciences économiques, gestion d'entreprise

Vol./Bd. 3174

PETER LANG

Frankfurt am Main · Berlin · Bern · Bruxelles · New York · Oxford · Wien

Wulf Alexander Kaal

Hedge Fund Regulation by Banking Supervision

A Comparative Institutional Analysis

PETER LANG
Europäischer Verlag der Wissenschaften

Bibliographic Information published by Die Deutsche Bibliothek
Die Deutsche Bibliothek lists this publication in the Deutsche Nationalbibliografie; detailed bibliographic data is available in the internet at <http://dnb.ddb.de>.

Zugl.: Berlin, Humboldt-Univ., Diss., 2005

11
ISSN 0531-7339
ISBN 3-631-54835-4
US-ISBN 0-8204-9843-2

Printed in Germany 1 2 3 4 5 7

www.peterlang.de

AMINA

Berlin, 14. September 2005

Danksagung

Vornehmlicher Dank gilt meinem ehemaligen Arbeitgeber, Doktorvater, Mentor und Vorbild, Herrn Professor Christian Kirchner, ohne den diese Arbeit nie vorgelegt worden wäre. Danken möchte ich ebenfalls Herrn Professor Schwintowski für die zeitige Erstellung des Zweitgutachtens. Besonderer Dank gilt natürlich auch Herrn Professor Richard Painter, der mich als Mentor und Freund immer mit Rat und Tat bei der Erstellung der Arbeit unterstüzt hat. Professor Thomas Ulen gebührt ebenfalls Dank, sowohl für die Durchsicht des amerikanischen Teils als auch für den ein oder anderen Tip zur ökonomischen Analyse der Problemstellung.

Außerdem möchte ich mich noch herzlich bei Herrn Dr. Andreas Philipp und Herrn Philipp Jaklin bedanken, deren Unterstützung besonders in der letzten Phase der Arbeit sehr hilfreich war. Gleiches gilt natürlich auch für Frau Karin Weber, die die administrative Koordination über zwei Kontinente vornahm.

Wulf A. Kaal

Table of Terms and Abbreviations

ASB	Accounting Standards Board
ACD	Authorized Corporate Director
ASC	Accounting Standards Committee
AuslInvestG	Auslandsinvestment Gesetz
AUTH	Authorization Sourcebook
AUTs	Authorized Unit Trusts
BAFin	Bundesanstalt für Finanzdienstleistungen
Basle	Committee Basle Committee on Banking Supervision
Board	Board of Governors of the U.S. Federal Reserve System
CEA	Commodity Exchange Act of 1974
CFR	Code of Federal Regulation
CFTC	Commodity Futures Trading Commission
CGFS	Committee on the Global Financial system of the G-10 central banks
CGFS	The Committee on the Global Financial System
CIS	Collective Investment Scheme
CNC	Conseil National de la Comptabilitè
COB	Conduct of Business Sourcebook
Code	Fund Manager Code of Conduct
Company Act	Investment Company Act 1940
COND	Threshold Conditions
CPO	Commodity Pool Operator
CRD	Capital Requirements Directive
CRMPG	Counterparty Risk Management Policy Group
CTA	Commodity Trading Advisers
DOL	Department of Labor
Exchange Act	Securities Exchange Act of 1934
EEA	European Economic Area
FAS	Financial Accounting Standards
FASB	Financial Accounting Standard Board
FCMs	Futures Commissions Merchants
FRS	Financial Reporting Standard
FS Act 1986	Financial Services Act, 1986
FSA	Financial Services Authority
FSF	Financial Stability Forum
FSMA	Financial Services and Markets Act 2000
HFIG	Hedge Fund Industry Group
HKMA	Hong Kong Monetary Authority
HLIs	Highly Leveraged Institutions

IAA	Investment Adviser Act of 1940
IAIS	International Association of Insurance Supervisors
IASC	International Accounting Standards Commission's
ICVCs	Investment Companies with Variable Capital
IFD	Investment Firms Division
IMF	International Monetary Fund
IMRO	Investment Management Regulatory Organization
InvG	Investmentgesetz
IOSCO	International Organization of Securities Commissions
IPO	Initial Public Offering
IPRU (INV)	Interim Prudential Sourcebook for Investment Businesses
IPRU	Interim Prudential Sourcebooks
ISD	Investment Services Directive
ISDA	International Swaps and Derivatives Association
KAG	Kapitalanlagegesellschaft
KAGG	Kapitalanlagegesellschaftsgesetz
LTCM	Long Term Capital Management
MAD	Market Abuse Directive
MAR	Market Conduct Sourcebook
MIFID	Markets in Financial Instruments Directive
ML	Money Laundering Sourcebook
MWGED	Multidisciplinary Working Group on Enhanced Disclosure
MWGED	The Multidisciplinary Working Group on Enhanced Disclosure
NASD	National Association of Securities Dealers
NAV	Net Asset Value
NFA	National Futures Association
NIE	New Institutional Economics
OEIC	Open-Ended Investment Company
OTC	Over-the-Counter
PFE	Potential Future Credit Exposure
PRIN	Principles for Business
PSB	Integrated Prudential Sourcebook
PWG	U.S. President's Working Group on Financial Markets
QEP	Qualified Eligible Persons
RDC	Regulatory Decisions Committee
REOC	Real Estate Operating Company
RIE	Recognized Investment Exchange
SEC	Securities Exchange Commission
Securities Act	Securities Act of 1933
SFA	Securities and Futures Authority Limited
SFC	Hong Kong Securities & Futures Commission
SRO	Self-Regulatory Organization

Summary Report	Financial Stability Forum Working Group on Highly Leveraged Institutions
SYSC	Systems Controls and Internal Arrangements
TC	Training and Competence Sourcebook
UCITS	Undertakings for Collective Investment in Transferable Securities
UKLA	UK Listing Authority
VAR	Value-at-Risk
VCOC	Venture capital Operating Company

Table of Contents

A. The Problem of Regulation

Hedge Fund regulation is an interesting paradox. If regulators do not regulate Hedge Funds, markets will be at risk and investors are insufficiently protected. However, if they over-regulate Hedge Funds, managers may decide to register their Hedge Funds offshore and evade regulation.

A short and naturally incomplete definition of Hedge funds defines them as investment schemes, which exploit various market opportunities with various strategies and instruments without direct regulation and constraint in order to achieve absolute return targets. Among the areas of concern regarding Hedge Fund regulation are systemic risk, moral hazard, transaction costs, and asymmetric distribution of information to name only the most important.

Firstly, systemic risk[1] is prevalent in connection with Hedge Funds because the sheer size of these funds has caused and may cause again disruptions in the world economy i.e. individual firms, market segments or settlement systems. This is a domino situation i.e. the knock on effect of the failure of one entity to pay its financial obligations causes insolvency that would result in other firms failing to meet their obligations and thus creating an inter-market disruption.

Secondly, besides the problem of systemic risk, moral hazard[2] problems arose in the case of LTCM. Here lenders to a Hedge Fund demanded repayment of their loans, this, in turn, would have prompted a collapse of the already fragile credit markets worldwide. Hence, the U.S. Federal Reserve deemed it necessary to orchestrate a bailout for LTCM in order to prevent a systemic collapse of the financial system[3]. Furthermore, a milder moral hazard problem is exemplified by the fee structure of Hedge Funds. This is highlighted by the fact that, even with "high water marks"[4] in place, a management fee of up to 30% constitutes an imbalance in incentives for investors, i.e. for any given risk taken, the manager's

---

1 Systemic risk defines the risk that a disruption in a firm, market segment or settlement system might cause at the level of the firm, market or entire financial system.

2 Tempel (2001), p. 7 -"The definition of moral hazard is a situation where one party to a contract has an incentive after the contract is made to alter his or her behaviour in such a way that can harm the other party to the contract. Or, put simply, that people behave in ways to satisfy themselves, but do not bear the full cost (or indeed any cost in some instances) if that behaviour is to the detriment of others"; others Furubotn/Richter (1996) pp. 181 ff. – define it as the approach that deals with "the problem of post-contractual opportunism of agents".

3 Holman Jenkins, in: Wall Street Journal, 15th of September 1998 - "Would Hedge Funds even exist without a fatty dollop of moral hazard somewhere along the great protein chain of lending?"

4 A "high water mark" is an incentive for higher performance. Given that a Hedge Fond starts investing with US $ 100 mill. and grows in the first year to US $ 200 mill.. The manager receives a significant performance fee. Now, if the manager does not enhance his performance in the second year to more than US $ 200 mil. he will obtain no performance fee at all. This regulation is called a "high water mark".

percentage loss will be less than the investor's if the investment goes wrong, and more than the investor's if it goes right. This is only a mild moral hazard problem because the desire of Hedge Fund managers to outperform their peers is a powerful incentive to make the right judgment calls in the markets, which, in turn, somewhat protects investors but cannot guarantee protection. Asymmetric information is, however, clearly not the only source of the moral hazard problem. Moral hazard can also occur because high enforcement costs might make it too costly for the lender, i.e. financial intermediaries to prevent moral hazard even when the lender is fully informed about the borrower's, i.e. Hedge Fund's activities.

Furthermore, these aforementioned risks and problems are combined with an asymmetric allocation of information. This asymmetric allocation of information is in part prompted by the secrecy under which Hedge Funds operate. This penchant for secrecy derives from the fact that the less information the market has about Hedge Fund's activities, the easier it is for them to steal a march on it. Or putting it different, the greater the secrecy the less the "market impact" of them dealing in a particular security, currency or other financial instrument. Furthermore, the very nature of high Hedge Fund performance used to be the fact that money flow, combination of strategies and diverse financial products as well as the enormous amounts of money, leveraged or not, could barely be traced in an internationally investing Hedge Fund. Thus, Hedge Funds will always trade up to the limits of what is allowed by the market, because it is very much in their financial interests – incentive fees make it so. One result is that transparency guidelines as well as regulatory initiatives threaten the Hedge Fund industry in their very existence. Hence, they are lobbying in order to try and preserve information asymmetries as far as possible. Regulators world wide, on the other hand, do not only not have the resources to investigate or regulate the activities of Hedge Funds they also had and have to deal with protectionist activities from their peers many of whom belong to the establishment investing in Hedge Funds themselves.

Information asymmetries are also a problem when banks acting as agents for undisclosed principals, i.e. Hedge Funds are not required to disclose who their clients are when transacting business with fund management groups. For the time being these information asymmetries can be expected to persist.

These aforementioned and combined scenarios become uncontrollable if not properly addressed by the involved parties[5] by way of contracting. The practical problem of not being able to address all imaginable contractual scenarios will not be discussed here. On the other hand, it has to be assumed, in case the parties should be able to address all these problems by way of contracting, that the costs involved, i.e. transaction costs would far outweigh the expected profits. Hence,

[5] I.e. Hedge Fund manager, administrator, prime broker, transaction brokers, financial intermediaries as well as accountants and attorneys.

there would be a strong disincentive and running Hedge Funds would not remunerate any more. This, in turn, would have disastrous effects on the Hedge Fund industry and, hence, the worldwide investing community, shareholder capitalism as well as various national economies, if not the world economy.

Thus, the thesis will emphasize the process of, on the one hand, willingly accepting incomplete contracts and, on the other hand, remedying the lack of regulation by providing rules and regulations for the market that are accepted by all participants[6], i.e. the necessity to regulate Hedge Funds has to be acknowledged.

A sensible regulatory approach has to take the aforementioned scenarios into account and will, thus, be required to address the resulting problems, risks, and demands of all involved parties. This will require exploring opaque areas such as the interconnections between all these problems and risks and their knock on effects. Hence, complexity is unavoidable because dynamic-, effect- and normative analysis will be involved, and many things formerly relegated to the category of the traditional legal regulatory approach will, thus, have to be shifted to an interdisciplinary comparative and institutional approach.

B. The Approach of the Dissertation

After seeing which problems are prevalent in Hedge Fund regulation, the author concedes that private ordering, i.e. leaving intentional gaps in private contracts - a substitute for legal protection in non-legal relationships, or in legal relationships that would be difficult or impossible to verify before a court[7]; is insufficient and regulatory gaps are to be closed by public ordering, i.e. rules and regulations which are obligatory for all market participants. The primary objective of regulation in the form of public ordering is the protection of the investing public.

This dissertation hypothesizes that an indirect regulatory approach via the banking supervision of various jurisdictions is the sensible approach to regulate Hedge Funds. In order to test this hypothesis the author examines the different regulatory approaches of nation states and international bodies. Once the gist of each approach has been underscored, the dissertation will commence with an effect analysis and emphasize the shortcomings of each approach.

- Thus, the thesis starts with a definition of Hedge Funds and addresses the many variations may have a common feature.
- Secondly, the thesis addresses the specific problems of the market for Hedge Funds that may affect investors.

---

6 I.e. NIE`s definition of regulation.

7 Furubotn/Richter (1996), pp. 160 ff.

- Following this, the author introduces the analytical tool, which is to be used, i.e. the theory of incomplete contracts as part of the New Institutional Economics (NIE). Here the author discusses the criteria for analyzing various regulatory approaches and combination of those approaches. Thus, the thesis differentiates between effect analysis and hypothetical effect analysis. Furthermore, the dissertation highlights the theoretical instruments that are to be used in order to test its hypothesis. Eventually the thesis concludes with the expected results.
- Furthermore, various possible approaches to Hedge Fund regulation will be analyzed. Among those are direct regulation, indirect regulation, so-called prudential Hedge Fund regulation, and eventually co-coordinated international co-operation.
- Moreover, the thesis evaluates, after explaining the Long Term Capital Management (LTCM) case and the historical factors that caused it, the different regulatory approaches of international bodies and authorities by way of effect analysis. This includes both general rules and regulation that were already in existence before LTCM as well as direct accounting measures and the various reports i.e. regulatory proposals in reaction to LTCM.
- After this effect analysis by way of normative analysis of Hedge Fund regulation, the thesis insinuates that the only sensible regulation is one via banking supervision. Basle II has an indirect self-regulatory effect not only on banks but also on Hedge Funds.
- The dissertation closes with a summary and conclusion.

It should be noted that the thesis focuses its analysis on the regulatory regimes in the UK and the United States. There are several reasons that precipitated the author to choose this weighting of the analysis. Firstly, Hedge Funds have been founded in the US and the US market for hedge funds has traditionally been among the strongest if not the strongest in international comparison. Given its competitive advantage, the regulation of hedge funds in the US is among the most advanced in the world followed closely by the regulatory regime for hedge funds in the UK. Secondly, the leading case, LTCM, and its repercussions in the markets as well as the inception of a need for more direct regulation of hedge funds has almost entirely been discussed by international and Anglo-American bodies. Thirdly, regulation of Hedge Funds in Europe is still in its infancy and existing regulation that touches upon Hedge Funds is still somewhat convoluted, sometimes contradictory, and not yet implemented in every European Member State. Fourthly, the German legislator has only recently addressed the demand for a coherent and modern regulatory framework of Hedge Fund regulation in Germany. At this point in time there is no relevant precedent or other legislative material that could be analyzed to determine whether the German legislator has addressed the concerns of the Hedge Fund industry in Germany appropriately. For the time being, analysis of the new German InVGO is relegated to mere conjecture. Only time will tell if the new law will enable the Hedge Fund industry in Germany to effectively compete with the regulatory regimes in the US and UK, thereby attracting more Hedge Fund promoters, managers, and eventually foreign Hedge Fund investors.

C. Hedge Funds and HLIs

I. *Definition of Hedge Funds*

The diversity of Hedge Funds makes it difficult to find a specific definition that fits all instances exactly. In general, a Hedge Fund is a private investment fund with far more flexibility than traditional funds in the choice of investment instruments, techniques and markets. Many authors have endeavored to define exactly what Hedge Funds are and what they do. However, most of them do not define the term but prefer to enumerate typical characteristics. The primary reason for the shortcomings of the definitions is that Hedge Funds are so heterogeneous that defining them accurately is almost impossible. The following definition, albeit lacking in elaboration on compensation and the internal structures of these funds, being as broad as possible and therefore obviously incomplete, seems to identify most of the central characteristics of Hedge Funds and shall be used for the purposes of this dissertation:

> *"Hedge Funds are investment schemes, which exploit various market opportunities with various strategies and instruments without direct regulation and constraint in order to achieve absolute return targets."*

In recognition of those key characteristics that are more likely to be found in Hedge Funds than in any other type of funds, they can be listed as follows:

- Choice of low-level regulation states: Hedge Funds tend to be incorporated 'offshore' and thus outside the legal jurisdiction of the countries in which their owners reside. This allows investment in the fund to be free of taxation or regulatory restriction.
- Leverage: Financial leverage is used to differing degrees according to the fund manager's investment process.
- Sophisticated investors: Hedge Funds are legally limited partnerships in which generally only wealthy individuals, i.e. so called sophisticated investors, and institutions can invest due to high minimum investment

levels resulting from legal restrictions on the number of investors permitted[8].

- Incentive fee: Hedge Fund managers charge a performance oriented incentive fee of typically 20 per cent. Being limited partnerships, managers (or general partners) can get a share in the profits earned on the limited partners' money.
- Absolute returns: Hedge Fund managers aim to achieve substantial absolute returns by engaging in aggressive trading tactics to profit from forecasting market swings. Performance is measured by absolute returns, which is essentially profit as opposed to a standard benchmark with traditional funds.

The advantages of these characteristics are more obvious when viewed in relation to mutual funds. However, generally speaking, a Hedge Fund is a fund that can take both long and short positions, use arbitrage, buy and sell undervalued securities, trade options or bonds, and invest in almost any opportunity in any market where it foresees impressive gains at reduced risk. Hedge Fund strategies vary enormously[9] -- many hedge against down turns in the markets -- especially important with volatility and anticipation of corrections in overheated stock markets. The primary aim of most Hedge Funds is to reduce volatility and risk while attempting to preserve capital and deliver positive returns under all market conditions.

There are approximately fourteen distinct investment strategies[10] used by Hedge Funds, each offering different degrees of risk[11] and return. However, gen-

---

[8] However, in recent years these tendencies have changed towards a focus group of mid to low level investors who can invest in Hedge Funds with a minimum investment of only Euro 1000 (DWS Hedge Select for example).

[9] A wide range of hedging strategies are available to Hedge Funds. For example: selling short - selling shares without owning them, hoping to buy them back at a future date at a lower price in the expectation that their price will drop; using arbitrage - seeking to exploit pricing inefficiencies between related securities – for example, can be long convertible bonds and short the underlying issuers equity; trading options or derivatives - contracts whose values are based on the performance of any underlying financial asset, index or other investment; investing in anticipation of a specific event - merger transaction, hostile takeover, spin-off, exiting of bankruptcy proceedings, etc.; investing in deeply discounted securities - of companies about to enter or exit financial distress or bankruptcy, often below liquidation value. Many of the strategies used by Hedge Funds benefit from being non-correlated to the direction of equity markets.

[10] MAR / Hedge Fund (2000): Hedge Fund Styles and investment strategies: 1. Aggressive Growth: Invests in equities expected to experience acceleration in growth of earnings per share. Tends to be "long-biased." Expected Volatility: High.; 2. Distressed Securities: Buys equity, debt, or trade claims at deep discounts of companies in or facing bankruptcy or reorganisation. Expected Volatility: Low – Moderate.; 3. Emerging Markets: Invests in equity or debt of emerging (less mature) markets that tend to have higher inflation and volatile growth. Expected Volatility: Very High.; 4. Funds of Hedge Funds: Mix and match Hedge Funds and other pooled investment vehi-

erally, Hedge Funds can be classified into two basic categories[12], based primarily on the nature of their trading strategies.

The first category of institutions comprises a macro or directional Hedge Fund. A macro Hedge Fund, invests in stock and bond markets and other investment opportunities, such as currencies, in hopes of profiting from significant changes in such things as global interest rates and countries' economic policies[13]. A macro Hedge Fund is more volatile but potentially faster growing than distressed-securities Hedge Fund that buys the equity or debt of companies about to enter or exit financial distress. Macro Funds are typically active in stock, bond or

---

cles. Expected Volatility: Low - Moderate – High.; 5. Income: Invests with primary focus on yield or current income rather than solely on capital gains. Expected Volatility: Low.; 6. Macro: Aims to profit from changes in global economies, typically brought about by shifts in government policy that impact interest rates, in turn affecting currency, stock, and bond markets. Expected Volatility: Very High.; 7. Market Neutral - Arbitrage: Attempts to hedge out most market risk by taking offsetting positions, often in different securities of the same issuer. For example, can be long convertible bonds and short the underlying issuers equity. Expected Volatility: Low.; 8. Market Neutral - Securities Hedging: Invests equally in long and short equity portfolios generally in the same sectors of the market. Expected Volatility: Low.; 9. Market Timing: Allocates assets among different asset classes depending on the manager's view of the economic or market outlook. Expected Volatility: High.; 10. Opportunistic: Investment theme changes from strategy to strategy as opportunities arise to profit from events such as IPOs, sudden price changes often caused by an interim earnings disappointment, hostile bids, and other event-driven opportunities expected Volatility: Variable.; 11. Multi Strategy: Investment approach is diversified by employing various strategies simultaneously to realise short- and long-term gains. Expected Volatility: Variable.; 12. Short Selling: Sells securities short in anticipation of being able to re-buy them at a future date at a lower price due to the manager's assessment of the overvaluation of the securities, or the market, or in anticipation of earnings disappointments often due to accounting irregularities, new competition, change of management, etc. Expected Volatility: Very High. 13. Special Situations: Invests in event-driven situations such as mergers, hostile take-overs, re-organisations, or leveraged buyouts. Expected Volatility: Moderate.; 14. Value: Invests in securities perceived to be selling at deep discounts to their intrinsic or potential worth. Expected Volatility: Low – Moderate.

11 There are many ways to define risk. For instance some may think it is the standard deviation of the daily returns, others may think it is value-at-risk (VAR-measured at the 95% confidence level), again others may think it is semi-variance, shortfall probability, or any other simple quantitative measure. These various measures may shed light on risk, and may help us to estimate risk, but they do not define the nature of risk. The nature of risk is not an issue which could be discussed extensively in this dissertation. Therefore, if we had to offer a simple definition of risk it should be "expected pain" – Robert A. Jaeger, Fund of Funds: Risk: Defining it, Measuring it and Managing it, in: Reynolds Parker (2000), p. 70. – which would combine a rough measure of the likelihood of various unfavourable outcomes with a rough measure of how unfavourable those outcomes are. This simple definition captures at least the fact that risk judgements depend on two elements: 1. The likelihood of various painful outcomes, and 2. The level of pain associated with those outcomes.

12 Basle Committee (1999), p. 9.

13 I.e. macro Hedge Funds take positions based on assumptions about the appropriate level and likely direction of fundamental economic indicators.

foreign exchange markets, both cash[14] and derivatives[15]. In recent years, directional and macro funds have focused on global trading strategies, with growing emphasis on emerging markets.

The second category comprises relative value or arbitrage funds. An arbitrage Hedge Fund attempts to hedge out most market risks by taking offsetting positions, often in different securities of the same issuer, thereby betting on changes in their relative value. For example an arbitrage Fund could go long on convertible bonds and short on the underlying issuer's equity. Similarly, this type of position could be replicated by using derivatives, going long on the swap[16] spread and short on the government futures contract[17].

Besides those aforementioned categories there are also equity Hedge Funds and relative value Hedge Funds that are of similar importance. An equity Hedge Fund may be global or country specific, hedging against downturns in equity markets by shorting overvalued stocks or stock indexes. A relative value Hedge Fund takes advantage of price or spread[18] inefficiencies.

A popular misconception is that all Hedge Funds are volatile -- that they all use global macro strategies and place large directional bets on stocks, currencies, bonds, commodities or gold, while using lots of leverage. In reality, less than 5% of Hedge Funds are global macro funds like Quantum, Tiger, and Strom. Albeit these Hedge Funds are the most influential in the global market.

1. The Jones Hedge Fund Model

In order to gain a basic understanding of the Hedge Funds of today, one must look at how the initial concept was defined and where it came from. The model for Alfred Winslow Jones's original fund is very simple and can be defined by three specific characteristics - leverage and short sales adapted to create a conservative investing system and a management incentive fee. It was the way that Jones combined these characteristics that made the fund unique.

---

14 I.e. cash balances held in a bank account and short-term, high-quality marketable securities, such as government bonds.

15 Basle Committee (1999), p. 9.

16 I.e.- in a swap, two parties trade the future returns on investments over a set period of time. For example, one party might pay a small amount to receive a fixed interest rate on a corporate bond in lieu of uncertain gains on the same corporation's stock. The counterparty accepts the payment and swaps the return on the bond for the return on the stock. Neither party actually needs to hold the underlying assets, as long as the payments are made.

17 Basle Committee (1999), p. 9.

18 I.e. the excess of the price or yield on a particular security or instrument relative to a benchmark. (e.g. the "spread over Treasury" is the difference between the yield for a certain fixed income instrument and the yield for a comparable U.S. Treasury security).

Short selling was typically used by investors as a speculative tool, as was leverage, that is, the amount of external[19] finance funding a project relative to the amount of internal[20] funding. The more leverage used by a firm, the more money is made in good times and lost in bad times. In the Jones model, short-selling was used to eliminate part of the market risk involved with holding long stock positions, thus shifting most of the exposure from market-timing to stock picking. Leverage used within a fund that employs a satisfactory level of short positions to hedge against unexpected movements in the overall market can boost returns while limiting risk. In controlling market risk, the Jones′ fund was free to pick stocks and amplify returns with leverage.

Jones quantified market exposure using the following formula:

Market exposure = (long exposure – short exposure)/capital

Jones would increase or decrease the net market exposure of his portfolio based on his perception of the state of the market. Seeing the market generally rose, his fund was predominately net long. Not only risk, but also performance within the hedge was dependent on stock selection. If the long positions are well selected then a rising market should see them increase by a greater amount than the market in general. Similarly if the shorts are well selected, they would rise less than the market and yield net profit, vice versa for a declining market. Realizing his limitations with regard to stock picking, Jones brought in some of the best Wall Street stars to pick stocks, which left him fulfilling solely an executive role.

Funds that follow the Jones model today often use a 70 per cent to 40 per cent split of long to short positions, the same as that most typically used by Jones. At 70 per cent net long, losses in a declining market would not be totally offset by profits from within the hedge, but the portfolio is designed to fall less than the market. It is this factor that provided the practical superior performance of the Jones fund over traditional long only funds. The third major characteristic, the incentive fee[21] structure, rewarded the general partner with 20 per cent of realized profits thus providing the incentive to pick winners.

---

19 I.e. debt

20 i.e. equity

21 In most Hedge Fund nowadays, the Investment Manager receives a quarterly Incentive Fee of up to 7.5% of the cumulative New Appreciation (if any) attributable to each Series of Shares, after reduction for all accrued but unpaid fees and charges (including the Portfolio Managers' management and performance fees and the Management Fee) other than the Incentive Fee itself. The Incentive Fee can be calculated on a "High Water Mark" basis in respect of the cumulative New Appreciation recognized by each Series of Shares. New Appreciation is only recognized with respect to Shares of a particular Series to the extent that the aggregate calendar quarter-end Net Asset Value per Share of such Series exceeds the highest such Net Asset Value per Share as of

2. The Evolution of Hedge Funds

Generally, 'Hedge Fund' is an industry term, not a legal term, coined to define the particular practice of investment managers who would take long positions in various securities and 'hedge' against the risk of decline in the general market by taking short positions in other securities. As it is used today, this term is misleading because not all Hedge Funds are hedged or free of risk. They instead encompass a diverse variety of non-traditional funds, hedged or not, using not only long, short and leveraged securities but futures, forwards, options and physicals[22].

Hedging is an old concept used for the purpose of protecting against the prospect of market swings. Last century commodities futures contracts were used to guard against unexpected movements in prices and short selling shares has been documented as having been practiced by individuals, institutional investors and securities brokers as early as the twenties[23]. The number of financial instruments available has grown exponentially since the 1980s, such that today there are a multitude of different hedging instruments in the way of futures, options and other derivatives at hand to use against price, interest rate and currency risk.

However, the first major rush into Hedge Funds came about in 1966, when many were introduced for the first time to the Hedge Fund concept through Carol Loomis's article 'The Jones Nobody Keeps Up With'[24] for Fortune magazine. The article outlined the superior performance of Jones' Hedge Fund over existing mutual funds, even after taking into account a considerable 20 per cent performance fee. The Jones fund bettered the best mutual funds of the time after all fees and expenses by 44 per cent over five years and 87 per cent over ten years[25]. With these results to provide inspiration and the article providing a blueprint of the operation, the number of Hedge Funds increased to a hundred within a few years.

However, the boom conditions were followed by a bust in the late 1960s and many inexperienced fund managers went bankrupt as the Hedge Fund bubble burst. Carol Loomis's article 'Hard Times Come to the Hedge Funds'[26], which

---

any previous calendar quarter-end, or $1,000, if the Series in question has been issued since the last calendar quarter-end or has been unprofitable. Another definition is - As of each calendar quarter-end, any cumulative increase ("New Appreciation") in the Net Asset Value per Share (prior to reduction for Incentive Fees paid or accrued) of each Series of Shares in excess of the highest Net Asset Value per Share as of any prior calendar quarter-end (after reduction for the Incentive Fee then paid or accrued) — or $1,000, if the Shares of the Series in question have been issued since the preceding calendar quarter-end or have been unprofitable — is subject to a 7.5% incentive fee (the "Incentive Fee") credited to the Investment Manager. Incentive Fees are calculated separately in respect of different Series of Shares.

22 See Crerend (1998).

23 See Caldwell (1995), p.6.

24 See Loomis, (1966).

25 See Caldwell (1995), p.10.

26 See Loomis (1970).

appeared in Fortune magazine's January publication in 1970, described the Hedge Fund phenomenon and its explosion, making reference to the fact that the bear market of 1969 was not foreseen by many managers. Well-managed funds survived but some, including Jones' fund, were forced to re-evaluate and change their strategies and models. The article, which is still considered as one the definitive articles on Jones and the industry, quotes Jones as having commented on the fact that the problems to arise from the bear market of 1969 were attributed to the overconfidence many money managers exhibited with regard to their money making abilities[27]. This view proved to have credence and applicability also in later years when the business cycle went through further movement from boom to bust.

Many in the industry thought that Hedge Funds would give way at this stage but slowly through the seventies and eighties the industry built itself back up. The industry operated in relative obscurity until the high performance years of 1987 to 1993 encouraged the spirited formation of new Hedge Funds.

The potential of Hedge Funds was reintroduced to investors in May 1986, when the article 'The red-hot world of Julian Robertson'[28] by Julie Rohrer appeared in the Institutional Investor. Robertson was an investor who hedged his portfolio with short sales in a textbook Jones fashion. The article reported that Robertson's Tiger Fund had been compounding, net of expenses and incentive fees, at 43 per cent in the first six years in comparison to 18.7 per cent for the S&P 500 for the same period. Robertson had been adopting new financial instruments since 1985 to improve on profits and it was in that year that he made his first global macro play. The article managed to outline the difference between traditional equity management and Hedge Funds that were well run – fodder to the investors who later joined the rush to try their hands at creating their own Hedge Funds.

Hedge Funds entered a new stage at the end of the eighties, capitalizing on the burgeoning variety of financial instruments that were becoming rapidly available. The numbers of Hedge Funds and the assets under management have exponentially grown since then and the Hedge Fund industry has subsequently entered a more mature stage. It is from this point that Hedge Funds diversified from the original Jones model to become the mixture of styles present today.

Up until the late nineties, particular funds were getting very large and powerful. Managers, such as George Soros of Soros Fund Management, Michael Steinhardt of Steinhardt Fine Berkowitz and Co, Julian Robertson of Tiger Fund, Paul Tudor Jones of Tudor Management and Louis Moore Bacon of Moore Capital Management, who amongst others built their vehicles into huge funds - some of which were managing up to $20 billion at their peaks and on occasion earning the title of super funds.

---

27 See Loomis (1970).

28 See Rohrer (1986).

Large amounts of leverage were being used by Hedge Funds in general and many funds were not sufficiently covering their positions. It is not a surprise that many in the industry thus found themselves in trouble during the volatile late nineties[29]. While the 1994 bond market crash in the US, led by the strong increase in US interest rates caused problems for many Hedge Funds and led to substantial losses the major drama arose during the late summer of 1998 in the form of a currency crisis in Asia, which spread to Russia, Europe and eventually to the United States. Volatility rocked the world's markets and although no one knew for certain the true size and scope of the losses that were resulting, it was clear that many of the most famous Hedge Funds were in trouble.

The financial crisis hit in more than one market simultaneously which meant an absence of profitable situations in the multiple markets in which many funds had placed trades to prevent losses. Many managers publicly announced that they had lost capital in considerable amounts and the losses turned out to be staggering. The most infamous collapse was obviously the aforementioned LTCM.

Many of the big players have more recently quit the industry because they got so large the market could see them coming, rendering their secretive strategies less effective than they should have been. A number of large fund managers, including Paul Tudor Jones and George Soros were known to have returned capital to investors facing their inability to continue to post superior returns with too much money to manage. More money at hand makes a fund harder to maneuver and it requires more ideas or a higher concentration on a smaller range of stocks. Now the tendency is for funds to remain small and out of the spotlight as this enables them to move in and out of positions quickly and without attracting unwanted attention from the media and other investors. The big funds, such as the Tiger Fund and others of Meriwether and Soros have been split up into smaller entities, which continue to call themselves Hedge Funds. Following this split, many former employees have set up their own, but significantly smaller funds with a preference for closing them at $500 million or $1 billion.

Early in 2000, following the millennium hype, the industry was hit by a tech sector crash but most Hedge Funds were generally better positioned to deal with the weakness in the sector. The majority of Hedge Fund managers that outperformed the market at this time were those who shorted overpriced technology and Internet related stocks taking advantage of the volatile stock market. Hedge Fund managers in both the US and Europe who specialized in event driven, convertible arbitrage[30] and equity market neutral generally experienced a rise in returns given

---

29 See Strachman (2000), p.74.

30 I.e. Arbitrage is a type of financial transaction or strategy that seeks to profit from a price differential perceived with respect to related or correlated instruments in different markets and typically involves the simultaneous purchase of an instrument in one market and the sale of the same or related instrument in another market.

heavy merger activity and plays on the ups and downs of biotech and large pharmaceuticals. Those in the emerging market and macro area did not perform so well. The popularity of many Asian oriented Hedge Funds came to an abrupt halt.

In general, it takes a downward slide in markets to separate funds that use true hedging strategies from those that are essentially speculative, but use Hedge Fund fee structures. The term 'Hedge Fund' is used as a catch phrase for private investment partnerships of any kind using almost any strategy, but given a volatile environment, 'real' Hedge Funds should perform better than the market. Net inflows to Hedge Funds totaled nearly $7 billion in the first quarter of 2001 - up to the levels found before the Long Term Capital Management crash in 1998, and most of that inflow has been into equity or equity linked funds. One of the major concerns that the industry faces today is the danger of the bubble bursting once more in the face of inexperienced fund managers.

In recent years the term Hedge Fund has become a generic term. Keeping in mind that estimates vary considerably given the problems of inadequate data and inconsistent definitions, research firms have released figures between $300-400 billion for the size of the total industry. The number of active Hedge Funds globally is estimated to range from 4,000 to 6,000. The global Hedge Fund industry is dominated by America with TASS Research[31] estimating that at least 80 per cent of Hedge Fund managers were based in the US, the UK coming in second.

Despite issues about the accuracy of the size of the industry, one thing that is clear is that Hedge Funds still comprise only a relatively small component of the finance industry in general. Still, there is also no denying that the Hedge Fund industry currently represents one of the fastest growing areas of the financial world. The larger percentage of funds with less than five year track records as shown in MAR/Hedge research[32] demonstrate this fact. TASS Research estimates that in the last five years, Hedge Fund assets in Europe have grown more than six-fold from $6 billion to $39 billion. Evident continual growth reflects the importance of Hedge Funds as an alternative investment group for both institutional and wealthy individual investors. People want superior returns but also sufficient protection for times of volatility and Hedge Funds profit regardless of market conditions. From the perspective of the many traders who are flocking to either set up or work for Hedge Funds, there is great freedom in being self employed and able to invest in anything and anywhere desired.

II. *Key Characteristics of Highly Leveraged Institutions*

Highly Leveraged Institutions (HLIs) are often organized in or operate from or through offshore jurisdictions that may be regulatory or tax havens. While

---

31 TASS report (1999).

32 MAR/Hedge research (2001).

HLIs, like other large institutional investors, can provide benefits to global financial markets, the combination of characteristics typically associated with HLIs and the legal and other uncertainties arising out of extensive operations in offshore centers pose particular challenges, which need to be managed carefully in order to avoid risks to the financial system.

HLIs are, for the purposes of this dissertation, institutions which are significant traders for their own account in financial instruments and which display a combination of the following characteristics:

1. Significant Leverage

HLIs take on significant leverage[33], which can expose creditors and/or investors to significant counterparty risk. This risk is a result of the increased exposure of HLIs' to large movements in market prices. There are various ways for HLIs to achieve leverage. One for instance is to obtain cash through unsecured or partially secured debt. However most of HLIs' leverage is a result of the transaction terms they receive form their counterparties and, of course, the types of trading strategies undertaken[34]. The fragility of leverage is, however, one of the problems. On the one hand leverage can provide benefits by reallocating risks, on the other hand, it is, when combined with insufficient transparency and little or no prudential supervisory oversight, problematic. Because of the latter, counterparties must perform the critical role of assessing the leverage employed in the risk-taking activities of HLIs and of understanding the concentration[35] of positions and trading strategies[36]. In order for counterparties to fulfill this role, a certain degree of transparency is indispensable and as long as there are no public disclosure requirements, such transparency must be achieved through private agreements between HLIs and their counterparties.

---

33 Leverage is the ratio between risk, expressed in some common denominator, and capital.

34 I.e. a HLI effectively leverages its activities when it sells treasury bonds short and uses the proceeds to establish a long position in corporate bonds against the short position in treasuries, thus adding basis risk to its position.

35 Concentration as a technical term referring to Hedge Fund operations arises when a significant percentage of a Hedge Fund's portfolio is exposed to the same or similar market factors or other risk factors, increasing the risk of losses caused by adverse market or economic events affecting such risk factors. Hedge Fund Managers may track concentration levels with respect to asset classes, industry sectors, regions or other relevant areas.

36 See Basle Committee (1999), p. 9.

2. Limited direct prudential regulation

They are subject to little or no direct prudential regulation. This limited direct regulatory oversight results, at least in the case of Hedge Funds[37], from the fact that those entities are in most cases structured as limited partnerships. Therefore, investors are either institutions or sophisticated high net worth individuals. Hence the securities issued take the form of private placements. Also most Hedge Funds operate via offshore financial centers, which make direct prudential regulation virtually impossible especially in the light of regulatory arbitrage.

Compared with regulated entities and financial institutions and/or publicly traded companies, HLIs are not subject to credit ratings by credit rating agencies. Which, in turn, has an effect with regard to transparency – without official rating and in the absence of any regulatory oversight HLIs can ignore investor protection and shareholder value – making them more flexible and easier to adapt to recent economic developments.

3. Limited disclosure requirements

HLI`s are subject to limited disclosure requirements. This is partly due to the fact that they are seldom public companies. They are, furthermore, structured to avoid registration and regulatory conditions imposed on other types of investment vehicles. This, in turn, enabled HLI`s to invest in world markets without much regulatory oversight.

D. Specific Problems of Hedge Funds and Investor Protection

The average sophisticated investor considers Hedge Funds to be a rather exclusive investment opportunity run by highly sophisticated financial experts, who invest their own money in the fund and whose skills and expertise may be used to exploit alternative investment strategies to produce absolute returns. In recent years, however, investors have discovered at their expense[38] that Hedge Funds are by no means immune from those problems that regularly befall those who venture into the complex and risky business of taking a position in today's financial markets.

There are several problematic scenarios associated with Hedge Fund investing and investor protection. It is not only the question of how to assess a Fund's investment strategies and, hence, the risks involved, but also how to distinguish fraudulent investment schemes from clean ones.

---

37 Hedge Funds are so far the ultimate example of HLIs. Albeit is should be noted that not all of them are highly leveraged and that HLIs are not necessarily confined to Hedge Funds.

38 The high losses of LTCM being only one, albeit the most significant example.

As to the involved risks investors should be encouraged to investigate the Hedge Funds strategies and risk measures with their lawyer and accountants. Hedge Funds are generally classified by the type of investment strategy they use and these can differ significantly in terms of investment returns, volatility and risk. The investment strategy, in turn, is dependent on the market analysis process[39]. However, the opportunity for profit hinges on whether traders are better informed of market movements than the majority and, in turn, the strategies managers develop to limit losses if the market moves against their expectations. There is no perfect formula as to how to pick Hedge Funds but eventually investors are well advised if their personal impressions of the Hedge Funds` representatives, trading records, SEC reports and the reputation of the Fund in the industry are used as primary indices. These should then obviously also be in conformity with the risks an investor is prepared to take on. The reason why Hedge Fund used to only attract wealthy and sophisticated investors are obvious in the light of the fact that most lay investors are not capable to understand the trading strategies and hence the risks involved.

---

39 Crerend, (2001), p. 122 "The Market Analysis Process, 1.) Within a strategy, fund managers can take different approaches to market analysis using different research techniques to achieve their ends. Fund managers make decisions on investment through thorough market analysis of which there are three main schools - fundamental, quantitative and economic. These market analysis techniques are not always right, but each has its merits and are used by managers to select long and short positions. A) Fundamental analysis - Fundamental analysis is the most widely practiced amongst managers. It attempts to identify the intrinsic worth of a company under consideration by looking at the company's accounting and financial position to see whether a stock is over or under valued, such as sales revenues, financial ratios and earnings. The problem with this method is that the analysis may lag behind price actions. B) Quantitative analysis - The quantitative, or market timing school of analysis is based on the study of the internal dynamics that are behind fluctuations in the price of a stock or the market as a whole. Essentially, all market timers are interested in is price and volume to determine the direction of trends and therefore spend their time analysing charts of stock prices, volume, moving averages, rate of change of prices and so on to achieve it. The focus is on market psychology and they study relative performance looking for group leadership. In observing an overall market trend, market-timers can determine when to buy and when to sell and after assessing relative performance, know which stock to focus on. This methodology is not recognised academically because of the lack of any systematic value to its reasoning. C) Economic analysis - Economic analysis involves looking at the performance of business as an indicator for anticipating phases of expansion and contraction of the economy. This is based on the idea that an economic situation can affect the rate of growth of many businesses and thus the approach involves measuring key business activities and examining their typical behaviour during the different cycles of the business cycle. The position of the aggregate is followed at any point in time to determine what is likely to happen next to stock and bond prices. Economic indicators can help anticipate major turning points in the business cycle. Some shortcomings are that the performance of specific stocks do not always follow general economic conditions and additionally, economic indicators give only a broad outline of the state of business and can not always detect the event of a meltdown."

However, if an investment should have gone wrong i.e. it turned out to be an investment scam, the situation is different. In most cases of investment fraud a Hedge Fund manager exploits public perception about the nature of Hedge Fund investments to lure unwary investors into fraudulent investment schemes. Managers do that by use of misrepresentations designed to solicit the initial investment and then keep investors on board. Among those fraudulent schemes are classic ponzi frauds as well as entirely non-existent funds. Thus, the Hedge Funds market is not immune to fraudsters. While widespread fraud is not common in the Hedge Fund industry, Hedge Fund fraud is on the rise as the industry has expanded rapidly[40]. Publicized cases include Michael Berger of the Manhattan Investment Fund, Mark Yagalla of Ashbury Capital fund and David Mobley the manager of the Maricopa fund. According to corporate security company Kroll, Hedge Fund investigation assignments have gone up from 2-3 a year to over 150 in the past 18 months. The experts say the best way to avoid Hedge Fund fraud is to invest in established Hedge Funds with a well-known track record and more importantly conducting due diligence. The Internet seems to be the optimal tool for fraudsters, which makes it even more difficult for regulators to address the issue since they cannot regulate the Internet as a whole. The future will show if regulators approach the aforementioned issues on a case-to-case basis or if they will try and regulate the use of Internet based applications and services as a whole.

Another problematic scenario associated with Hedge Fund fraud are unexpected or new market conditions such as the Russian default of August 17, 1998 or the Asian crisis. Those special market situations can cause catastrophic scenarios with specialist alternative investment strategies that Hedge Fund manager often employ[41]. When faced with those appalling market situations, some fund managers may be tempted to mislead investors in order to make sure that at least the funds keep coming so they may be able to turn the situation around when the market starts to move in a more favorable direction.

Furthermore, given the scenario that a fund's assets are frozen by authorities due to money laundering accusations, money laundering is not only a problem for fund managers and their advisor but also for investors. An innocent investor may have to face a lengthy period of time with no immediate control over his fund, which could result in severe losses not only due to lost interest but also missed investment and credit opportunities.

Probably the worst of all problems for investors is the secrecy and, thus, the asymmetric allocation of information surrounding Hedge Fund investing. Hedge Funds are more likely to display high net returns if they operate in secrecy. Inves-

---

40 See Financial Times, 7 Feb. 2002.

41 Such as arbitrage, use of derivatives and leverage, short selling, special situations, ceteris paribus.

tors do, on the one hand, benefit from the secrecy and, thus, the increased profit, which prompted them to choose Hedge Funds in the first place, on the other hand, however, they have to give up regulatory protection because it would rule out secrecy. It has, thus, been conjectured that investors in the Hedge Fund environment, who are generally people of substantial means, should not trouble the regulators to protect them. Free market proponents[42] argue that since the purpose of regulation is to protect investors from excessive risk-taking, and loss regulation does not apply to Hedge Funds, they are invested precisely for their risk strategy outside the regulated sector. Hence, because investors willingly accept not to be regulated there can be no imposition to force them into regulation. They further point out that the average long/short equity Hedge Fund is less risky than a long-only portfolio in the current market environment and that the use of leverage is at an all-time low[43]. Regulatory regimes do, thus, to a considerable degree, recognize that wealthy individuals are to be treated differently. This is exemplified by the fact that different levels of protection are provided for investors depending on their level of financial sophistication. In the U.K., for instance, an experienced investor can contract out of much regulatory protection by being classified as an expert investor[44]. Moreover, to avoid any requirements under various acts in the U.S. Hedge Funds generally do not raise funds through public offerings, advertise broadly or engage in general solicitation[45]. Consequently, shareholders may not have the benefit of the investor protection provisions of some of these statutes.

The various regulatory approaches by legislators and international bodies are at least partly motivated, apart from systemic risk implications, by investor protection objectives. Therefore, the dissertation details how rules and regulations in the various jurisdictions as well as various reports by international bodies and authorities suggest remedying this problematic situation for investors.

---

42 See Mr. Sorros' interview with FT of 16th February 1999.

43 Meropi on Friday 15. Feb. 2002, from Reuters – "The Hedge Fund industry says it is being made a scapegoat for problems in financial markets, following recent comments by Hans Eichel, German finance minister, reports Reuters. Mr. Eichel had called for international supervision of Hedge Funds and for a temporary ban on the short selling of shares, as a means to reduce threats to the world financial system. Hedge Fund executives at a conference organised by the Alternative Investment Management Association, said that Mr Eichel misunderstood the industry..."

44 Under the rules of the SFA, for example, an investor can be so classified provided that he may be "believed on reasonable grounds to have sufficient experience and understanding to waive SFA private protection". Ismene Larussa-Chigi v. CS First Boston Ltd. QBD Commercial Court Dec. 18, 1997.

45 Some exemptions from this general rule can be seen in Germany, i.e. DWS Xavec Hedge Select was one of the first public offering with broad advertising (even on private television).

E. Theory of Regulation

As seen above, the problem of Hedge Fund regulation demands an applicable theory of regulation. A pure theoretical legal approach is deemed incapable of presenting a clear message regarding the possible regulatory alternatives and thc necessarily associated systemic risk-, transaction cost-, moral hazard-, and adverse selection analysis and how to avoid wasting of resources[46]. Therefore, an approach via the social science[47] is deemed more beneficial. Such a comparative, regulatory and analytical approach is the theory of incomplete contracts as part of New Institutional Economics (NIE). Hence, the hypothesis of this dissertation is to be tested by way of comparative institutional analysis via the theory of incomplete contracts.

I. *The Theory of Incomplete Contracts*

The theory of incomplete contracts explores the nature of contractual arrangements when certain specialized assumptions hold[48]. The assumptions in question include: incomplete foresight by decision makers, asymmetric information between the contractual parties, and the inability on an individual to verify a breach of contract to third parties[49]. The incomplete contract theory devotes its attention to cases in which private information is shared by the contracting parties but unavailable to outsiders[50]. Hence, the situation is one of observable but unverifiable information[51]. A characteristic problem considered is whether some

46 Holmes (1897), p 474 - "For the rational study of the law the black-letter man may be the man of the present, but the man of the future is the man of statistics and the master of economics ... We learn that for everything we have to give up something else, and we are taught to set the advantage we gain against the other advantage we lose, and to know what we are doing when we elect."

47 Posner (1993), p. 76 -"To me the most interesting aspect of the law and economics movement has been its aspiration to place the study of law on a scientific basis, with coherent theory, precise hypotheses deduced form the theory; and empirical tests of the hypotheses. Law is a social institution of enormous antiquity and importance, and I can see no reason why it should not be amenable to scientific study. Economics is the most advanced of the social science, and the legal system contains many parallels to and overlaps with the system that economists have studied successfully. "

48 Furubotn/Richter (1996), pp. 232 ff.

49 E.g. the courts.

50 Hart (1987), p. 755 "Take, for example two parties – B agrees to rent A`s concert hall for a particular price. A`s hall burns down. The contract will usually not mention what is meant to happen under these conditions. Thus, in the event of a dispute, the courts will have to fill in the "missing provisions". Hence, the original contract is incomplete."

51 Furubotn/Richter (1996), p. 259.

"specific investments"[52], designed to increase the probability of a later improvement of product, should be undertaken or not. A second-best optimum may be reached if the parties agree about some distribution of property rights. Thus, the model of the relational or incomplete contract provides that parties do not attempt to find an answer to all contingencies at the time the relation commences[53]. The objective is to build a governance structure that will allow the parties to solve problems when, and if, they arise. The ultimate goal of incomplete contracts is to reinforce the relation itself. The hope is that concord and collaboration become embedded standards of the association, and that the parties will maintain to deal with one another in good faith even when facing intricate modification problems[54].

II. *Theory of Regulation – New Institutional Economics*

The core of the theory of regulation of the New Institutional Economics (NIE) is the aforementioned concept of an incomplete contract. Considering the uncertainties of future events contracting parties leave intentional gaps in their agreements. They agree instead explicitly or implicitly on the procedures by which they intend to accommodate themselves to new situations. Public regulation is such a procedure.

The regulator has two functions in this adapting - procedure:

- To establish, further develop, monitor and help to enforce a constitution or order of a relational contract accepted by principals and agents.[55]
- To initiate the continuously necessary renegotiations with the agents and help to enforce the corresponding day-to-day agreements.

1. Basics of New Institutional Economics

Before discussing the assumptions of NIE from the perspective of the theory of incomplete contracts, the basic assumptions fundamental to NIE have to be pointed out. The central message of NIE is that institutions matter for economic performance[56]. The relevant factors for NIE are the traditional "economic" factors and institutions[57]. Actors in NIE are individual citizens who co-operate in nation

---

52 Id. at 128ff – a specific investment is an investment that generates higher returns in a particular employment (i.e., in a transaction – specific relation) than elsewhere.

53 O'Kelley/Thompson (1999), p. 10.

54 See id.

55 Ex ante guarantee against ex post opportunism.

56 Furubotn/Richter (1996), p. 1.

57 I.e. a set of rules together with the system to enforce the rules.

states or private organizations. The basic assumptions of NIE are: self-interested opportunistic behavior, bounded rationality and imperfect information.

a) Institutions

An institution may be defined as a set of formal, or informal, rules, including their enforcement arrangements[58]. These constraints are, in effect, the rules of the game whose purpose is to steer individual behavior in some particular direction[59].

Another definition understands an institution to be a partial order for community life which serves specific purposes and which has the capacity to undergo further evolution independently. It offers a firm basis for shaping social actions over long periods of time; as for example property, slavery, serf hood, marriage, guardianship, market system, coinage system, freedom of trade[60].

The purpose of an institution is to steer individual behavior in a particular direction. And, insofar as it is successful in realizing this objective, an institution provides structure to everyday activity and thus reduces uncertainty[61]. Therefore, a `good` institution is one, which creates stable conditions for growth while at the same time not obstructing change [62]. In effect, institutions define the incentives structure of societies and specifically economies[63].

It is a deficit of the abovementioned definitions not to take into account the individual who uses or leads the institution. Hence, institutions so defined can be compared to the rules of the game without the players. The function of an institution, though, depends in part on the individual who uses the institution. Thus, it follows that one cannot construct a foolproof institution[64].

b) Bounded rationality

Bounded rationality[65] refers, broadly, to rational choice behavior that is conditioned by the cognitive limits of decision makers[66]. From this perspective,

58 Frurubotn/Richter (1996), p. 6.

59 Examples are ownership, marriage, guardianship, market system, monetary system, the state, the firm, etc.

60 Schmoller (1990), p. 61.

61 North (1990), p. 239

62 Gunnarsson (1991) p. 52.

63 North (1994) p.4.

64 Popper (1957), p. 66.

65 Bounded rationality originates with Herbert Simon, who has defined bounded rationality as behaviour that is "inherently rational, but only limitedly so" Simon (1957). Kreps (1990), p. 156, interprets the ramifications of bounded rationality for modelling in the following way: "in building a model, one must balance the tractability and cost of analysis of the model with the amount of detail put in, a trade-off that itself is not amenable to analysis; the balance must be struck accord-

the preferences of decision makers are recognized as incomplete and subject to change over time[67].

A boundedly rational individual attempts to maximize profit but finds it costly to do so. Since the individual is unable to anticipate all contingencies, and of this inability, he or she provides ex ante for the almost inevitable time ex post when an unforeseen contingency will arise. This highlights that the situation under bounded rationality[68] is such that it is impossible to deal with complex reality in all contractual relevant respects. Therefore, inter alia, bounded rationality means that all economic exchange cannot be organized by market contracting[69].

c) The economic paradigm

As seen above, NIE is an economic approach. The characteristic feature of the economic approach is the so-called economic paradigm, which is a set of theories and a definite decision in favor of the methodological individualism. The basic theoretical assumptions are: limited resources, opportunistic behavior and rational choice[70].

d) Methodological Individualism

Methodological individualism emphasizes that people are different and have different live objectives[71]. Hence, the implication is that organizations are not to be perceived as collective entities that behave as though they were individual agents. The organization per se is no longer the main focus. On the contrary, the views and behaviors of the individual members whose actions give rise to the phenomena being studied serve as a starting point and basis in the process of analysis.

---

ing to intuition (i.e., heuristically)". The term bounded rationality also refers to the impossibility of thinking through complex but well- structured problems – such as describing the complete decision tree of chess – Simon, (1973) – it can also be used to describe "misconceptions" – such as myopia of the inability to correctly process low probability events. Another relates to the limitation of language – Polanyi (1962). The idea of mind as a scarce source – Simon (1978), p. 12 – is an especially productive way to think about bounded rationality. It immediately suggests the need to economise on bounded rationality

66 Furubotn (1994), p. 15.

67 North, (1978), p. 972f.

68 and non-zero-transaction costs

69 Williamson (1985).

70 Kirchner (1988); Furubotn/Richter (1996), p. 2-5.

71 Furubotn/Richter (1996), p. 2.

e) Maximizing profit

Individuals are assumed to seek their own interests as they perceive them and to maximize utility subject to the constraints established by the existing institutional structure. Contrary to conventional practices in neo-classical theory, the dichotomy between the theory of consumer choice and the theory of the firm is ended by extending the utility maximization hypothesis to all individual choices. Therefore, a decision-maker is presumed to make his own choices and pursue his own goals within the limits allowed by the organizational structure in which he is operating.

f) Transaction costs

A distinguishing feature of the New Institutional Economics is its insistence on the idea that transactions are costly. Indeed, the "discovery" of transaction costs by Ronald Coase[72] gave major impetus[73] to the development of NIE.

One way to define transaction costs is to consider, first, the meaning of the basic term transaction. A transaction occurs when a good or service is transferred across a technologically separable interface. One stage of activity terminates and another begins[74]. According to this interpretation, the term is restricted to situations in which resources are actually transferred in the physical sense of delivery.

Another way to define transaction costs is via the basic term property rights. Transaction costs are the costs of establishing and enforcing property rights and protecting these rights in transactions. Therefore, transaction costs are the costs of control[75].

A more fundamental approach could be seen in an explanation of bounded rationality. Bounded rationality means that, as seen above, because of their human limitations, their restricted knowledge, and their tendency to make errors, real world decision makers will always function inefficiently. Therefore, it is not unreasonable to say that human beings are, in a significant sense, boundedly rational in their behavior. But, insofar as people are conceived as possessing limited or bounded rationality, it is clear that they must incur "transaction costs". Therefore, non-zero transaction costs will be incurred no matter what sector of an economy decision maker are conducting operations.

Others define transaction costs as the costs of running the economic system[76]. But transaction costs embrace, in addition to such routine costs, the cost of

---

72 Coase (1937).

73 after an incubation period of some twenty-five years

74 Williamson (1985), p. 1.

75 Eggertsson (1998), p. 5.

76 Arrow (1969), p. 48.

establishing, maintaining, or changing a system's basic institutional framework. Thus, relative to formal institutions, it can eventually be said that transaction costs are the costs that arise from establishment, use, maintenance, and change of:

- institutions[77] in the sense of law
- institutions in the sense of rights[78]

Typical examples of transaction costs are the costs of using the market and the costs of exercising the right to give orders within a firm. In the first case it is to be spoken of market transaction costs, in the second case of managerial transaction costs. As far as institutions in the sense of law are concerned, what must be considered is the array of costs associated with the running and adjusting of the institutional framework of a polity. In order to use a better term, it shall in this case be referred to political transaction costs.

Having seen that transaction costs do exist it should be added that they are, in fact, quantitatively substantial. According to some estimates, transaction costs in modern market economies comprise as much as 50 to 60 percent of net national product. And these figures do not include the set up costs of new institutions and organizations.

2. Differences between NIE and neo-classic Theory

The Neo-classic approach is useful because it enables the theorist to show the basics of economic efficiency under ideal-typical conditions. These ideal-typical conditions are: perfect information and foresight and zero-transaction-costs. Hence, the implication is that institutions[79] are perfect and individuals act with complete rationality.

However, in real live are neither institutions perfect nor do individuals behave with complete rationality. As a result of the imperfections found in the real world, formal institutional arrangements[80] are inevitably incomplete. This inherent limitation has to be recognized. Thus, NIE has placed increasing emphasis on the need to view institutional design from the perspective of unavoidable incompleteness.

The basic concept of NIE can be described as well as distinguished from neo-classic theory by the following factors[81]:

---

77 E.g., a constitution or civil code.

78 E.g., a concrete claim based on a voluntarily agreed upon labor contract.

79 Including perfect constitutions, laws, individual contracts, etc.

80 Such as constitutions, laws, contracts and charters

81 Kirchner (1997a), p. 37.

- The analytical focus must remain with the individual decision maker rather than on the organization. Individuals have different goals, but each person can be conceived as maximizing his utility subject to the limits imposed by the existing institutional structures.
- Institutions are no longer to be regarded as neutral elements that exercise no significant effect on economic behavior.
- The economic system is not a frictionless one. Transaction costs arise in connection with the exchange process and their magnitudes affect the way in which economic activity is organized and carried out.
- More than one pattern of property rights exists and profit maximization is not assured.
- There is no such thing as complete and absolute information.
- Human beings and therefore decision-makers do behave boundedly rational.
- There is an emphasis on the analysis of processes her than

3. Differences between Relational Contract and Classical Contract

The classical contract, applied in microeconomics, has to be contrasted with the relational contract[82]. The classical contract assumes that the parties to the contract execute the contract as agreed and that the parties agree ex ante about all possible scenarios. Hence, the classical contract is assumed to set a system of rules dealing and legally guaranteeing all future eventualities. This is a construction of a comprehensive regulation, which leaves no discretion to the agents and, thus, excludes opportunistic behavior. The ex post supervision and enforcement of the obligations is assumed to work perfectly. The cost of initiating, concluding and enforcing the contract, i.e. transaction costs, are not considered[83]. Here, the analogy in the discrepancies between NIE and neo-classic theory is detectable. This is further exemplified by the fact, that, in the classical contract model the parties, although they cannot describe the state of the world or quality characteristics, they are still supposed to be able to write a contract which is unambiguous and which anticipates all eventualities[84]. This is highly unrealistic.

The incomplete contract model, on the other hand and more realistically, leaves room for opportunistic behavior of agents because it assumes that in a world with transaction costs, the ideal typical construction of the classical contract applies best to simultaneous transactions among strangers. Take, for example two parties – B agrees to rent A`s concert hall for a particular price. A`s hall burns down. The contract will usually not mention what is meant to happen under these

82 Richter (1989), p. 136.
83 Id.
84 See Hart (1987), p. 755.

conditions. Thus, in the event of a dispute, the courts will have to fill in the "missing provisions"[85]. Hence, the original contract is incomplete. This is particularly true for transactions, which require transaction-specific investment. The model of the incomplete contract is tailored to such cases. And since information is asymmetrical either after contracting or before, the concept might generally be seen as part of the principal – agent approach. Here, in turn, the agent has a certain amount of discretion and opportunistic behavior is possible. Regulation is, hence, only possible in the form of "private ordering"[86], i.e. the parties concerned regulate themselves and their dealings with each other. Since continuous negotiations between the parties are expensive, one of the parties or a third party, i.e. in the agency model the agent or regulator is given the power of decision[87]. The relevant markets, on the one hand, provide the external discipline of the agents. The internal discipline, on the other hand, is provided by the principal-agent model.

III. *Incomplete Contract Theory and modern Institutionalism*

Generally, the incomplete contract concept might be seen as part of the principal agent approach[88], i.e. information is asymmetrical either after the contract is agreed upon (moral hazard) or before (adverse selection), or both.

1. Principal Agent Model

The basic assumption of the principal-agent approach, in which the agent enjoys some informational advantage over the principal, is asymmetric information. The principal may be, for instance, the owner of a firm and the agent his manager. More general, the principal may be the employer, the agent the employee. Two types of asymmetric information are to be distinguished in this connection, depending on whether the parties are asymmetrically informed before and up to the moment of contract conclusion of thereafter. The two types are referred to as moral hazard[89] and adverse selection[90]. The better-informed party is tempted

---

85 Id.

86 Furubotn/Richter (1996), p. 160 (elaborating that:"Private ordering, as opposed to court ordering, is a substitute for, or a supplement to, legal protection in non-legal relationships, or in legal relationships that would be difficult or impossible to verify before court. Private ordering is not to be confused with self-help. It consists of the choices of a suitable governance structure to help resolve disputes. E.g.: Enforcement by the explicit or implicit threat to terminate an agreement; the agreement to use arbitrators to resolve disputes, the "union" of contractual parties as, for example, vertical integration.").

87 See Richter (1998), p. 140.

88 See id. at 136.

89 Post-contractual asymmetric information.

90 Pre-contractual asymmetric information .

to engage in post contractual opportunism in the first case and pre contractual opportunism in the second case. Furthermore, in the first, moral hazard case, one distinguishes between hidden information[91] and hidden action[92].

However, unlike the principal – agent models, in a relational contract[93]:

- The contracting parties do not know the nature or the probable occurrences of all future events, i.e. it exists genuine uncertainty;
- The principal does not know the utility function of the agent;
- It is not assumed that the execution of the obligations can be enforced by the courts without costs and with absolute certainty.

a) Moral Hazard

Principal Agent Model of the moral hazard type deals with ex post opportunism[94] of agents[95]. Two sub-cases can be distinguished:

- Hidden action: The actions of the agent are unobservable by the principal[96].
- Hidden information: The agent has information which the principal has not.

The principal, however, is not satisfied, by some exogenously determined profit payment. Rather he tries actively to some as close as possible to his first-best utility maximum. For that purpose, the principal offers the agent, on a take it or leave it basis, a contract that requires the agent to maximize, the principal's utility together with his own. Granted certain assumptions, the principal can realize in this manner his first-best optimum when no uncertainty surrounds the agent's activities. In the case of uncertain results, a second-best optimum obtains.

---

91 The agent has acquired some information that the principal has not.

92 E.g.: the effort level of agent, which is unobservable by the principal.

93 See Richter (1998), p. 136.

94 See Williamson (1985), p. 47 (defines "opportunism" as "self-interest seeking with guile." - In other words, individuals are likely to be less than completely trustworthy in the sense that they may disguise preferences, distort data, deliberately confuse issues, etc. in order to gain advantage.

95 E.g.: managers etc.

96 For example: The shareholders are unable to observe the effort levels of their managers. Under certain assumptions, however, the shareholders (i.e. the principals) are able to offer incentive contracts to their managers (i.e. the agents) that induce the managers to act so as to maximize the stockholders' utility together with their own utility. In the case of uncertain results only a second best optimum obtains.

b) Adverse Selection

The principal-agent model of the adverse selection type deals with ex ante opportunism of agents. Here, the principal[97] cannot observe fully the qualities of the individual agent[98] before contract conclusion. The agent, in these circumstances, is tempted to misrepresent his qualifications. To avoid this outcome, the principal proposes a menu of contracts that lead the individual agent, under certain conditions, to reveal his type or qualities and at the same time promotes the principal's welfare. However, the behavior induced brings about only the second-best utility optimum for the principal.

2. Property Rights

Transaction costs, property rights and contractual relations constitute basic elements of NIE and, thus, incomplete contract theory. Analysis in this dissertation is based on the elementary basic insight that the creation of institutions and organizations, and their day-to-day use, requires the input of real resources. In short the existence of the aforementioned transaction costs is recognized. And, in turn, none-zero-transaction cost means that resources have significance at several levels. Resources serve as transaction inputs in production and distribution activities and as necessary factors in maintaining the framework within which all economic operations take place. Accordingly, assignment and formation of individual property rights in resources have direct influence on the economic results achieved by a society. Hence, property rights are one element for incomplete contract theory.

The prevailing structure of property rights in a society can be understood as the set of economic and social relations defining the position of each individual with respect to the utilization of resources. But, from a practical standpoint, the crucial requirement for the property–rights approach is to show that the content of property rights affects the allocation and use of resources in specific and statistically predictable ways[99]. Since the allocation of property rights influences incentives and human behavior in ways that are generally predictable, a basis exists for studying the impact of property rights arrangements on economic outcomes.

---

97 E.g.: the employer.

98 Eg.: job applicant.

99 Furubotn/Pejovich, (1972), p. 1139.

IV. *Prudential Bank Regulation*

Given that this dissertation argues that Hedge Fund regulation is to be achieved by banking supervision, i.e. banking regulation, the approach of New Institutional Economics to banking regulation has to be explored.

The theory of public regulation of the New Institutional Economics can be applied to bank regulation in a wide sense, including both the regulation of central banks and commercial banks. In light of the fact, that not central banks but commercial banks interact with Hedge Funds, the regulation of commercial banks shall remain the focus henceforth.

The regulation of commercial banks, specifically of deposit banks, is considered necessary primarily for three reasons: ensuring the safety of banks; control of the currency, including safeguarding the value of money; and preserving competition within the banking industry[100]. Considering that primarily banks interact with Hedge Funds i.e., provide credit/leverage and various other services, it is also banks which are exposed to the associated risks in dealing with Hedge Funds. When discussing banking supervision/regulation from the perspective of Hedge Fund regulation the primary concern pertains to the safety of banks. Bank safety can be seen as important from two perspectives: the protection and safety of the bank customer[101] on the one hand, and the avoidance of banking panics and crises on the other hand. The former relates to the safety of individual banks and their customers and is comparable to concerns for consumer protection in other areas. The latter, requiring primary attention for purposes of this dissertation, relates to the safety of the banking- and financial system as a whole. The distinction is often made between prudential[102] regulatory measures on the one hand, and protective measures on the other[103]. Both concern the capacity of the system to handle bank failures.

Prudential measures are those aimed at controlling the levels of risk assumed by banks and thus affecting the probability of banks failures. Generally, prudential measures can include capital adequacy requirements, liquidity requirements, interest[104] regulations, asset diversification rules[105], restrictions on permissible business activities, restrictions on market entry[106], and general banking su-

---

100 Baltensperger, (1990), p. 2.

101 Especially the depositor.

102 I.e. preventive.

103 Baltensperger, (1990), p. 6.

104 Especially deposit rate.

105 Including foreign exchange exposure.

106 An important kind of control which can be employed in banking as well as in other areas of business is the control market entry through some sort of authorisation procedure and licensing practice. At least in form this kind of control exists in the banking area in every country. As a formal check of adherence to the law and of the professional reputation of prospective manage-

pervision and inspection. For the purpose of this dissertation the focus shall remain on capital adequacy requirements.

Capital adequacy requirements are a type of control existing in most countries is some form and can take a variety of forms. Most countries know a minimum level of required capital[107]. Beyond that many countries require the maintenance of some capital – or solvency- ratio; that is, a minimum ration between capital and an overall balance sheet magnitude, such as total assets or liabilities, or some weighted measure or risk assets. Important problems in the implementation of such capital adequacy controls are the definition of "capital"[108] on the one hand, and the determination of "adequacy"[109] of capital on the other. In relation to capital adequacy and solvency controls, it has to be distinguished between countries[110] that disclose information[111] and those[112] which rely heavily on hidden reserves to smooth reported profit and equity.

F. Model Approaches to Hedge Fund Regulation

After having seen how to evaluate the regulatory problems with NIE, the dissertation will continued with an overview of theoretical model approaches to Hedge Fund regulation. These are co-coordinated international co-operation, direct regulation, indirect regulation, and prudential regulation.

I. *Co-coordinated International Co-operation*

One model approach to Hedge Fund regulation is the setting up of an international body to control worldwide Hedge Fund investment strategies and actual investing. The first and foremost reason for this initiative is the problem of establishing jurisdiction over Hedge Funds as a significant number operate through offshore financial centers[113]. And, in turn, imposing national direct regulatory requirements may drive more Hedge Funds offshore[114]. U.S. regulators have there-

---

ment, this may be seen, along with general banking supervision, as an obvious and unobjectionable part of any prudential, safety-oriented policy.

107 An absolute amount.

108 Treatment of subordinated debt; hidden reserves, including franchise value of established firms under restricted competition and appropriate valuation of assets.

109 Appropriate evaluation of the different risks assumed by banks and their potential consequences.

110 E.g. the United States.

111 Such as non-performing loans, off-balance sheet business and country exposure.

112 E.g. Germany, Belgium and Switzerland.

113 Eichel (2002).

114 So called jurisdictional arbitrage.

fore called for co-operation and the adoption of international regulatory standards[115] at least by the key jurisdictions[116].

Proponents of this international authority have claimed that this initiation of a co-operative and comprehensive international co-coordinated action would ensure proper standards and timely international surveillance. Supposedly, it would also, while inherently costly, be the most effective way to maintain integrity of the markets[117] and hedge against the risks posed by Hedge Funds. It would further serve the collective interest of the markets, its intermediaries, investing public and the international community. It has been conjectured that the objective of such an exercise is not just to identify weaknesses but also rather to ensure the identified material weaknesses are addressed in a prompt and effective manner by the regulators which could ultimately reduce systemic risk to the global financial system.

II. *National direct Regulation*

Despite the fact that regulators generally favor letting market forces discipline Hedge Funds, there is a certain amount of pressure to consider direct approaches to reduce creditor and systematic risk associated with investment in Hedge Funds. The objective of direct regulation would be to prevent the excessive expansion in the size and risk-taking by Hedge Funds that could lead to disruption in financial stability. Licensing requirements, fit and proper tests and minimum standards for capital and risk management have been proposed. And, all but the smallest Hedge Funds may be required to file quarterly reports.

The purpose of national direct regulation ensures that markets are fair, efficient and transparent and reduce systematic risk. The threat of the latter was made evident on the near-collapse of LTCM.

III. *Indirect Regulation*

In most jurisdictions regulators do not have regulatory authority over Hedge Funds. However, they can use the regulatory authority over their respective regulated entities[118] in order to regulate Hedge Funds indirectly. Regulators can use a number of regulatory tools including capital, margin and reporting requirements to regulate Hedge Funds.

Regulators are also relying on private sector practices by counterparties and creditors to constrain Hedge Funds' degree of leverage and potential systematic

115 Eichel (2002).

116 Ie. Europe: England, Germany; Asia: Hong Kong, Tokyo

117 Eichel (2002).

118 E.g. securities regulators over broker-dealers, prime brokers, material affiliates of broker dealers.

failure. They recommend that banks and institutional investors tighten credit standards, limit counterparty credit exposure, improve procedures for estimating potential future credit exposures and stress testing and use collateral.

The risk management process, however, poses a challenge to banks and financial institutions given the opaqueness of the activities of Hedge Funds, the absence of a common measure with which to calculate leverage and exposure and the dynamic nature of Hedge Funds′ trading strategies. Competition among creditors also lends to compromising on important elements of the risk management process and agreeing generous credit conditions.

IV. *Prudential Hedge Fund Regulation*

Prudential Hedge Fund Regulation is a combination of indirect and direct measures intended to enhance regulatory possibilities. Prudential control measures include improved supervision and regulation of HLI credit providers, a firmer market infrastructure, increased HLI disclosure, enhanced national market surveillance and good practice guidelines for foreign exchange trading. However, there are at present no precise formulas for devising an effective integrated prudential Hedge Fund regulation. Comprehensive prudential controls, are, according to this model's assumptions, supposed to cover the entire process of a transaction and should include controls and systems, risk management, internal audit and the compliance functions. The model further assumes that effective supervision is considered to increases the effectiveness of controls[119] on conduct and is therefore deemed to be one of the major tools employed to prevent systemic instability in the market. However, proponents of prudential Hedge Fund regulation opine that one of the major constraining factors that constricts effective supervision is the complex trading-, investing- and corporate structure of active international Hedge Funds. Because of these complex structures, both of Hedge Funds and financial intermediaries, most supervisory authorities base their judgment on somewhat inadequate information. Therefore, it is this model's assumption that, in order to be effective, supervisors should adopt a multi-dimensional assessment of risks of their intermediaries and supervise its intermediaries, where possible, on a group basis rather than as a stand-alone registered entity. The model's other ingredient in improving supervision is an expansion of what is being reviewed. Rather than restricting supervision to merely sales practices, a Hedge Fund's controls and systems, risk management policies and products, conduct, capital adequacy, its fit-

---

119 As shown by the Hong Kong experience, as that of other countries. When the Asian financial crisis started, focused inspections were conducted frequently in Hong Kong. The inspections were conducted by applying systematic scrutiny of market and prudential data, so as to identify specific points which need inspection and intervention. This has proved to be very successful in Hong Kong to minimise contagion effect of any closures of intermediaries.

ness and properness and also systemic implications should be assessed. Information collection from these supervisory activities should also be made available to other co-supervisors if legally permitted to. Furthermore, the model of prudential regulation assumes that in order to monitor effectively the financial position of a Hedge Fund, a supervisor needs to be able to assess the potential impact of key affiliates on the registered entity. This means, information about a Hedge Fund's conditions, decisions and actions needs to be made accessible to the supervisor. Additionally, to prevent the build-up of financial and economic imbalances, the gathered information needs to be visible and understandable to other regulators and public[120]. In short, transparency is deemed to help improve systemic stability and effective supervision. In this context, a broad international effort will need to be initiated for supervisors to collect and collate consistent, comprehensive information with adequate disclosure on strategies and system on a regular and timely basis for dissemination. The use of such an approach is deemed to augment market pressures on intermediaries to harmonize their disclosures and hopefully, an increase in capital through the competitive and market process.

However, the model of Prudential Hedge Fund Regulation indicates that the following qualitative regulatory approaches need to be considered when assessing the adequacy of current prudential Hedge Fund regulation:

- Improvements in financial intermediaries` risk management
- Improving the role of regulators in individual firms` risk management
- Improvements in market practice at industry and firm level
- Improved transparency – reporting and disclosure

V. *Hypothesis*

Having elaborated on the theoretical tools of the dissertation and the different theoretical model approaches to Hedge Fund regulation, the hypothesis that is to be tested can be summarized as follows.

A sensible approach to Hedge Fund regulation is one via banking supervision and, thus, an indirect one. Here, the capital adequacy standards in Basle II are the future basis for lending practice to Hedge Funds.

And, because this new framework will align regulatory capital requirements more closely with underlying risks, and provide banks and their supervisors with several options for the assessment of capital adequacy the resulting proposition comprises both, the notion that indirect regulation is most appropriate but also that capital adequacy standards and, thus, its regulatory influence on the credit market and credit policies of banks and Hedge Funds play an increasingly important role

120 If such disclosures are permitted and do not compromise confidentiality.

for this type of Hedge Fund regulation and should eventually become the prevailing model.

G. Regulatory Approaches

In this chapter the thesis will address what happened to Long-Term Capital Management, L. P. ("LTCM"), i.e. the reason for an increasing demand for Hedge Fund regulation. Here, the author analyzes the various factors and their influence to bring down LTCM. Secondly, he analyzes the historical and practical implications, as well as the role of the various participants to the case.

After analyzing the reasons to bring down LTCM, the dissertation proceeds with an analysis of regulatory approaches, both implemented and non-implemented, as well as regulators conclusions by way of effect analysis. Here, the author conjectures which results are to be expected from various approaches to Hedge Fund regulation. This is done by way of systemic risk-, transaction cost-, moral hazard-, and adverse selection analysis.

I. *Long Term Capital Management, L.P.*

LTCM is the most well publicized case of a Hedge Fund that got into severe difficulty when faced with extreme market volatility[121], specifically because its collapse almost brought world financial markets down with it. 1998 was a tumultuous time for many Hedge Funds, but LTCM's collapse in particular exposed the risks that Hedge Funds were taking and raised awareness concerning the risk tolerance of banks, prime brokers[122] and investors. Here, the author points out the factors that combined to bring down what was considered to be a low risk, successful fund with a strong reputation and how that event bled into the financial industry at large.

The LTCM Cayman Islands fund, Long-Term Capital Portfolio, LP used trading strategies, which included convergence trading[123] and dynamic hedging[124].

---

121 Volatility is a measure of risk based on the standard deviation of an asset's return. In the context of assets - the greater the degree of an asset's volatility, the greater the risk of the asset.

122 Like most Hedge Funds, LTCM centralised much of its custodial, record-keeping, clearance, and financing services with a single firm. This bundle of services is typically referred to as prime brokerage and generally includes the following: providing intraday credit to facilitate foreign exchange payments and securities transactions; providing margin credit to finance purchases of equity securities; and borrowing securities from investment fund managers on behalf of Hedge Funds to support the Hedge Funds' short position (thus allowing investment funds to avoid direct exposure to Hedge Funds). LTCM's prime broker was, and still is, Bear Stearns.

123 Convergence traders take risky positions against noise trading. When they face capital losses from unfavourable stocks, they liquidate positions due to their reduced risk bearing capacity, resulting in amplification of the original shocks. Although convergence traders reduce asset price volatility and provide liquidity most of the time, in certain extreme circumstances the wealth

The fund had around 80 per cent of the balance sheet positions in government bonds of G7 countries and these government bond positions were supported with repo and reverse repo agreements with a variety of counterparties.[125] The fund traded on and off-exchange derivatives[126] in interest rates and equity[127] products

---

effect can cause them to be destabilising, i.e. they can trade in exactly the same direction as noise traders when they are liquidating losing positions. Xiong (2002), p. 1 - 'convergence trading strategies were made popular by the Hedge Fund Long-Term Capital Management (LTCM). A typical convergence trading strategy is to be that the price difference between two assets with similar, but not identical, characteristics will narrow in the future...'.

124 See Benninga/Wiener (1998), p. 1 - 'A dynamic hedging strategy typically involves two positions: Firstly, a static positions in a security or a commitment by a firm. For example - a financial institution has written a call on a stock or a portfolio - this call expires some time in the future and is held by a counterparty which has the choice of either exercising it or not... ; secondly, an offsetting position in a financial contract. Typically, this counter-balancing position is adjusted when market conditions change; hence the name dynamic hedging strategy. To hedge its written call, the issuing firm decides t buy shares of the underlying stock or portfolio. The number of shares purchased at time t will depend on the price of the underlying stock at t and on the amount of time remaining until the expiration of the call. Another way of viewing this is that the amount of stock held against the call position depends on the probability that the option will be exercised.'.

125 See Dunbar (2000), p. 45.

126 Generally a derivative is a financial instrument whose value depends on, or is derived form, the value of an underlying asset, index, rate or instrument, There are four basic types of derivative instruments: 1. Forward contract: A contract that obligates one party to sell and the other party to buy a financial instrument or commodity at an agreed price with delivery and payment occurring at a specified future date (commodity). Forward contract are privately negotiated in the over-the-counter markets (rather than on organised exchanges) and incorporate terms that are tailored to the requirements of the parties (OTC).; 2. Futures Contract: Like a forward contract, a future contract involves the sale of a financial instrument or commodity with delivery and payment occurring at an agreed price on a specified future date. Unlike forward contracts, futures are traded on exchanges and are standardised as to their terms. In addition, future contracts may provide for the making of cash payments based on the value or level of an asset, rate, instrument or index. Exchanges seek to minimise the risk of default on such contracts by requiring buyers and sellers to deposit assets (e.g., cash, Treasury securities) as margin. An amount of "initial margin" is generally required upon establishment of a futures contract position. Additional "variation margin" is required (or repaid), if the value of a futures contract position declines (or rises). 3. Swap Contract: An agreement by two parties to exchange currencies, commodities, interest payments or cash flows based on these or other underlying assets, rates or indices on one or a series of future dates. The most common form of swap is an interest-rate swap, in which two parties agree to exchange two cash flows that are determined by two different interest rates. (E.g. one party agrees to pay a fixed rate of interest to the other party in exchange for a variable rate of interest. 4. Option contract: Generally, a contract, that gives a holder the right, but not the obligation, to buy or sell the underlying asset to a fixed price on or before a specified date or time. An example of an option is the right to buy the stock of a company over a two-months period for a set price. Certain options (e.g., options on stock indices) are settled in cash rather than through physical delivery of that asset or other instrument which underlies it.

and also engaged in foreign exchange dealing to support these other activities[128]. The fund had $4.8 billion in capital prior to the crash and controlled $160 billion in stocks and bonds. In addition, derivatives of the fund had a notional value of $1 trillion[129].

LTCM performed strongly in the bull market of the mid and late 1990s. It produced returns, net of fees, of approximately 40 per cent in 1995, and slightly less than 20 per cent in 1996 and 1997. In 1997, the managers of the fund increased the fund's balance sheet leverage[130] by reducing its capital base[131] to $4.8 billion rather than increase its equity positions. On 1 January 1998, the fund had a balance sheet leverage ratio of more than 25 to 1[132].

In one particular investment, LTCM went long[133] large amounts of the 29-year Treasury bond and large amounts short[134] the 30-year Treasury bond in a non-directional bet that the yields would converge.[135] The spread between the two yields was minute - in June 1998, a 29 year $1,000 bond yielded just 50 cents a year more than a 30 year bond and leverage was used to make the bet worth-

---

127 Equity and equity products are in the context of investing, a synonym for stocks or shares of companies. When used in connection with accounting, equity refers to the amount by which the assets of an entity exceeds its liabilities.

128 See Leach (1998), p. 5-6.

129 See Edwards (1999), p. 201.

130 Leverage is the ratio between risk, expressed in some common denominator, and capital. It is also defined as a factor (rather than an independent source of risk) that influences the rapidity with which changes in market risk, credit risk or liquidity risk change the value of the portfolio.

131 By 36 per cent.

132 See Jorion (1999), p. 34.

133 Going Long or a long positions means an excess of purchases over sales of the relevant commodity, currency or investment instrument, e.g. if a trader is said to be long on Yen, the he or she has bought Japanese Yen. A long position i.e. going long is the opposite of going short or a short position. Krugman (1999), pp. 119 – 120 – "The terminology of 'short' versus 'long' positions is jargon . . . Basically, to go long in something is to put yourself in a position to gain if its price rises- which is what the ordinary investor does when buying sock, real estate, or anything else."

134 Short sales involve borrowing securities and selling them in hopes of repurchasing them at a lower price at a later date. Krugman (1999): pp.119-120 "To go short in something is to put yourself in a position to gain if its price falls. To sell a stock short, one borrows the stock from its owner with a promise to return it later – then one sells it. This means that the stock must be repurchased before the due date; the short-seller is betting that its price will have fallen by then. Meanwhile, the short-seller has acquired extra cash, which can be invested in something else- that is, he takes a long position in some other asset. Of course, the owner of the borrowed assets have be reassured that the short –seller will actually have enough cash to buy the asset back, so they will want some kind of reassurance that he has enough wealth to deliver on his promise. When investors who engage in a lot of short-selling suffer heavy losses, they typically find that they are no longer able to borrow as much as they could before.".

135 See Dowd (1999), p. 65.

while.[136] When the currency crisis hit the market, the Treasury issues went against this bet and drifted apart.

This alone would not have brought the fund down, but many of LTCM's trades went wrong at the same time. It became obvious that while the fund was diversified in terms of markets, its overall strategy was not diversified[137]. When the risk spreads continued to widen, the losses LTCM suffered in individual markets greatly exceeded what conventional risk models suggested were probable, but these were estimated during more stable periods.[138] Investors globally sold risky investments for safer ones, liquidity premiums increased, market liquidity declined and the fund was unable to reduce its trading positions.[139] The situation was exacerbated by the enormous leverage used by the fund in its drive to capture profits from the smallest market movements. LTCM's leverage was achieved in various ways, including derivatives transactions, short sales, repurchase agreements[140] and direct financing loans. Its negotiating power led LTCM to increase its leverage by obtaining favorable terms for these transactions. Among these preferential terms were credit enhancements, including re-hypothecation rights[141], zero initial margin[142] and two-way collateral requirements[143]. In spite of the fact that leverage was key to LTCM's high returns, it also magnified LTCM's losses.

Right after the announcement of the Russian debt moratorium in mid August 1998, investors began to seek superior credit quality and higher liquidity[144]. Hence credit spreads[145] widened in markets around the world, creating ma-

136 See Dunbar (2000), p. 47.

137 See Lowenstein (2000), p. 54.

138 See Dunbar (2000), p. 45.

139 Lowenstein (2000), p. 58.

140 Repurchase agreements are agreements between buyers and sellers of securities, whereby the seller agrees to repurchase the securities at an agreed-upon price and, usually, at a stated time.

141 Hypothecation means offering assets owned by a party other than the borrower (e.g., collateral held by the borrower form another transaction, such as a derivatives contract) as collateral for a loan without transferring the title. Re-hypothecation is the reuse of posted collateral.

142 Margin generally is a certain amount of assets that must be deposited in a margin account in order to secure a portion of a party's obligations under a contract. Initial margin is the amount of cash or eligible securities required to be deposited with a counterparty before parties engage in a transaction. A party will be required to post "variation margin" if the futures contracts change in value. Margin is also required in connection with the purchase and sale of securities where the full purchase price s not paid upfront or the securities sold are not owned by the seller.

143 Two-way collateral means that both parties to a contract are required to post collateral, depending on the direction of the credit exposure.

144 There are two separate but related types of liquidity. Funding liquidity is the ability of a Hedge Fund to hold its market positions and meet the cash and/or collateral demands of counterparties, other credit providers and investors. Asset liquidity, on the other hand, refers to the ability to liquidate an asset quickly, and in large volume, without substantially affecting the asset's price. An asset that cannot be liquidated in a short period of time without substantially affecting the asset's price is considered an illiquid instrument.

jor losses for LTCM and other market participants. The Bank for International Settlements ("BIS")[146] describes the events of the summer of 1998 as follows[147]:

> *"In mid-August 1998 [...] financial markets around the globe experienced extraordinary strains, raising apprehension among market participants and policy makers of an imminent implosion of the financial system. As investors appeared to shy away from practically all types of risk, liquidity dried up in financial markets in both industrial and emerging economies, and many borrowers were unable to raise financing even at punitive rates. Prices for all asset classes except the major industrial country government bonds declined and issuance of new securities ground to a halt."*

During the month of August 1998 alone the fund suffered losses of US$1.8 billion, bringing the loss of equity for the year to over 50 per cent. As its condition worsened, LTCM's credit arrangements became more rigid and the daily market-to-market valuation for collateral calls[148] became more contentious. Significantly, prior to the crash the banks and brokers were lending LTCM 100 percent of the value of collateral[149] for the fund. When the banks began to make their margin calls the $4.8 billion capital[150] kept in the bank for the purpose of the odd call dwindled quickly.[151]

The fund required a large capital injection to stay afloat and the amount of money that LTCM owed other companies was so large that these companies may have also been pushed to the edge of insolvency if LTCM were left to go bank-

---

145 A credit spread is the difference between the yield (the percentage rate of return) of a treasury security and a non-treasury debt security (e.g. corporate bonds) that are identical in most respects (particularly the term of the obligation), except with respect to credit rating.

146 BIS was established in 1930 in Basle, Switzerland, by European central banks. The Federal Reserve joined the BIS board in 1994. The objectives of BIS are to promote the co-operation of central banks and to provide additional facilities for international operations.

147 See BIS (1999), p. 43.

148 A collateral call is a notice given by a secured to the provider of collateral informing the latter that the change in the market value of a position has required the posting of collateral.

149 Collateral in general is an asset that is pledged as security, or whose title is transferred to a secured party, in order to secure payment or performance obligations. If the party providing collateral defaults, the asset pledged or transferred may be taken and sold by the secured party to satisfy the obligations of the pledgee/transferee. Instruments that are typically accepted as collateral include government securities, cash and, to a lesser extent, corporate debt and equities. Collateral generally serves to mitigate counterparty credit risk.

150 Capital is the total assets of a Hedge Fund net of liabilities but including assets such as deferred compensation owed to the Hedge Fund Manager. Capital and Equity are often used interchangeably.

151 See Dowd (1999), p. 55.

rupt. The positions of a bankrupt Hedge Fund are generally liquidated, but the already unstable world credit markets would have collapsed if lenders sold LTCM's collateral to the value of $1 trillion to recoup their costs. After initial prompting from the Federal Reserve, Wall Street's elite met and fourteen firms, such as Goldman Sachs, Merrill Lynch, Salomon Smith Barney and JP Morgan eventually agreed to participate in a consortium to bail out LTCM by committing between $100 million to $350 million each[152]. In total, the consortium injected[153] US$3.6 billion in private equity in the Fund and received a 90 per cent stake in LTCM's portfolio and operational control in return.

Many of Wall Streets top executives suffered personal losses when the firm went down and the rescue plan reduced investor stakes to less than 10 per cent of what they had originally been. The risk profile of the firm was reduced by nearly 90 per cent and by early autumn of 1999, the fund's financial situation had turned around and almost three quarters of the bailout had been paid back.

LTCM was able to reach its position pre August 1998 because of the degree of secrecy surrounding the business and its activities. LTCM was considered unique because of the large scale of its activities and size or its positions in certain markets[154]. BIS considered LTCM to be "market-maker" in some markets[155]. According to some in the industry[156], LTCM's counterparties often treated it more like an investment bank than a Hedge Fund. Counterparties were not provided with specific information regarding the fund's risk profile in either the balance sheet or income statements supplied. Long-Term Capital's strategies were supposedly low risk and at the time they would have seemed conservative to LTCM's banks. The LTCM case essentially illustrates the risks arising from utilizing high leverage, managing very large positions, inadequate risk management strategies, investor redemptions[157], funding liquidity, insufficient monitoring of fund credit quality by counterparties and insufficient provision of information to counterparties rendering monitoring ineffective.

A direct result of the crisis was a general shift from Hedge Fund activity and for those who stayed invested in the industry, towards less risky forms of Hedge Funds. Investing has become more of a buyer's market, which is slowly encourag-

---

152 See Strachman (2000), p. 21.

153 Allan Greenspan, Testimony before the Committee on Banking and Financial Services, U.S. House of Representatives, Private–sector refinancing of the large Hedge Fund, Long-Term Capital Management, Federal Reserve Board, p. 4.

154 See United States General Account Office (1999), p. 5.

155 See Basle Committee (1999), p. 10.

156 Hedge fund of funds manager Mike Dubin of Powers & Dubin LLP (a leading boutique hedge fund of funds management firm) in an interview with the author, Wulf A. Kaal, at the Yale Club, Manhattan, NY, 16th of June 2001.

157 I.e. the redemption of shares or other interests in, or withdrawals of funds from a Hedge Fund by an investor.

ing a higher degree of information disclosure, and risk control and risk management have also become a higher priority for many Hedge Funds. The amount of leverage used by Hedge Fund managers[158] has fallen by choice and also because, until relatively recently, credit was not as readily available. This latter factor was due to another important development in the form of restrictions placed on lending to Hedge Funds.

The commercial relationships between lenders and Hedge Funds were exposed following LTCM's crash. LTCM made some bad investment decisions, but Wall Street and the banks also played a large part in the collapse. Hedge Funds are significant clients and counterparties to banks, particularly because they uniquely take on risks that other financial participants would not, borrow massive amounts and are willing to pay a premium for borrowing. Given this, banks management viewed, and still does, business from Hedge Funds as being desirable. LTCM grew as large as it did because it was lent money without regard for whether this money could be paid back. Banks put their own existence at risk with their lending practices during this time.

In summary, a far too high leverage ratio, non-existing trading strategy diversification and excess of available funds prompted the demise of LTCM.

II. *Measures in Response to LTCM*

1. Regulatory Measures

In the aftermath of the near-collapse of LTCM and the prolonged regional economic crises[159], regulators have started to revise the regulatory framework relating to Hedge Funds.

Generally, regulators are considering whether to bring Hedge Funds under their regulatory authority. Regulator's initial approach was to call into question the risk management systems of banks and securities firms and to recommend various changes to them. In fact, they have increased the disclosure requirements applicable to financial institutions that are counterparties or creditors of Hedge Funds and considered imposing disclosure requirements on Hedge Funds to enhance transparency.

Whether this flurry of activity by regulators is an over-reaction or action long overdue remains unclear. However, regulators have assumed that the risk

---

[158] Hedge Fund managers are an entity that serves as investment advisor to a Hedge Fund and manages its assets and investments. Offshore Hedge Funds typically have Hedge Fund Managers that are separate legal entities, while many U.S. Hedge Fund Managers my be part of the Hedge Fund structure (e.g., as general partner of a limited partnership or managing member of a limited liability company). Hedge Fund Mangers are often investors in the Hedge Fund they mange and are compensated in part based on the performance of the Hedge Fund.

[159] I.e. Asian contagion and Russian debt market.

models used by financial institutions including LTCM do not take the right snap shot of the economy. They are recommending changes to the regulatory framework as well as the risk models. These recommendations include: improvements in public disclosure by HLIs through both regulations, and where necessary new legislation, and good practices guidelines for foreign exchange trading; stronger counterparty risk management by institutions providing credit to HLIs; stronger risk management by all Hedge Funds; enhanced regulatory oversight of banks and securities firms which provide credit to HLIs; and finally measures to improve the market infrastructure to facilitate the liquidation of large, leveraged Hedge Funds. Uniting these regulatory measures as a key topic is the importance of promoting adjustments in firm behavior and enhancing market discipline. Regulators are about to take the necessary steps to implement many but surely not all of these recommendations. However, continued efforts, pro-activity, diligence and vigilance will be necessary to try and implement the recommendations and thereby address the risk problems.

On the other hand, however, there is the risk and this cannot be emphasized enough, that the revised regulations could overburden the market participants once the regional economic crises correct themselves or even hamper the correction. And, of course, there is the issue of cost. For example, the cost of implementing FAS 133[160], is estimated to range between US$5000,000 to US$2,500,000 or half that if certain functions such as matching hedging relationships can be performed by the complicated system.

Hedge Funds are exempt from U.S. SEC reporting requirements, as well as from regulatory restrictions on leverage or trading strategies[161]. Generally unsupervised is also their structure and size of fees they may charge.

Whilst trading desks of major banks and securities firms are constrained by internal risk management functions, by risk-based capital requirements and by public disclosure of the firm's overall trading activity, Hedge Funds are subject to fewer public disclosure requirements and less monitoring. Disclosure by Hedge Funds to counterparties and investors are often made by using balance-sheet concepts, which are not informative about the nature of the exposures to market risk and credit risk[162].

---

160 Until the adoption of Financial Accounting Standards Board's Statement 133 (FAS 133), most derivatives had been treated as off-balance-sheet transactions. Off-Balance-Sheet Transactions are transactions entered into by a Hedge Fund that does not appear on its balance sheet.

161 At least as long as they comply with requirements to remain exempt from relevant legislation.

162 Credit risk is the risk that an issuer of a security (asset credit risk) or a counterparty (counterparty credit risk) will not meet its obligations when due. Asset credit risk also includes sovereign risk where the potential loss is related to the financial solvency of a sovereign issuer of a security. Counterparty credit risk is frequently broken down into component risks for monitoring purposes.

Furthermore, regulators face on the one hand the problem of jurisdictional arbitrage, i.e. if they directly regulate, Hedge Funds may relocate offshore and escape from regulation altogether. On the other hand, if regulators weakly regulate, investors may not be afforded adequate protection. In order to remedy this problem, regulators appear to be adopting a middle ground by taking an indirect regulatory approach[163], which when rigorously applied by banks and financial institutions that are counterparty[164] to Hedge Funds is hoped to prevent systematic disruption.

For practitioners[165] it is, however, clear that if another disaster comparable to the LTCM case should take place[166], there will be mounting pressure both by politicians and market participants as well as lobby groups to further regulate Hedge Funds, even in a more direct way.

In the following chapter, the author analyzes what various jurisdictions i.e. the regulators of various countries as well as international bodies and regulatory authorities proposed to regulate Hedge Fund. Each positive analysis will be followed by a summary and either a hypothetical or an actual effect analysis.

a) U.S. Securities Exchange Commission

Hedge Funds are exempt from U.S. SEC reporting requirements, as well as from regulatory restrictions on leverage or trading strategies as long as they comply with certain requirements to remain exempt form relevant legislation. The SEC proposed a rule, which was finalized in January 1997[167] requiring specific quantitative and qualitative disclosures about market risk and institution's accounting policies relating to derivatives and reason for material quantitative changes in market risk exposures between the current and previous years. Albeit the rule was published in 1997, i.e. before the Fed bailed out LTCM in 1998, it can still be labeled "a regulatory measure in reaction to LTCM" because these measures applied to LTCM later. U.S. regulators have also recommended that Hedge Funds disclose their portfolios′ financial condition in quarterly filings that

---

163 E.g. by regulating counterparties of Hedge Funds.

164 A counterparty is a third party that enters into transactions with a Hedge Fund.

165 Mike Dubin of Powers and Dubin LLP N.Y. (a firm specialised to develop financial products and Hedge Funds for private as well as institutional investors) in an interview conducted on 15th of August 2001.

166 There is strong evidence that this could happen because the various regulatory proposals have not yet been implemented and there does not seem to be a unilateral, coherent approach, which makes it even more difficult.

167 See 17 CFR Parts 210, 228, 229, 239, 240, and 249; [Release Nos. 33-7386; 34-38223; IC-22487; FR-48; International Series No. 1047; File No. S7-35-95] - Disclosure of Accounting Policies for Derivative Financial Instruments and Derivative Commodity Instruments and Disclosure of Quantitative and Qualitative Information about Market Risk Inherent in Derivative Financial Instruments, other Financial Instruments, and Derivative Commodity Instruments.

are available to the public but have not proposed new direct regulation of the industry. The public reports, possibly to the CFTC, would include comprehensive measure of market risk without disclosing proprietary information on strategies and positions.

b) U.K. Financial Services Authority

In the aftermath of the LTCM debacle, the U.K. Financial Services Authority (FSA) proposed a new ruling to monitor counterparty risk[168]. Under the ruling, banks acting as agents for undisclosed principals are required to disclose who their clients are when transacting business with fund management groups. It was the lack of such disclosure that left counterparties and lenders quite unable to develop a realistic view of counterparty risk. They had no picture of the overall risk in spite of the fact that most of their individual trades with the fund were adequately collateralized. The ruling was applied to banks in March 1999 and has been extended to securities firms in June 1999.

In the Memorandum by the Financial Services Authority to the Treasury Select Committee, 28th of October 1998, the FSA also expressed concern that regulators' should demand more information from banks and regulated firms on their dealings with and exposure to Hedge Funds. Their conclusion, however, emphasized that there was no case for direct regulation of Hedge Funds for the sake of the investors[169]. The FSA opines that investors who have the monetary possibility to invest in Hedge Funds are on the one hand mostly aware of their risks and wealthy enough to find solutions for their own protection, on the other hand regulatory protection does not make sense if those who are to be protected, as in the case of Hedge Funds investors, do not demand to be protected. However, they state that the one imaginable justification of direct regulation was the promotion of systemic safety[170].

---

168 See FSA (1998).

169 See id at 29.

170 Perry/Grant: Plumbers, Gurus and Global Markets: The Financial Services Authority and the Regulation of Hedge Funs, in: Cullen/ Parry (2001), pp. 131-132. "Any such measures addressing such issues would only be applicable to a few funds whose sheer size and levels of leverage meant that they were in a position, either alone or acting with others, threaten such safety. Even direct regulation of such funds raises difficult problems, such as the inevitable attractive option of offshore regulatory arbitrage, and the fact that many regulated institutions display similar characteristics and would, therefore, also potentially be in the frame. Most reports on the LTCM crisis, including the Treasury Second Report on the World Economy have endorsed the FSA view that investor protection would not be an appropriate basis on which to regulate Hedge Funds. Current thinking favours the approach of leaving the question of general direct regulation in abeyance for the time being to allow time for industry based voluntary measures to work through. There is a general recognition that such direct regulation with authorisation requirements and prudential con-

c) Conclusion

The direct regulatory response to LTCM remains minimal. If this is a result of the fact that LTCM was bailed out successfully which resulted in a slow recovery of the worlds credit market remains unclear. Both, the SEC and the FSA take an indirect, i.e. prudential approach by, on the one hand requiring disclosure of accounting policies for derivative financial instruments and, on the other hand, proposing a rule to monitor counterparty risk.

Event though the SEC introduced the rule on "Disclosure of Accounting Policies for Derivative Financial Instruments and Derivative Commodity Instruments and Disclosure of Quantitative and Qualitative Information about Market Risk Inherent in Derivative Financial Instruments, other Financial Instruments, and Derivative Commodity Instruments,"[171] before LTCM`s demise it may have been too late at that point. Saving LTCM and preparing it for the events to come would have demanded a lot more than disclosure of its accounting policies for derivatives and this especially since only a fraction, albeit a significant one, of LTCM`s investments were derivatives. Hence, this measure could only have prompted earlier warnings for the derivative part of the portfolio. This may have been a first step to get to grips with the problems at hand but the overall systemic risk-, moral hazard- and transaction cost- problems have not been addressed.

The same applies to the FSA approach. Proposing a rule to monitor counterparty risk[172] under which banks acting as agents for undisclosed principals, i.e. Hedge Funds, are required to disclose who their clients are when transacting business with fund management groups, may have been a step in the right direction to try and resolve the aforementioned information asymmetries and, hence, moral hazard problems. Despite the fact that the asymmetries are one of the major problems demanding regulation, the other aforementioned problems are not addressed by the FSA. It is, furthermore, questionable why the FSA only applies this rule to transactions with fund management groups and not with other parties. It might have been preferable to choose a more flexible wording and, therefore, allowing greater discretion in its application.

trols, may eventually become necessary but only on systemic and not consumer protection grounds."

171 See 17 CFR Parts 210, 228, 229, 239, 240, and 249; [Release Nos. 33-7386; 34-38223; IC-22487; FR-48; International Series No. 1047; File No. S7-35-95].

172 See FSA (1998).

2. Legislative Measures

Apart from the measures taken by the SEC and FSA the U.S. legislator introduced two bills before Congress in response to the near-collapse of LTCM. These were the Hedge Fund Disclosure Act 1999[173] and the Derivatives Market Reform Act 1999[174].

a) Hedge Fund Disclosure Act 1999

Hedge Funds are required under the Hedge Fund Disclosure Act to make certain public disclosures[175]. The essence of the Act is a quarterly disclosure that would apply to the largest Hedge Funds. The Hedge Funds that would be subject to these disclosure rules are those that are defined as unregulated Hedge Funds[176]. Among the information that is to be quarterly reported to the Federal Reserve[177] are balance sheet leverage ration of assets to liabilities, total notional amount of derivatives, as well as "meaningful and comprehensive measures of market risk such as VaR or stress test results."[178]

However, after fierce lobbying by the Hedge Fund industry, demanding to lower the threshold for reporting requirements, the Act was revised at a subcommittee hearing held on 16th of March 2000. Thus, the definition of "unregulated Hedge Fund" has been changed to "any pooled investment vehicle, or any group or family of pooled investment vehicles, with aggregate total assets of U.S.$3 billion or more or aggregate net assets of U.S.$1 billion or more"[179]. Therefore, in effect, "unregulated Hedge Funds" are pooled investment vehicles with a net asset value of $1 billion or more that are professionally managed and not available to the general public and not regulated as public mutual funds under the Investment Company Act of 1940.

However, the vast majority of Hedge Funds would not be affected by the enactment of the Act. Only Hedge Funds whose failure could move markets are among the few large funds that would be covered by the disclosure requirement,

---

173 Dubbed the "Baker Bill" since on 23rd of September 1999, Representative Richard Baker introduced H.R. 2924, a bill to enact the "Hedge Fund Disclosure Act".

174 Dubbed the "Markey/Dorgan Bill" since on 19th of November 1999, Representative Edward J. Markey (D-Ma.) and Senator Byron Dorgan (D-ND) introduced H.R. 3483 and S. 1968, respectively, i.e. bills to enact the "Derivatives Market Reform Act 1999". – The Baker Bill and the Markey/Dorgan Bill take different snap shots at the problem, i.e. the Markey/Dorgan Bill is considerably more expansive than the Baker Bill in that it includes, among other things, registration and/or reporting requirements for "derivatives dealers".

175 See U.S. House of Representatives (2000), p. 2.

176 Section 3 of the Hedge Fund Disclosure Act 1999.

177 These reports are later disclosed to the public.

178 See U.S. House of Representatives (2000), p. 45.

179 See Roth (2001), p. 165.

i.e. about 25 of those that actually are covered by the Act[180]. The Act further provides a compulsory summary in the financial statement of public companies` detailing the direct material exposure to highly leveraged institutions[181] and, thus, also addresses the suppliers of leverage to hedge funds and other highly leveraged institutions.

b) Derivatives Market Reform Act 1999

The Derivatives Market Reform Act 1999 is part of a comprehensive bill intended to address issues relating to the use of over-the-counter derivatives, as well as matters raised by the near collapse of LTCM. With respect to Hedge Funds, Title II of the Derivatives Market Reform Act, entitled "Hedge Fund Reporting", proposes certain amendments to the Investment Company Act of 1940 for every "unregistered Hedge Fund". The "unregistered Hedge Fund" is defined as any pooled investment vehicle or group of pooled vehicle that:

- has total assets under management of $ 1 billion and
- relies on Section 3(c)(1) or 3(c)(7) of the Investment Company Act 1940 or is a foreign company that would be required to obtain an SEC order if it conducted a public offering of securities.

Under the reporting requirements, each "unregistered Hedge Fund" would be required to file a quarterly report with the SEC prepared in accordance with generally accepted accounting principles. Upon receipt of such a report, the SEC would transmit copies to the aforementioned regulators and, subject to the protection[182].

c) Conclusion

One objective, and probably the most important one for the U.S. legislator, was to minimize the size of speculative positions. As seen earlier, there are two ways to limit the size of speculative positions, by direct regulation, by limiting capital reserve requirements such as those that apply to banks and securities brokers, or indirectly by reinforcing market mechanisms that ought to constrain excessive leverage. The Hedge Fund disclosure Act 1999 takes the second approach. Instead of directly regulating Hedge Funds, the Act takes an indirect approach of reinforcing the market mechanisms that ought to constrain excessive leverage and speculation in the absence of regulation. In other words, improving transparency

180 See U.S. House of Representatives (2000), p. 3.
181 Section 6 of the Hedge Fund Disclosure Act 1999.
182 See Roth (2001), p. 100.

through enhanced disclosure to the public is intended to help market participants make better, more informed judgments about market integrity and creditworthiness of borrowers and counterparties[183].

Upon closer inspection the premise of the legislation seems to be that the markets do not work in the sense that markets and sophisticated investors are not capable of determining what information they need adequately to assess the risk they choose to take. Therefore, there seems to be the need for the Government to impose disclosure.

In the real world, however, markets do work and the market forces may be called the favorable tools for constraining excessive leverage and the highly sophisticated institutions that are involved in this are quite capable of defining and receiving the information that they need. Also, Hedge Funds only exist because their entire stock in trade is their ability to pursue and exploit very sophisticated strategies of finding market inefficiencies. In some ways, it is inherently a proprietary business that contributes to the well functioning of markets. Requiring Hedge Funds to disclose the risks they are taking reveals the nature of their business. Hence, this legislation with its focus on disclosure and, thus, transparency could put an onerous burden on the Hedge Fund industry and could put American financial institutions at a competitive disadvantage relative to competitors from Europe and Asia in particular.

It has, moreover, to be pointed out that a number of so-called new measures have already been put in place. For instance, the institutions that extend credit to Hedge Funds have already implemented extensive and rigorous new forms of analysis in their credit departments. Eventually, this legislation can be said to encourage hedge fund activity to take place offshore, beyond the reach of American regulators, i.e. jurisdictional arbitrage is inevitable.

Perhaps to a lesser extent, there is the question about whether this legislation imposes a moral hazard problem in the sense that the illusion that the Federal regulation exists where, in fact, there is no meaningful Federal regulation, thereby sending out a signal, that some of Hedge Funds might be "too big to fail". Arguably, the Federal Reserve has already sent this signal by bailing out LTCM.

---

183 See U.S. House of Representatives (2000), p. 2. In his opening remarks before the U.S. House of Representatives` Subcommittee on Capital Markets, Chairman Richard H. Baker remarked that the purpose of the Hedge Fund Disclosure Act 1999 was not to regulate Hedge Funds, but "to enhance market discipline and allow market participants to make better and more informed judgements about the creditworthiness of Hedge Funds. More Disclosure will aid in constraining excessive leverage, particularly in the largest Hedge Funds, and help limit risk exposure to the broader financial markets." Thus, we can see that the motivating concept underlying the Baker Bill is that market discipline will be enhanced by public disclosure.

d) International Accounting Standards Committee

In December 1998, the International Accounting Standards Committee (IASC)[184] adopted International Accounting Standard (IAS) 32[185], which includes requirements for the disclosure of terms, conditions and accounting policies for financial instruments, interest rate risk and credit risk data and the fair value[186] of on- and off-balance-sheet financial instruments. The IASC has also announced

---

184 The IASC and its International Accounting Standards Board (IASB) is an independent, privately-funded accounting standard setter based in London, UK. Board Members come from nine countries and have a variety of functional backgrounds. The Board's objective is to establish a single set of high quality, understandable and enforceable global accounting standards that require transparent and comparable information in general purpose financial statements. In addition, the Board co-operates with national accounting standard setters to achieve convergence in accounting standards around the world. The current structure and organisation of the IASB came about as a result of a strategy review undertaken by its predecessor body, the Board of the International Accounting Standards Committee, between 1997 and 1999. Eventually, in March 2001, the IASC Foundation was formed as a not-for-profit corporation incorporated in the State of Delaware, USA. The IASC Foundation is the parent entity of the International Accounting Standards Board, and independent accounting standard setter based in London, UK. Effective 1. April 2001, the IASB assumed accounting standard setting responsibilities from its predecessor body, the International Accounting Standards Committee. This was the culmination of a restructuring based on the recommendations of the report Recommendations on Shaping IASC for the Future. The IASB structure has the following main features: the IASC Foundation is an independent organisation having two main bodies, the Trustees and the IASB, as well as a Standards Advisory Council and the International Financial Reporting Interpretations Committee. The IASC Foundation Trustees appoint the IASB Members, exercise oversight and raise the funds needed, whereas IASB has sole responsibility for setting accounting standards.

185 IAS 32, Financial Instruments: Disclosures and Presentation - was approved by the IASC Board in March 1995. In December 1998, certain paragraphs were amended and a paragraph inserted to reflect the issuance of IAS 39: Financial Instruments: Recognition and Measurement. In October 2000, the Standard was amended to eliminate disclosure requirements that become redundant as a result of IAS 39. The changes to IAS 32 become effective when an enterprise applies IAS 39 for the first time. Summary of IAS 32: Presentation - Financial instruments should be classified by issuers into liabilities and equity, which includes splitting compound instruments into these components; - Classification reflects substance, not form; - An obligation to deliver cash or other financial asset is debt; -Mandatorily redeemable preferred stock is debt, - Split accounting is required for compound financial instruments (such as convertible securities); - The cost of a financial liability (interest) is deducted in measuring net profit or loss; - The cost of equity financing (dividends) are a distribution of equity; - Offsetting on the balance sheet is permitted only if the holder of the financial instrument can legally settle on a net basis. Disclosures: Terms and conditions; - Interest rate risk (re-pricing and maturity dates, fixed and floating interest rates, maturities); - Credit risk (maximum exposure and significant concentrations); - Fair values of financial instruments; - Financial assets carried at a value in excess of fair value.

186 Fair value generally refers to the price at which a single unit of an instrument would trade between disinterested parties in an arm's length transaction. Fair value does not generally take into account control premiums or discounts for large or illiquid positions.

IAS 39[187], which, like U.S. FAS 133, covers derivatives and hedge accounting but also conventional assets and liabilities such as cash, trade receivables and securi-

[187] IAS 39, Financial Instruments, Recognition and Measurement; Summary of IAS 39: - Under IAS 39, all financial assets and financial liabilities are recognised on the balance sheet, including all derivatives. They are initially measured at cost, which is the fair value of whatever was paid or received to acquire the financial asset or liability. An enterprise should recognise normal purchases and sales of financial assets in the market place either at trade date or settlement date. Certain value changes between trade and settlement dates are recognised for purchases if settlement date accounting is used. Transaction costs should be included in the initial measurement of all financial instruments. Subsequent to initial recognition, all financial assets are re-measured to fair value, except for the following, which should be carried at amortised cost: (a) loans and receivables originated by the enterprise and not held for trading; (b) other fixed maturity investments with fixed or determinable payments, such as debt securities and mandatorily redeemable preferred shares, that the enterprise intends and is able to hold to maturity; and (c) financial assets whose fair value cannot be reliably measured (generally limited to some equity securities with no quoted market price and forwards and options on unquoted equity securities). An enterprise should measure loans and receivables that it has originated and that are not held for trading at amortised cost, less reductions for impairment or uncollectibility. The enterprise need not demonstrate an intent to hold originated loans and receivables to maturity. An intended or actual sale of a held-to-maturity security due to a non-recurring and not reasonably anticipated circumstance beyond the enterprise's control does not call into question the enterprise's ability to hold its remaining portfolio to maturity. If an enterprise is prohibited from classifying financial assets as held-to-maturity because it has sold more than an insignificant amount of assets that it had previously said it intended to hold to maturity, that prohibition expires at the end of the second financial year following the premature sales. After acquisition most financial liabilities are measured at original recorded amount less principal repayments and amortisation. Only derivatives and liabilities held for trading (such as securities borrowed by a short seller) are remeasured to fair value. For those financial assets and liabilities that are remeasured to fair value, an enterprise will have a single, enterprise-wide option either to: (a) recognise the entire adjustment in net profit or loss for the period; or (b) recognise in net profit or loss for the period only those changes in fair value relating to financial assets and liabilities held for trading, with the non-trading value changes reported in equity until the financial asset is sold, at which time the realised gain or loss is reported in net profit or loss. For this purpose, derivatives are always deemed held for trading unless they are designated as hedging instruments. IAS 39 requires that an impairment loss be recognised for a financial asset whose recoverable amount is less than carrying amount. Guidance is provided for calculating impairment. IAS 39 establishes conditions for determining when control over a financial asset or liability has been transferred to another party. For financial assets a transfer normally would be recognised if (a) the transferee has the right to sell or pledge the asset and (b) the transferor does not have the right to reacquire the transferred assets. With respect to de-recognition of liabilities, the debtor must be legally released from primary responsibility for the liability (or part thereof) either judicially or by the creditor. If part of a financial asset or liability is sold or extinguished, the carrying amount is split based on relative fair values. Hedging, for accounting purposes, means designating a derivative or (only for hedges of foreign currency risks) a non-derivative financial instrument as an offset in net profit or loss, in whole or in part, to the change in fair value or cash flows of a hedged item. Hedge accounting is permitted under IAS 39 in certain circumstances, provided that the hedging relationship is clearly defined, measurable, and actually effective. Hedge accounting is permitted only if an enterprise designates a specific hedging instrument as a hedge of

ties investments. IAS 39 came into effect on 1. January 2001, but earlier adoption had been allowed for financial years completed after 15 March 1999. In October 2000, the IASC Board approved five limited revisions to IAS 39 and other related International Accounting Standards[188] to improve specific paragraphs and help ensure that the Standards are applied consistently. These changes become effective when an enterprise applies IAS 39 for the first time. The revisions include: to require consistent accounting for purchases and sales of financial assets for each category of financial assets using either trade date accounting or settlement date accounting; eliminated a requirement in IAS 39 as originally approved for a lender to recognize collateral received from a borrower in its balance sheet; provide more explicit requirements for impairment recognition; require consistent accounting in the consolidated financial statements for temporary investments in equity securities in accordance with IAS 39 and other International Accounting Standards; and eliminated redundant disclosure requirements for hedges in IAS 32.

e) U.S. – Financial Accounting Standard Board

The U.S. Financial Accounting Standard Board (FASB)[189] issued a Statement of Financial Accounting Standards (FAS) No. 133 effective since 15 June

a change in value or cash flow of a specific hedged item, rather than as a hedge of an overall net balance sheet position. However, the approximate income statement effect of hedge accounting for an overall net position can be achieved, in some cases, by designating part of one of the underlying items as the hedged position. For hedges of forecasted transactions that result in the recognition of an asset or liability, the gain or loss on the hedging instrument will adjust the basis (carrying amount) of the acquired asset or liability. IAS 39 supplements the disclosure requirements of IAS 32 for financial instruments. The new Standard is effective for annual accounting periods beginning on or after 1 January 2001.Earlier application is permitted as of the beginning of a financial year that ends after issuance of IAS 39. On initial adoption of IAS 39, adjustments to bring derivatives and other financial assets and liabilities onto the balance sheet and adjustments to re-measure certain financial assets and liabilities from cost to fair value will be made by adjusting retained earnings directly.

188 IAS 27, IAS 28, IAS 31, and IAS 32

189 Since its foundation in 1973 it has been FASB`s objective to establish and improve standards of financial accounting and reporting for the guidance and education of the public, including issuers, auditors and users of financial information. Those standards govern the preparation of financial reports. They are officially recognized as authoritative by the SEC and the American Institute of Certified Public Accountants. The SEC has statutory authority to establish financial accounting and reporting standards for publicly held companies under the Securities Exchange Act of 1934. Throughout its history, however, the Commission's policy has, however, been to rely on the private sector for this function to the extent that the private sector demonstrates ability to fulfil the responsibility in the public interest. FASB acts to: Improve the usefulness of financial reporting by focusing on the primary characteristics of relevance and reliability and on the qualities of comparability and consistency; keep standards current to reflect changes in methods of doing

1999. FAS 133[190] established accounting and disclosure standards for derivative instruments and for hedging activities. It requires that all derivatives be recog-

---

business and changes in the economic environment; consider promptly any significant areas of deficiency in financial reporting that might be improved through the standard-setting process; promote the international convergence of accounting standards concurrent with improving the quality of financial reporting; and improve the common understanding of the nature and purposes of information contained in financial reports. The FASB also develops broad accounting concepts as well as standards for financial reporting. It also provides guidance on implementation of standards. Concepts are useful in guiding the Board in establishing standards and in providing a frame of reference, or conceptual framework, for resolving accounting issues.

[190] U.S. FASB, Summary of Statement No. 133 Accounting for Derivative Instruments and Hedging Activities (Issued 6/98): "Summary: This Statement establishes accounting and reporting standards for derivative instruments, including certain derivative instruments embedded in other contracts, (collectively referred to as derivatives) and for hedging activities. It requires that an entity recognise all derivatives as either assets or liabilities in the statement of financial position and measure those instruments at fair value. If certain conditions are met, a derivative may be specifically designated as (a) a hedge of the exposure to changes in the fair value of a recognized asset or liability or an unrecognized firm commitment, (b) a hedge of the exposure to variable cash flows of a forecasted transaction, or (c) a hedge of the foreign currency exposure of a net investment in a foreign operation, an unrecognized firm commitment, an available-for-sale security, or a foreign-currency-denominated forecasted transaction. The accounting for changes in the fair value of a derivative (that is, gains and losses) depends on the intended use of the derivative and the resulting designation. For a derivative designated as hedging the exposure to changes in the fair value of a recognized asset or liability or a firm commitment (referred to as a fair value hedge), the gain or loss is recognized in earnings in the period of change together with the offsetting loss or gain on the hedged item attributable to the risk being hedged. The effect of that accounting is to reflect in earnings the extent to which the hedge is not effective in achieving offsetting changes in fair value. For a derivative designated as hedging the exposure to variable cash flows of a forecasted transaction (referred to as a cash flow hedge), the effective portion of the derivative's gain or loss is initially reported as a component of other comprehensive income (outside earnings) and subsequently reclassified into earnings when the forecasted transaction affects earnings. The ineffective portion of the gain or loss is reported in earnings immediately. For a derivative designated as hedging the foreign currency exposure of a net investment in a foreign operation, the gain or loss is reported in other comprehensive income (outside earnings) as part of the cumulative translation adjustment. The accounting for a fair value hedge described above applies to a derivative designated as a hedge of the foreign currency exposure of an unrecognised firm commitment or an available-for-sale security. Similarly, the accounting for a cash flow hedge described above applies to a derivative designated as a hedge of the foreign currency exposure of a foreign-currency-denominated forecasted transaction. For a derivative not designated as a hedging instrument, the gain or loss is recognised in earnings in the period of change. Under this Statement, an entity that elects to apply hedge accounting is required to establish at the inception of the hedge the method it will use for assessing the effectiveness of the hedging derivative and the measurement approach for determining the ineffective aspect of the hedge. Those methods must be consistent with the entity's approach to managing risk. This Statement applies to all entities. A not-for-profit organisation should recognise the change in fair value of all derivatives as a change in net assets in the period of change. In a fair value hedge, the changes in the fair value of the hedged item attributable to the risk being hedged also are recognised. However, because of the format of their statement of finan-

nized as either assets or liabilities and that they are measured at fair value. It also requires that the objectives for holding or issuing derivatives be disclosed. The accounting treatment is based on the designated use of the derivatives and requires disclosure of the resulting earnings effects.

f) U.K. – Accounting Standards Board, FSA

The U.K. Accounting Standards Board (ASB)[191] issued its Financial Reporting Standard (FRS) 13[192] in September 1998, with effect from March 1999. The

---

cial performance, not-for-profit organisations are not permitted special hedge accounting for derivatives used to hedge forecasted transactions. This Statement does not address how a not-for-profit organisation should determine the components of an operating measure if one is presented. This Statement precludes designating a non-derivative financial instrument as a hedge of an asset, liability, unrecognised firm commitment, or forecasted transaction except that a non-derivative instrument denominated in a foreign currency may be designated as a hedge of the foreign currency exposure of an unrecognised firm commitment denominated in a foreign currency or a net investment in a foreign operation. This Statement amends FASB Statement No. 52, Foreign Currency Translation, to permit special accounting for a hedge of a foreign currency forecasted transaction with a derivative. It supersedes FASB Statements No. 80, Accounting for Futures Contracts, No. 105, Disclosure of Information about Financial Instruments with Off-Balance-Sheet Risk and Financial Instruments with Concentrations of Credit Risk, and No. 119, Disclosure about Derivative Financial Instruments and Fair Value of Financial Instruments. It amends FASB Statement No. 107, Disclosures about Fair Value of Financial Instruments, to include in Statement 107 the disclosure provisions about concentrations of credit risk from Statement 105. This Statement also nullifies or modifies the consensus reached in a number of issues addressed by the Emerging Issues Task Force. This Statement is effective for all fiscal quarters of fiscal years beginning after June 15, 1999. Initial application of this Statement should be as of the beginning of an entity's fiscal quarter; on that date, hedging relationships must be designated anew and documented pursuant to the provisions of this Statement. Earlier application of all of the provisions of this Statement is encouraged, but it is permitted only as of the beginning of any fiscal quarter that begins after issuance of this Statement. This Statement should not be applied retroactively to financial statements of prior periods."

191 The ASB took over the task of setting accounting standards from the Accounting Standards Committee (ASC) in 1990. The ASB has up to ten board members, two board members (the Chairman and the Technical Director) are full-time, and the remainder, who represent a variety of interests, are part-time. Accounting standards developed by the ASB are contained in the FRSs. Soon after it started its activities, the ASB adopted the standards issued by the ASC, so that they also fall within the legal definition of accounting standards. One of ASB`s objectives is to develop principles to guide it in establishing accounting standards. These are contained in the ASB's "Statement of Principles for Financial Reporting". Unlike its predecessor body, the ASC, the ASB can issue accounting standards on its own authority, without the approval of any other body. The ASB collaborates with accounting standard-setters from other countries and the IASB in order to ensure that its standards are developed with due regard to international developments. www.fasb.org.

192 FRS 13 Issued September 1998, amended December 1998: Derivatives and other Financial Instruments: Disclosures. Some financial instruments, such as cash, debtors and creditors, gener-

standard requires U.K. listed companies (other than insurance companies) and all banks to provide a comprehensive range of information about risks arising from their financial instruments and their response to such risks. The main disclosures are interest rate risk disclosures, currency disclosures and liquidity and maturity disclosures, information on fair values and the effect of hedge accounting.

g) France

Offshore Hedge Funds do not qualify as EU UCITS and therefore are not subject to specific tax regulations in France. French individual investors in an offshore fund are taxed either at the applicable personal income tax rate on income received from a distribution by the fund of its revenue or at the capital gains tax rate upon disposal of their interest in the fund. If an individual French investor holds more than 10 per cent of the voting or financial rights of the fund either directly or indirectly, he will be taxed an amount on the profit of the fund proportionate to his financial rights. A minimum lump sum payment based on the net assets will be also required should the fund not be located in a tax treaty country. On the other hand, institutions that are subject to French corporation tax are taxed only on distribution of a fund's revenue. Like the individual investor, if a French corporation owns over 10 per cent of the voting or financial rights of a fund it may be taxed on accumulated profits of the fund, an amount in proportion to its holdings at yearend.

---

ally arise as part of an entity's operating and financing activities and tend to be highly visible in the financial statements. Others (such as swaps, forwards, caps and collars, and other derivatives) are entered into in order to manage the risks arising from the operating and financing activities of the entity and are generally less visible. FRS 13 seeks to improve the disclosures provided in respect of all financial instruments and it does this by focusing on the way in which they are used by the reporting entity. The objective of its disclosures is to provide information about: a. the impact of the instruments on the entity's risk profile; b. how the risks arising from financial instruments might affect the entity's performance and financial condition; and c. how these risks are being managed. FRS 13 applies to all entities, other than insurance companies and groups, that have one or more of their capital instruments listed or publicly traded on a stock exchange or market and all banks and similar institutions. The FRS requires both narrative and numerical disclosures. The narrative disclosures should include an explanation of the role that financial instruments play in creating or changing the risks that the entity faces in its activities. The directors' approach to managing each of those risks should also be explained, and this should include a description of the objectives, policies and strategies for holding and issuing financial instruments. The numerical disclosures are intended primarily to show how these objectives and policies were implemented in the period. They focus on: a. interest rate risk; b. currency risk; c. liquidity risk (except for banks and similar institutions, which are covered by existing requirements); d. fair values; and e. hedging activities. Although all entities falling within the scope of FRS 13 are required to provide the same type of narrative disclosures, the standard requires different numerical disclosures for each of: a. entities that are not financial institutions; b. banks and similar institutions; and c. other types of financial institution. FRS 13 is effective for accounting periods ending on or after 23 March 1999.

Where an offshore Hedge Fund has a substantial amount of French investors, the French tax authorities may 'look-through' the fund if it is established in any jurisdiction outside the European Economic Area (EEA). In this case each French investor will be treated as if it had invested directly in the underlying assets. Such a situation could be avoided if a Hedge Fund manager established an Irish feeder fund into, say, a Cayman master fund in which non-French investors could directly invest or instead, an Irish fund into which all investors would directly invest.[193]

However, the "Conseil National de la Comptabilitè" (CNC - National Accountancy Council)[194] issued two documents on market risk disclosure in 1998. Advice no. 98.05 requires banks and investment firms supervised by the Banking Commission to disclose information on accounting principles and rules, profitability of banking activities, counterparty risk in derivative activities and off-balance sheet items. Recommendation no. 98.R.01 requires information relating to business strategies, interest rate risk and foreign exchange risk, as well as qualitative and quantitative information relating to market risk exposures.

h) Conclusion

All four accounting authorities, i.e. IASC, FASB, ASB and the French CNC used in their reaction to the LTCM case a set of prudential accounting measures focusing on disclosure, especially of derivatives. This approach may partly be based on a common misperception, i.e. Hedge Funds are risk exposed because they take on extreme leverage and use derivatives to enhance their performance.

---

193 Cullen (2001), p.10.

194 France, as all countries, has a specialized set of laws defining accounting principles and procedures that require all companies to keep up a journal, a ledger and a balance-sheet book. Such laws are determined by the "Conseil National de la Comptabilitè" (CNC - National Accountancy Council) and are, on the whole, comparable to those in the U.S., though they tend to be more restrictive than in other countries in terms of methodological consistency. Companies have an obligation to maintain a journal, a ledger and a balance-sheet book. The first two must be kept on a monthly basis in accordance with the Chart of Accounts. The Chart of Accounts (Plan Comptable Gènèral) contains accounting definitions and principles which industrial and commercial firms must obey in the keeping of accounts. Computerized accounting systems are subject to specific regulations designed to facilitate checking procedures, particularly with regards to taxation procedures. French accounting principles are defined by the law (law of 30 April 1983 dealing with the financial statements of companies and the law of 3 January 1985 on consolidated financial statements), by decisions of the CNC and the recommendations of professional bodies. Fundamental principles such as the principle of prudence, operational continuity, impartiality and consistency of methods thus have a legal basis. The principle of methodological consistency is more restrictive in France than in other countries. In principle, accounting methods can only be changed if the company can demonstrate that the new method is more appropriate to its business. In practice, the only way the method can be changed is if the company's business changes, if errors need to be rectified or if exceptional circumstances arise.

From that perspective it is surely right to emphasize disclosure requirements in accountancy policy. In the real world, however, leverage has been decreased significantly[195] and derivatives only play a minor role in general investing and diversification strategy. Thus, one not too significant element in the conglomerate of problems surrounding Hedge Fund regulation may have been addressed, the aforementioned core issues, however, remain to be examined. Furthermore, by introducing these reactionary disclosure requirements the authorities insinuate that periodical disclosure of derivatives positions may minimize general risk exposure. Here the authorities take the wrong snap shot at Hedge Fund regulation. General risk exposure can only successfully be minimized by precautionary measures. Otherwise regulators will continually be forced to adjust their reactionary measures to an increasingly changing Hedge Fund environment. The Hedge Fund industry, on the other hand, can be expected to always be one step ahead in their reaction to regulatory measures, be it by running Hedge Funds from tax- and offshore havens or lobbying. This, in turn, bears significant transaction costs, which could be avoided. Market forces with the right incentive structure may be a preferable approach.

Moreover, the erroneous assumptions of the aforementioned authorities are exemplified when looking at the relationship between the effort and costs of regulation and expected regulatory attainments. The cost of implementing FAS 133, for instance, is estimated to range between US$500,000 to US$2,500,000,[196] the expected regulatory attainments like the fair value of on- and off-balance-sheet financial instruments, on the other hand, seem insignificant especially in the light of the fact that FAS 133 only precipitated Hedge Funds to treat off-balance-sheet transactions, i.e. derivatives, as on-balance sheet transactions. Even assuming that total derivative transactions of all U.S. Hedge Funds exceeded US$2,500,000, only a fraction of those transactions could possibly have a detrimental effect for a Hedge Fund's financial health. Hence, the fair value of on- and off-balance-sheet financial instruments does not counterbalance these costs.

III. *Rules and Regulation in Major Hedge Fund Jurisdictions*

Hedge Funds are generally structured to avoid the registration and regulatory conditions imposed on other types of investment vehicles, but must adhere to certain requirements to remain exempt from relevant legislation. For instance, neither Hedge Funds nor any of the Portfolio Funds are registered as investment companies under the U.S. Investment Company Act of 1940; most Portfolio Managers will not be registered as investment advisers under the U.S. Investment Advisers Act of 1940 or any comparable legislation; Hedge Funds can achieve ex-

---

195 See MAR report (2000).

196 FASB website: http://www.fasb.org/

emption from registration and prospectus delivery requirements of the U.S. Securities Act of 1933 through Regulation D, a non- exclusive safe harbor provided under section 4(2) of the U.S. Securities Act of 1933[197]; also, there are various exemptions under the U.S. Securities Exchange Act of 1934 to ensure that a general partner or partnership must not register with the SEC. Furthermore, sponsors of Hedge Funds that trade on organized futures exchanges and that have U.S. investors are required to register with the U.S. Commodity Futures Trading Commission (CFTC) as a Commodity Pool Operator (CPO)[198]. Registered CPOs are subject to periodic reporting, record-keeping and disclosure requirements. To avoid any requirements under these mentioned acts, Hedge Funds generally do not raise funds through public offerings, advertise broadly or engage in general solicitation. Consequently, shareholders may not have the benefit of the investor protection provisions of some of these statutes. Regulations could be imposed in the future on the operations of Hedge Funds or Portfolio Funds which adversely affect the ability of Hedge Funds to implement their strategies. It is uncertain in what respects future regulatory interpretations, in respect of United States or other jurisdictions, may require Hedge Funds to alter the manner in which they do business.

Here, the dissertation will explore the requirements for Hedge Funds to remain exempt from relevant legislation and their importance for the Hedge Fund Industry. Therefore, this section is broken down into three parts, which offer most relevant details of the regulatory constraints operating in the United States, United Kingdom and other jurisdictions.

1. Regulatory Provisions in the United States

A large proportion of the regulatory issues affecting Hedge Fund structure are related to US legislation. The term "Hedge Fund," is not defined or used in the U.S. federal securities laws but has come to mean a pooled investment vehicle[199] that is not registered under the federal securities laws as an investment company, a broker-dealer or a public corporation. The two main US governmental agencies under which Hedge Funds are subject to regulatory requirements are the Securi-

---

197 § 4 (2) of the 33 Act provides: "The provision of section 5 [Prohibition Relating to the Interstate Commerce and the Mails] shall not apply to - ... (2) transactions by an issuer not involving any public offering.".

198 A CPO is defined under the U.S. Commodity Exchange Act of 1974 (CEA) as a person who either directly or through capital contributions solicits, accepts or receives from other funds, securities or other property for the purpose of trading in commodity futures contracts or commodity option contracts- see further part Rules & Regulation.

199 I.e. and investment entity, such as a limited partnership, trust, corporation or similar form of enterprise operated for the purpose of trading securities or other investment instruments, and which is exempt from registration under the U.S. Investment Company Act of 1940.

ties Exchange Commission (SEC)[200] and the Commodity Futures Trading Commission (CFTC)[201], which may in turn be subject to guidelines issued by the Department of Labor (DOL). All Hedge Funds are indirectly regulated through transactions with counterparties and those funds structured as partnerships must also follow statutory and common law partnership principles to protect interests of the limited partners[202].

a) Securities Laws

The SEC is the main regulator administering federal securities laws, but it is estimated that between 60-70 per cent of Hedge Funds are exempt from regulation by the SEC[203]. The most important thing to keep in mind when establishing a domestic Hedge Fund is SEC registration requirements and structuring the fund to take advantage of exemptions. Registration of funds requires a large investment of both time and money given the rigorous regulatory provisions of the Acts and if a fund does not qualify for exemptions, sanctions can be very serious for failing to register under them.

---

200 The U.S. Congress established the Securities and Exchange Commission in 1934 to enforce the newly-passed securities laws (i.e. Congress passed the Securities Act of 1933 and the Securities Exchange Act of 1934. These laws were designed to restore investor confidence in the US capital markets by providing more structure and government oversight., to promote stability in the markets and, most importantly, to protect investors. With the Securities Act of 1934, however, Congress created the Securities and Exchange Commission. The Act empowers the SEC with broad authority over all aspects of the securities industry. This includes the power to register, regulate, and oversee brokerage firms, transfer agents, and clearing agencies as well as the nation's securities self regulatory organizations (SROs). The various stock exchanges, such as the New York Stock Exchange, and American Stock Exchange are SROs. The National Association of Securities Dealers, which operates the NASDAQ system, is also an SRO. The Act also identifies and prohibits certain types of conduct in the markets and provides the Commission with disciplinary powers over regulated entities and persons associated with them. The Act also empowers the SEC to require periodic reporting of information by companies with publicly traded securities) President Franklin Delano Roosevelt appointed Joseph P. Kennedy, President John F. Kennedy's father, to serve as the first Chairman of the SEC. The SEC is comprised of five Commissioners, who are appointed by the President, four Divisions, and 18 Offices. With approximately 2,900 staff, the SEC is small by federal agency standards. Headquartered in Washington, DC, the SEC has 11 regional and district Offices throughout the country.

201 The US CFTC was created by US Congress in 1974 as an independent agency with the mandate to regulate commodity futures and option markets in the United States. The agency protects market participants against manipulation, abusive trade practices and fraud. Through oversight and regulation, the CFTC is supposed to enable the markets to serve better their important functions in the US economy--providing a mechanism for price discovery and a means of offsetting price risk.

202 Press (2001), p.110.

203 See id. at 112.

The key statutory provisions common to Hedge Funds[204], which are enforced by the SEC are the Securities Act of 1933[205], the Securities Exchange Act of 1934[206], the Investment Company Act 1940[207] and the Investment Advisers Act of 1940[208] as well as the Commodity Exchange Act of 1974. The securities laws are in place to protect investors and prevent market place manipulation while both the Company and Advisers Acts are specifically used by the SEC to regulate Hedge Funds and prevent pool operators from taking advantage of investors[209]. Currently, SEC officials are discussing new rules that would force hedge funds to submit to regular examinations by the agency.[210] The SEC is also considering making hedge funds provide investors and regulators with more accurate and timely information about their operations, including their performance, leverage and holdings[211].

b) The Securities Act of 1933

If an offshore fund is to engage in a public offering of securities either in the US or to US investors it must comply with the registration and prospectus delivery requirements of the Securities Act. Hedge Funds tend to offer securities on a private placement basis in order to achieve exemption through Regulation D, a non-exclusive safe harbor provided under section 4(2) of the Securities Act. Section 4(2) essentially restricts the number and nature of offerees, prohibits public solicitation of investors and restricts the resale of such securities. However, section 4(2) has always been subject to a degree of uncertainty given that a precise definition of the 'private placement' exemption had not been provided under it through the various court decisions. In consequence, Regulation D[212] was released to establish non-exclusive safe harbor criteria from the requirements of the Securities Act[213]. In particular, rule 506 provides standards by which it can be deter-

---

204 Inclusive of sponsors and advisers

205 Hereinafter the 'Securities Act".

206 Revised 1996-hereinafter the 'Exchange Act'.

207 Hereinafter the 'Company Act'.

208 Hereinafter the 'Advisers Act'.

209 See Press (2001), p.110.

210 *See* 69 FR 72054, SEC Release No. IA-2333, File No. S7-3-04, RIN 3235-AJ25 – Rules and Regulations Securities and Exchange Commission, 17 C.F. R. Parts 275 and 279 (December 10, 2004) ("The Commission is adopting an new rule and rule amendments under the Investment Adviser Act of 1940. The new rule and amendments require advisers to certain private investment pools ("hedge funds") to register with the Commission under the Adviser Act. The rule and rule amendments are designed to provide the protections afforded by the Advisers Act to investors in Hedge fund, and to enhance the Commission's ability to protect our nation's securities markets.").

211 WSJ (2002).

212 I.e. 501 through to 508, 1933 Act Rules.

213 See Hazen (2002), p. 213.

mined when offers or sales of securities do not constitute a public offering and therefore qualify for exemption under section 4(2) of the Securities Act[214].

(1) Private Placement Exemption - Accredited Investors

Rule 506 in Regulation D is made for the sophisticated investor and was adopted by the SEC in 1982 to provide standards that parallel the requirements of the private offering exemption. It permits the sale of interests to an unlimited number of 'accredited investors' and limits the sale of such securities to 35 'non-accredited', but sophisticated investors[215]. Most private investment funds in the US will accept only accredited investors for practical business reasons and to avoid the necessity for particular information delivery and other requirements of Regulation D. While there is no limit to accredited investors under the Securities Act, section 3(c)(1) of the Investment Company Act of 1940 effectively limits investor numbers to 100[216]. In particular, under section 3 (c) (1) and 3(c) (7) of the Investment Company Act, hedge fund advisers were able to rely on the so-called "private investment adviser" exemption, if they have fewer than 14 clients in the preceding 12 months, whereby an investment fund counted as one client only.

Accredited investors as defined under Regulation D, at the time of investment, include[217] as:

- Any specified institutional investors[218].
- Any employee benefit plans within the meaning of Employee Retirement Income Security Act 1974 (ERISA), which have total assets in excess US$5 million or have a bank, savings and loan association, insurance company or registered investment adviser as the plan fiduciary or if it is a self directed plan in which investment decisions are made solely by persons who are accredited investors.
- Any corporation, partnership, limited liability company or foundations[219] with total assets in excess of US$5 million and not formed for the specific purpose of acquiring the securities offered and whose purchase is directed by a sophisticated person as defined in rule 506(b)(2)ii of the 33 Act.

214 See Van Grover (2001), p. 41.

215 Rule 506 (b) (2) (i) 1933 Act Rules.

216 Hazen (2002), p. 237.

217 Id at 240f.

218 I.e. banks, savings and loan associations, broker-dealers, insurance companies and investment companies.

219 And other entities exempt from federal taxes under section 501(c)(3).

- Any persons with a net worth[220] greater than US$1 million or an income of US$200,000, or US$300,000 joint income with a spouse in each of the preceding two years with a reasonable expectation of earning the same level of income in the current year.
- Any director, executive officer, or general partner of the issuer of the securities being offered or sold, or any person holding any of those positions in a general partner of the issuer.
- Any entity in which all the equity owners are accredited investors.

An issuer that sells securities to US purchasers who are not accredited investors must have reasonable belief that such persons have a sufficient knowledge and experience in financial and business matters to enable them to evaluate the risks of a prospective investment.

(2) Private Placement Exemption

While there is no dollar limit on the amount of money that can be raised, the second requirement for exemption from the Securities Act is that no issuer nor any person acting on its behalf may offer to sell the securities by means of any form of general solicitation or general advertising[221]. Regulation D does not specifically define the terms 'general solicitation' or 'general advertising' and thus SEC focus in analyzing these factors has been on the relationship between the one who makes the offer and those who receive the offer and the means of communication to the latter.

The securities must be privately placed, that is, the issuer - an offshore fund, its adviser, or respective affiliates or placement agents - must have a substantive relationship with the US offeree predating the particular transaction and the offering must not have been undertaken through general solicitation or public circulation, but personally directed to the offeree[222]. Essentially, the relationship should be such that it enables the issuer, or body acting for the issuer, to determine whether the investor is sophisticated and if the securities are suitable for them. Additionally, the relationship must be of a decent duration, such that the offer is not considered to have been made through general solicitation or advertising,

---

220 Or joint net worth with spouse.

221 17 C.F.R. § 230.502(c); Hazen (2002), p. 229.

222 Generally, the SEC has indicated that any "public advertising is inconsistent with a claim of private offering." - Non-Public offering Exemption Sec. Act. Rel. No. 33-4552, 1962 Wl 3573, 1. Fed. Sec. L. Rep. (CCH); 2781 (Nov. 6, 1962). Accord , e.g., Waterman v. Alta Verde Indus., Inc., 643 F. Supp. 797, 807 (E.D.N.C1986). Cf. Texas Capital Network, Inc., [19993-1994 Transfer Binder] Fed. Sec. L. Rep (CCH); 76,857 (SEC No Action Letter Feb. 23, 1994) (non-profit corporation`s matching of business ventures with potential investors did not constitute a general solicitation).

which includes mass mailing, cold calling and advertising in any medium, such as print, television, radio or the internet[223]. General solicitation or general advertising also includes sponsoring seminars or conferences where attendees have been invited through such means and where offshore funds are discussed as part of the conference content.

(3) Disclosure Requirements

An issuer appealing for exemption from section 4(2) or Regulation D must provide investors with all material information concerning the securities and ensure that these do not contain materially false or misleading statements[224]. An offering document is not required under Regulation D if an offering is made solely to US persons who are accredited investors, but it is highly recommended that one be provided due to fact that the anti-fraud provisions of the US securities laws still apply[225]. A private placement memorandum, if properly drafted, can be used as a marketing document for the fund and from a legal viewpoint, can also provide the general partner with protection against 'failure to disclose' claims. Disclosure materials issued to non-accredited US investors must parallel the standards required for a registered offering in the US.

(4) Resale Restrictions

In a Regulation D private placement in the US, securities acquired cannot be resold by the investor unless this follows registration of the entity under the Securities Act or follows exemption from such registration. To ensure the private placement exemption of an offshore fund is not threatened, an offshore fund must take steps to assure that purchasers of its securities understand resale restrictions under Federal securities law and therefore do not purchase the securities with the aim of transferring them to the public[226]. The subscription agreement contains an outline of resale restrictions to which investors must comply[227].

---

223 Hazen (2002), p. 231.

224 17 C.F.R. § 230.502(c) provides in detail: "The information contained in any reports or documents required to be filed by the issuer under sections 13(a), 14(a), 14(c), and 15(d) of the Exchange Act since the distribution or filing of the report or registration statement specified in paragraph (b)(2)(ii)(A) or (B), and a brief description of the securities being offered, the use of the proceeds from the offering, and any material changes in the issuer's affairs that are not disclosed in the documents furnished.".

225 Hazen (2002), p. 241 – adding that: "Accordingly, the failure to deliver an offering memorandum to accredited investors will not destroy the safe harbour exemption".

226 Van Grover, (2001), p. 43.

227 Id.

(5) Private Placement and Offshore Public Offerings

An offshore fund can sell securities to non-US investors in non-private placement transactions alongside private offerings to US investors provided these offerings do not integrate and thereby violate the private placement exemption under rule 506 or section 4(2) of the Securities Act. Integration will not occur if the non-US offering complies with Regulation S under the Securities Act, which requires that an offshore fund does not have a substantial US market interest, the offers and sales are made in offshore transactions and that there are no directed selling efforts in the US[228].

(6) State Legislation - Blue Sky Requirements

A Hedge Fund being distributed in any particular state must meet certain requirements as set out in statutes referred to as 'Blue Sky' law[229] and the filings associated with the law are similarly referred to as Blue Sky filings[230]. If a filing is necessary it is usually required within 15 days from the date of the first sale in that state, however there are exceptions. There are exemptions from Blue Sky registration and qualification requirements for issuers relying on rule 506 under section 18 of the Securities Act, although state notice and fee requirements would still apply, which would remove the need for a Hedge Fund to submit a filing to a particular state. While state authorities are still permitted to investigate fraud, section 18 prohibits individual states from regulating the substance of offering documents and the conditions on securities that are part of offerings.

c) Securities Exchange Act of 1934

The Exchange Act requires that a Hedge Fund determine whether the general partner or partnership is required to register as a securities broker or dealer[231]. Broker-dealers must register with the SEC if they are either physically located in the United States or if, no matter where they are situated, they effect, induce or attempt to induce securities transactions with investors in the United States.

---

228 Id. (adding that: "private placement activities in the US are not considered as directed selling efforts.").

229 Blue Sky Laws are state statutes that regulate the sale of securities to the public within the state. Most blue-sky laws require the registration of new issues of securities with a state agency that reviews selling documents for accuracy and completeness. Blue-sky laws also may regulate securities brokers and salesmen. A federal statute enacted in 1995, the National Securities Markets Improvement Act, pre-empts a significant portion of blue sky law regulation.

230 Van Grover (2001), p. 44.

231 Hazen (2002), pp. 411f; See also Sections 12 and 15 Securities Exchange Act 1934.

(1) Brokers-Dealers and the Issuer Exemption

Investment partnerships, in general, do not practice the actions of a broker or dealer to a large enough extent to qualify for registration[232] as either one, but as this is not always the case each situation must still be assessed to determine the necessity.

A broker under the Exchange Act[233] is any person engaged in the business of carrying out transactions in securities for the account of others. In most cases Hedge Funds will trade for their own account rather than effecting transactions for other parties and hence will not need to undergo broker registration.

A dealer is defined under the Exchange Act[234] as 'any person engaged in the business of buying and selling securities for his own account, through a broker or otherwise, but does include a bank or any person insofar as he buys or sells securities for his own account, either individually or in some fiduciary capacity, but not as part of a regular business.'

The SEC has identified through a series of no-action letters[235] a number of situations that encapsulate the actions of a dealer, such as acting as an underwriter or taking part in a selling group in any distribution of securities, quoting a market in any security, advertising or holding out to the public as a dealer or willing to buy or sell any security on a continuous basis[236]. A Hedge Fund will not have to undergo dealer registration provided its personnel do not practice any of these actions to an extent that they will qualify as dealers under the Exchange Act definition.

(2) The Agent Exemption

An offshore fund's officers or directors, owners or employees of the investment manager to the offshore fund and independent solicitors who sell securities of the offshore fund to US persons may be subject to registration as brokers in the US. A sponsoring investment manager and its employees can avoid broker-dealer registration by using a placement agent that is already registered as a broker-dealer[237]. An independent solicitor would normally be required to register if engaged by a Hedge Fund to place interests in it. However, a partner or employee

---

232 See on general Registration Requirements of the Securities Exchange Act 1934 – Hazen (2002), pp. 411f.

233 Section 3(a)(4) Securities Exchange Act 1934.

234 Section 3(a)(5) Securities Exchange Act 1934.

235 E.g. SEC No-Action letter – Davenport Management, Inc. (publ. avail. April 13, 1993) ("Davenport"); Letter from Charles M Horn, SEC Division of Market Regulation, to David R. Burton, President Burton Securities, 5th December 1977.

236 See Roth (1995), p.150.

237 See Van Grover (2001), p. 44.

whose key role is to raise money from investors may claim exclusion from the definition of broker if they are 'associated persons' under rule 3(a)(4)-1 of the Exchange Act. This rule outlines provisions specifying associated persons of an issuer of securities who will be exempt from registration as brokers provided that they do not receive payment of commissions or other compensation based either directly or indirectly on transactions in securities, are not associated persons of any broker or dealer and are not subject to statutory disqualification for prior acts as set forth in section 3(a)(39).

An associated person's activities must meet one of the following requirements under the rule's safe harbor:

- The sale of securities of the offshore fund must be restricted to registered broker-dealers, registered investment companies, insurance companies, banks, trust companies or registered advisers with investment discretion given in writing or who are acting as trustees.
- The sales of offerings of securities for an issuer must be sporadic and not occur more than once every 12 months; the person must have other substantial duties with or for the issuer except in association with transactions in securities; and no association with a broker dealer for the preceding 12 months, or
- Activities must be restricted to particular ministerial and clerical work involved in carrying out transactions.

Under rule 15(a)(6) of the Securities Act, the SEC will exempt foreign investment managers and other associated personnel that effect transactions with US customers from registering as broker-dealers if their US customers initiated transactions outside the US without solicitation. Foreign broker-dealers that solicit transactions with US persons are required to register as broker-dealers in the US unless a US registered broker-dealer is used in conjunction with solicitation, subject to additional restrictions and conditions[238].

(3) The Finder Exemption

An intermediary that places securities of an issuer may on very limited occasions escape broker registration as a 'finder', that is, a person not engaged in the business of effecting securities transactions. The exemption looks at how frequently a person acts as intermediary in securities transactions, their degree of involvement in the transactions, their receipt of transaction-based compensation and their contact with outside investors[239].

---

238 See id. at 45.

239 See id.

(4) Registration

If registration as a broker-dealer is required there are a number of SEC regulations and fiduciary and disclosure rules to be met under section 15(a)(1) of the Exchange Act and other self-regulatory organizations. The requirements under section 15(a)(1) include a minimum net capital, financial reporting, the filing of financial statements and Form B-D, the retention of specific records, and client confirmation and reporting. A registered broker-dealer must also become a member of a self-regulatory organization, such as the US National Association of Securities Dealers (NASD). Additionally, a registered broker-dealer must register with the state securities authorities in all of the states connected by a fund's offer or sale of securities, that is, the states from which offers or sales are made/received.

As previously mentioned, an offshore fund could avoid registration by engaging a US registered broker-dealer in connection with its offering of securities to US persons, but even in such a case it is necessary for a fund to monitor the activities of its personnel to ensure the fund does not risk losing the exemption from broker-dealer registration under the Securities Act.

(5) Soft Dollaring

Soft dollar fees are a means of paying brokerage firms for their products or services through commission revenue rather than direct payments. The SEC defines the practice as arrangements under which all products or services, with the exception of the execution of securities transactions, are obtained by an adviser from or through a broker-dealer in exchange for the direction of client brokerage transactions by the adviser to the broker-dealer. Section 28(e) of the Exchange Act is a safe harbor, which allows an investment adviser to use client commissions to purchase research from a broker-dealer on the premise that the arrangement is disclosed to clients.

d) Investment Company Act 1940

Hedge Fund operators are exempt from the provisions of the Company Act if they can stay outside the statutory meaning of an 'investment company', which is subject to registration[240]. The definition of an investment company is contained

---

[240] See Lybecker, Goldfus & Mackey (1980) (elaborating that: "The Act's great detail and prima facie inflexibility might have proved particularly problematic in light of the many innovations in the industry for which provisions had not been made in the Act. However, Congress chose to temper the Act's inflexibility through the broad exemptive powers it granted the Commission. Through the exemption process interested persons have been permitted to modify the Act's restrictions to suit their own circumstances. Over the years, the exemption process has loomed as an in-

in section 3(a)(1) of the Company Act, that is, 'is or holds itself out as being engaged primarily, or proposes to engage primarily, in the business of investing, reinvesting, or trading in securities'. Additionally, under section 3(a)(3) a fund will be classified as an investment company if it engages in the business of investing, reinvesting, owning, holding or trading securities and if it owns or intends to acquire investment securities exceeding 40 per cent of its total assets.

Given the restrictions placed on investment companies, a private investment partnership should attempt to come under the 'private' investment exclusion. Basically, exemption from this Act is based on definition and the most common exclusions from this definition are through satisfying the requirements of section 3(c)(1), the 100 or less beneficial owner exemption and section 3(c)(7), the qualified purchaser exemption[241].

(1) Section 3(c) (1) Exemption

In order to fall outside the definition of an investment company and thus gain exemption under section 3(c) (1) a fund must not have more than 100 beneficial owners, nor must a fund engage in a public offering of its shares in the US[242].

An issuer must continuously monitor the number of beneficial owners to ensure it does not exceed the 100 investor limit and thus forfeit the exemption. Each US person that has a beneficial interest, either directly as a shareholder or indirectly as a participant in particular profit sharing with a partner is counted in the 100 investor's total. The general partner or investment manager will not be counted in this total because they have no securities interest. With respect to an offshore fund there are no restrictions on the number of non-US investors permitted to invest in because this SEC rule applies only to US investors.

While US shareholders in a corporation or other partnerships are usually counted as single beneficial owners there may be additional restrictions if a Hedge Fund itself invests in Hedge Funds. The process is not always a straightforward one when determining if an entity investor should be counted as a single beneficial owner for the 100 investor test or if it should be looked-through and each partner or holder of securities of the entity investor be counted as beneficial owners of interests in the investment partnership. A two part test is used to determine if it should be looked-through. The first part is ongoing and involves determining whether the entity investor owns 10 per cent or more of the outstanding voting securities of the issuer. In general, each entity investor that holds more than 10 per

---

creasingly major avenue for addressing problems in regulating investment companies [. . .] [M]any people argue that the [complex and expensive] application process has encouraged 'regulation by exemption' in which the scope and complexity of certain exemptions have begun to eclipse the Act itself in importance.").

241 See Hazen (2002), p. 930.

242 See id.

cent will be counted as a single US beneficial owner of the fund if its interests are not deemed to be voting securities[243].

If limited partnership interests are reckoned as voting securities, a look-through is generally only required if a second condition is met. To avoid being considered more than a single beneficial owner the entity investor must satisfy the condition that it does not invest more than 10 per cent of the entity investor's assets in funds that are themselves reliant on section 3(c)(1) for exclusion from the definition of an investment company. For example, if a fund of funds limited partnership interest exceeds ten per cent of a fund's capital the fund may be subject to the look-through rules in which case the partnership will be required to count each of the investors in the fund of funds as if they were individual investors in the partnership[244]. Limited partnership interests in an investment partnership may not technically be voting securities, but it is the policy of the SEC to treat limited partnership interests as voting securities where an entity investor acquiring more than 10 per cent of the interests in a limited partnership also depends upon an exclusion from the definition of an investment company[245]. This condition was implemented by the SEC to allow investments that do not constitute a significant portion of an entity investor's assets to be made in private funds without being subject to look-through. It is assessed only at the time when an entity investor makes each investment.

There is actually another provision for look-through to be avoided and it is that an entity investor cannot have been created specifically to invest in a fund nor use the fund to avoid the 100 beneficial owner restrictions. The entity investor is not permitted to opt in and out of particular investments given section 48(a) of the Company Act, which prohibits anything done indirectly that cannot be done directly[246].

Security-holders of the entity investor will be counted as part of the 100 beneficial owner total when a look-through is required; however there are certain classes of investors who will not be considered as security-holders for the purpose of the 100 investor limit. Some examples include those interests in an involuntary or non-contributory employee benefit plan. The beneficiaries of such plans do not make any investment decisions and therefore cannot be deemed security-holders. Similarly, charities, foundations and academic institutions are also not deemed security-holders, which allow them to acquire more than 10 per cent of interests in a Hedge Fund.

---

243 See Roth (1995), p. 156.

244 See Press (1995), p. 204.

245 See Weiss, Peck, & Greer Venture Associates II, LP, SEC No-Action Letter - pub. avail. Apr. 10, 1990; Roth (1995), p. 156.

246 See Van Grover (2001), p. 47.

If an investment manager desires to create more than one fund there are certain circumstances where the SEC may call for the separate funds to be integrated, treated as one and forced to comply with the 100 or fewer beneficial owner's requirement. Integration will be necessary if an investor qualified to invest in both funds views the funds as being similar in economic terms, the analysis of which is based upon the differences in investment objectives, portfolio holdings and risk/return characteristics[247]. The exclusions to this analysis, which will not need to be integrated are two funds structured to cater for the needs of different types of investors although they may possess similar investment objectives. Essentially, the different tax treatments for different investor types creates a significantly different investment for US taxable, US tax-exempt and non-US investors. Additionally, if appropriately structured, it is not expected that a domestic partnership with US investors and a parallel non-US fund with non-US investors will have to integrate due to tax differences despite the fact that they share the same investment adviser.

The restrictions associated with failing to meet the classifications of the Company Act makes it important for a fund to keep an accurate count of investor types to stay within the specified limits.

(2) Section 3(c) (7) Exemption

In this section a fund will be exempt from registration as an investment company provided all investments[248] and, thus, all investors in the fund are "qualified purchasers"[249] and that the fund does not engage in a public offering of its

---

[247] See id.

[248] Investments by definition include securities publicly traded and listed on a US national securities exchange or traded on NASDAQ; shares in registered investment companies such as mutual funds and money market funds; interests in private investment companies such as Hedge Funds, commodity pools and similar private investment companies; cash and cash equivalents held for investment purposes; real estate held for investment purposes; shares of non-public companies, which have total shareholder equity of US$50 million or more; commodity interest, including commodity futures contracts and options thereon, swaps and other financial contracts; investment held jointly with the subscriber's spouse; investments held in any IRA, 401(k) or similar retirement account directed by the subscriber and held for the subscriber's benefit; and investments that exclude the principal amount of any outstanding debt, including margin loans, incurred by the subscriber to acquire for the purpose of acquiring the investment. Investments should be valued at either their fair market price as of most recent practicable date or cost.

[249] The term 'qualified purchaser' refers to: Any individual who owns at least US$5 million in, -Any family-owned company that owns at least US$5 million in investments, -Any trust not created for the specific purpose of acquiring the securities being offered provided the trustee or other person with the authority to make decisions with respect to the trust and other persons who contributed assets to the trust is a qualified purchaser, -Any person who has capital to invest of no less than US$25 million, -Knowledgeable employees of an offshore fund and its investment manager, -Transferees of qualified purchasers if the transferees received their interests from the qualified

interests in the US. This section is a relatively recent addition to the Act - in 1996, the National Securities Markets Improvement Act increased the number of investors allowed from 100 to 500, provided that all investors accepted by a fund post September 1996, met the qualified purchaser requirement[250].

The Company Act does not limit the number of qualified purchasers that may participate in a fund. In fact, offshore funds applying for this exemption need only have reasonable belief that all of its US shareholders are qualified purchasers. This criterion does not apply to non-US investors who are not required to be qualified investors.

The additional requirement for obtaining exemption from the Company Act through 3(c)(1) and 3(c)(7) is in section 7(d) where a fund must be a private investment vehicle, that is, must not be, or planning to make, a public offering of shares in the US. Thus, even if a fund has less than 100 beneficial owners who are all qualified investors the fund must register under the Company Act if it has plans to make, or has made a public offering.

This public versus private offering is also part of the principles of the Securities Act. While assessing the financial components of whether a fund qualifies for exemption is objective, it is totally subjective whether a fund qualifies for private placement under either the Company Act or the Securities Act. In general, however, if a fund does not qualify for private placement exemption under the Securities Act then it is unlikely that it will qualify for exemption under the Company Act[251].

The limitations created by the Company Act, particularly the restriction to 100 US investors, have implications for fund managers[252] establishing both an offshore corporation and US limited partnership in terms of the most appropriate structure by which they should be managed. If the funds are operated side by side it is important to ensure that US tax-exempt investors are limited to the offshore fund and US taxable investors to the US limited partnership with no overlap. If US taxable investors are allowed to participate in the offshore fund, the 100 beneficial investor limit will apply to total US investors as aggregated across both funds rather than for each fund independently. If the limited partnership and offshore corporation are established as feeder funds it will also be necessary to aggregate all US investors across both funds to satisfy the 100 limit, but this is irrespective of whether there are US taxable investors invested in the offshore fund. Similar requirements exist if one of the feeder funds restricts US investors to qualified purchasers and the other does not although in this case the aggregate

---

purchaser either as a gift, bequest, result of separation, divorce, death or any other unforeseen event, -Any organisation if each beneficial owner of the company's securities is a qualified purchaser

250 See Hazen (2002), p. 930.

251 See id. at 935.

252 See Van Grover (2001), p. 47.

limit of 100 applies and the advantage from having an unlimited number of US investors as qualified purchasers in a company is lost[253].

(3) Registration

Registration under the Company Act involves a number of rigorous constraints in terms of arduous reporting requirements and restrictive trading and finance rules that are essentially inconsistent with Hedge Fund operation. For example, funds registered as investment companies under the Company Act must have a board of directors with a minimum number of disinterested directors, which must approve the investment advisory contract, custodial arrangements and other matters that affect the fund's operations. Particular associated transactions would be restricted by statute, which might, however be permitted with disclosure and consent with unregistered funds. Other examples of the requirements include distributions to equity owners each year, investment diversification rules, a minimum amount of initial seed capital and a maximum usage placed on liquidity and leverage, which would effectively limit short sales, futures, forwards and margin transactions.

e) Investment Advisers Act of 1940

Section 202(a)(11) of the Advisers Act of 1940[254] defines an investment adviser as any person 'who, for compensation, engages in the business of advising others...as to the advisability of investing in, purchasing or selling securities...'. This definition, however, excludes certain banks, accountants, lawyers, broker-dealers, publishers and others that have no direct or incidental involvement with the provision of investment advice. Some advisers run their own funds while others act as advisors to Hedge Fund investors and provide recommendations for particular funds[255].

(1) The Adviser Exemption

The section most commonly relied on for exemption from SEC registration as an investment adviser is under section 203(b)(3) of the Advisers Act. Within this section an adviser is exempt if it has had less than 15 clients in the past 12 months, if it does not 'hold out' to the public, that is, does not offer investment

253 See Cullen (2001), p. 8.

254 Amended 1996.

255 In the case of the latter type of adviser, it is important to ensure that the adviser is paid only by clients and not by funds so that the potential for a conflict of interest is removed.

advisory services to the general public, nor act as investment adviser to a registered investment company or business development company.

In calculating the number of clients a US fund manager has, both their US and non-US clients must be taken into account. Non-US fund managers need only count their US clients. Under rule 203(b)(3)-1 a limited partnership itself may be counted as a single client of the general partner or any other person acting as the investment adviser, provided investment advice to the partnership is based on the partnership's objectives rather than on the needs and objectives of the limited partners. This rule also applies to an offshore fund in the corporate form, which may in general be treated as one client by an adviser.

An adviser participating in a private placement of limited partnership interests will be classified as holding itself out to the public and therefore be subject to registration if it advertises its offer of investment advisory services, uses letterhead or business cards to indicate such interests, or even uses telephone listings. Similarly, a private investment adviser may still be called on to register with the SEC if it is affiliated with a registered investment adviser and cannot prove it is a separate entity. Sufficient proof for a private adviser as a distinct entity can be achieved through satisfying certain SEC requirements, which include adequate capitalization of the private adviser, a governing body with members independent of the registered adviser and employees behind investment advice that have no involvement in the registered advisers investment management business. Additionally, a private manager must make its own investment decisions using information provided by sources that are not limited to the registered adviser and the advice should be kept confidential until such time that clients are briefed. Foreign affiliates of US registered advisers are not subject to the same level of restriction as there is no requirement for the investment staff to be independent[256].

(2) Registration

To register under the Advisers Act, an investment adviser must file an application on Form ADV with the SEC and keep the information current by updating around once a year. Form ADV must include details on the investment adviser's owners and business practices, such as types of accounts, affiliate relationships, solicitation arrangements and the extent of their authority over client's funds and accounts. It must also give an account of the investment adviser's personnel including information on their background, such as their disciplinary history.

Registration will involve a number of requirements including the need for extensive record keeping under rule 204(2) whereby books and records must, in general, be kept in an office of the adviser for two years and in an accessible place

---

256 See Uniao de Bancos de Brasileiros AA, SEC No-Action Letter; Van Grover (2001), p.50.

for three years after this period. Additionally, organizational documents linked to the business of a registered adviser must be held in the main office of the adviser and preserved for three years after termination of the adviser's business. Rule 204-2(a)(10) requires a registered adviser to keep a copy of all written agreements entered into by the adviser with any client or otherwise relating to the business of the adviser.

Other restrictions include sporadic SEC examinations, restrictions on the payment of referral fees[257] and the filing, updating and delivery of a written disclosure statement to each advisory, or prospective advisory client[258]. This latter requirement for a disclosure statement may be either a copy of Part II of the adviser's Form ADV or a written document that includes the information listed in Part II of the Form ADV and it should be delivered to each prospective investor. While an adviser must deliver a written disclosure statement to each prospective investor prior to entering into an advisory contract it must additionally deliver or at least offer in writing to deliver its written disclosure statement to each advisory client no less than annually[259].

Registered investment advisers are also generally prohibited from receiving payment of performance fees under section 205(a). In this section a registered investment adviser is not permitted to enter into an investment advisory contract where compensation is based on a portion of either the capital gains or capital appreciation of the funds of a client. There are exemptions from this restriction provided in rule 205(b) (5) which permits the receipt of performance fee compensation from a non-resident of the US and rule 205-3 whereby investment advisers may receive the payment of performance fees from an 'eligible investor'. An eligible investor is any person or company with a net worth of over US$1.5 million who invests US$750,000 or more with the adviser or persons who are qualified purchasers as defined in the Company Act.

Rule 205-3 also contains a number of other requirements with regard to performance compensation. Firstly, the performance compensation must be calculated based upon the performance of the client's account over a minimum period of 12 months. Both realized and unrealized capital losses over the period for securities with readily available market quotations are required in the calculation, or just realized capital losses of the securities over the period if market quotations are not readily available. If an entity investor is registered as an investment company under the Company Act, or would be defined as an investment company bar qualifying for the exclusion from section 3(c)(1) of that Act, rule 205-3 of the Advisers Act requires that each beneficial owner of the entity be an eligible investor as defined above. Additionally, for rule 205-3, mandatory disclosure is re-

257 Rule 206(4)-3.

258 Rule 204-3.

259 See Roth (1995), p. 160.

quired on a number of factors, such as how a performance based fee may encourage an adviser to make more risky investments than would normally be the case; the period over which investment performance will be measured throughout the contract and how important it is in the calculation of the fee; details on any index used as a comparative measure of performance and why it is considered appropriate; and in the case where investment adviser compensation is based partly on the unrealized appreciation of securities for which market quotations are not readily available, an adviser must state how the securities will be valued and to what degree the valuation will be independently determined[260].

Additionally, as long as particular procedures are followed, it is generally possible for a non-US adviser registered under the Adviser Act to apply the laws of its home jurisdiction to its non-US investors[261].

Registered advisers' use of solicitors is regulated by rule 206(4)-3 including the payment of cash fees to such solicitors with regard to their solicitation activities in an effort to highlight the amount paid for solicitation activities and thus indicate if there is any conflict of interest. In determining the suitability of an investor the subscription document is particularly important under this Act as it allows the fund manager to determine if an investor is appropriate for the fund.

(3) State Law

The provision of investment advice to US persons also calls for compliance with laws of the states where advisers do business. However, there is a provision in section 203A(b)(1)(A) of the Advisers Act which dictates that advisers under the Advisers Act will not be subject to state laws that require registration, licensing and qualification of investment advisers. Also, section 222(d) of the Advisers Act will only allow states to impose regulation, licensing or qualification requirements on advisers if they have a place of business in the state or if the adviser has more than five clients resident in that state.

Performance compensation fees for both registered and unregistered investment advisers are subject to state regulatory and statutory provisions, which tend to vary from state to state. Generally the acceptance of performance compensation is permitted on satisfying conditions based on the eligible client criteria for all investors in the entity in question. A number of states prohibit investment advisers from accepting performance fees by statute or regulation as a fraudulent practice. Other states qualify their restrictions on the acceptance of performance fees through regulation or statute, but this generally brings state law into line with rule 205-3 of the Advisers Act through containing some reference to the rule.

---

260 See id. at 162.

261 See Van Grover (2001), p. 49.

f) The Commodity Exchange Act of 1974

Funds that invest in and trade commodities will be classified as 'commodity pools' and the commodity pool operators (CPO) and commodity trading advisers (CTA) will be subject to registration under the Commodity Exchange Act of 1974 (CEA).

According to the CEA, a commodity[262] includes goods and articles and all services, rights and interests in which contracts for future delivery are dealt in, in the present or the future[263]. The Commodities Futures Trading Commission (CFTC) regulates any transaction in, or contract for the purchase or sale of a commodity for future delivery with the exception of certain exemptions listed in the CEA including hybrid instruments, swap and forward transactions[264] and exchange-trading requirements for transactions involving foreign currencies[265].

A CPO is defined under the Act as a person who either directly or through capital contributions solicits, accepts or receives from other funds, securities or other property for the purpose of trading in commodity futures contracts or commodity option contracts. No matter how small or infrequent such transactions by an investment fund may be, the fund will still be classified in the eyes of CFTC as a commodity pool and the manager/sponsor of the fund a CPO. Any person who solicits funds or supervises soliciting for a commodity pool must register as an associated person of the CPO unless they are already registered in an assured capacity in which case they will be exempt from this Act.

Operators and advisers of offshore funds, unless exempt, must register with the CEA if they trade commodity interests on either US futures exchanges or non-US futures exchanges that function from inside the US.

(1) Exemptions

A CPO is exempt from registration under the Adviser Act through Section 4.13 if either the CPO receives no compensation and manages only one commodity pool, or if the total gross capital contributions to all commodity pools for which it operates is less than US$200,000 and there are no more than 15 participants in any one commodity pool. Section 4m of the CEA, provides an exemption

---

262 A commodity is generally, an article of commerce or a product that can e used for commerce. In the U.S. the term is often narrowly used to refer to financial products underlying futures contracts traded on regulated futures exchanges. The types of "commodities" that underlie such contracts include both physical and financial commodities such as agricultural and energy products, metals, foreign currencies, and interest rate and equity instruments. Commodities are also traded in the forward or cash markets.

263 7 U.S.C. 4; Van Grover (2001), p.51.

264 Section 4(c).

265 Section 2(a)(1)(A).

from registration as a CTA if it has 15 or fewer clients in any 12 month period and does not hold itself out to the public as a commodity trading adviser. CTAs who only provide commodity trading advice to commodity pools will also be exempt from registering as CTAs if they are already registered as CPOs or exempt from registering as CPOs under rule 17 Code of Federal Regulation (CFR) section 4.14, which provides exemption for a broad group of investment advisers[266].

Non-US CPOs of offshore funds can find exemption from registration through CFTC rule 30.4 provided their commodity trading activities are restricted to non-US futures exchanges; US investors comprise less than 10 per cent of the offshore fund's participants; and less than 10 per cent of the fund's assets are held by or on behalf of US investors. Of course, the offering of the offshore fund to US investors must also comply with exemption requirements of both the Securities Act and Company Act.

Both non-US CPOs and CTAs of offshore funds will be exempt from registration through CFTC rule 30.5 if their commodity trading activities are restricted to non-US futures exchanges and all trades in non-US commodity interest contracts are taken through qualifying futures commissions merchants (FCMs)[267]. There are a number of conditions to satisfy in order for the exemptions to carry through. Both the CPO and CTA must appoint either a US FCM or US broker-dealer through a written agreement with the designated entity as their agent for service of process in legal proceedings in the US. The agreement must contain a list of all FCMs through which the transactions in non-US commodity interest contracts will be effected and the FCM must carry the offshore funds account on a fully disclosed basis. A copy of the agreement must be forwarded to the National Futures Association (NFA) by the agent.

Those CPOs and CTAs who are exempt from registration under the CEA will still be subject to the anti-fraud provisions of the Act. The CFTC or aggrieved investors are able to take action if antifraud provisions are violated by the activities of a fund, for example, through insufficient disclosure of the range of a fund's commodities trading activity. Additionally, while exempt they are still required to supply each pool participant with a copy of the monthly statement for the pool received from a FCM and a supplemental statement, if necessary, clearly showing the net profit or loss of all commodity interests closed since the last monthly statement.

(2) Limited Relief

There are two CFTC rules that allow registered CPOs and CTAs limited relief from the CEA provisions on disclosure reporting and record keeping. Rules

266 See Van Grover (2001), p.51.

267 See id.

4.12 and 4.7 generally provide relief, but not exemption from registration unless claims to the rules are filed before the solicitation of investors take place.

Filing a claim of exemption with the CFTC under rule 4.12 offers a registered CPO limited relief from the certain disclosure, reporting and record keeping restrictions subject to satisfying conditions that essentially require commodity trading be incidental to securities trading. These conditions include the offering and sale of interests pursuant to registration with, or exemption from registration under the applicable securities regulations. A pool must generally and routinely trade in securities, commit no more than 10 per cent of the fund's assets as initial margins or premiums for commodity interest trading and trade commodity interests in a manner incidental to its securities trading activities. Relief under rule 4.12 removes some disclosure requirements applicable to a pool, but a pool must still provide an offering memorandum to investors, pre-cleared with the CFTC, containing many of the disclosure requirements mentioned above. Similarly, financial statements must still be filed with the CFTC and NFA, however there is less information required in the financial statements and annual report than would be the case for a normal commodity pool.

A registered CPO can avoid the bulk of the disclosure required under the CEA by restricting US investors to 'qualified eligible persons' (QEP) as defined in the Act under rule 4.7. A qualified eligible person is generally an accredited investor under Regulation D of the Securities Act and an investor who owns and controls in his own account at least US$2 million in securities or other investment assets or alternatively has deposited at least US$200,000 initial margin and option premiums with a futures commission merchant for commodity interest trading. For rule 4.7, persons comparable to accredited investors include certain investment companies, banks, insurance companies, employee benefit plans, tax-exempt organizations, private business development companies, corporations, partnerships[268] and high-net worth individuals. Qualified eligible persons also generally include registered FCMs, registered broker-dealers, registered CPOs managing pools with greater than US$5 million in assets, registered CTAs managing commodity accounts with greater than US$5 million in assets and both the CPO and CTA of the pool being offered. Finally, QEPs under this rule also include entities in which all of the equity owners are QEPs and non-US persons as defined in the rule.

Rule 4.7 provides more extensive relief than 4.12 in that there is no limit on commodity interests to hold to and the investments in commodities need not be incidental. The main benefit, however, if the requirements for rule 4.7 are met and a claim is filed with the CFTC for exemption, is that the CPO is exempt from providing a disclosure document to pool participants or having to file a CEA disclosure document with the CFTC or NFA. However, the offering memorandum must

---

268 All with total assets exceeding US$5 million.

be used in conjunction with the offering, which apart from containing all necessary disclosure to prevent the information from being misleading must also contain a prominent statement on its front cover indicating the pool is operating under rule 4.7 exemption.

Unless they qualify for an exemption, it will always be necessary for a non-US pool that sells shares to US investors to register as a CPO. It will, however, be possible for such a registered CPO to also gain some relief from compliance issues associated with US investors under the terms of the provisions of the CFTC Advisory Opinion 18-96. Offshore funds that are commodity pools, which have no US investors and that do not carry out any marketing activity that might solicit investments from US persons may also find relief in the CFTC Advisory Opinion 18-96. Through this they can file a claim with the CFTC and NFA for relief from a portion of the requirements generally imposed on CPOs in the way of record keeping, reporting and disclosure. An operator of an offshore fund that has no US connection in terms of investors, directors and sources, but purchases commodities on US commodity exchanges through US FCMs should not be subject to registration as a CPO.

(3) Registration

Registration under the Commodity Exchange Act means that CPOs and CTAs must adhere to various requirements, one of which is the provision of a written disclosure document to prospective investors on the investment risks in each commodity pool. The disclosure document must contain detailed information on a number of issues including the CPO and its principals, CTAs, FCMs and introducing brokers; commodity interests to be traded; a record of performance of the CPO and principals; conflicts of interest; minimum investments; expenses; restrictions on redemption and transferability; and risk. The disclosure document must be filed with both the CFTA and NFA and the CPO must receive written acknowledgement from each participant confirming receipt of the document prior to accepting a contribution from that participant.

Other registration requirements include the avoidance of conflicts of interest and protection of customer funds, advertising restrictions within the applicable NFA compliance guidelines and reporting and record-keeping requirements. Upon registration with the CFTC, both CPOs and CTAs are required to become member firms of the NFA, the nominated self regulatory organization of the CFTC, which will undertake sporadic inspections of registered CPOs. The Hedge Fund must also keep particular books and records located at their main office that are to be made available for inspection upon request by the CFTC[269].

---

269 17 C.F.R. 4.23.

The CFTA also imposes position limits on the maximum net long and net short positions that any one person may hold or control in each commodity futures contract and each put and call option on futures traded on the exchange, however these contract market limits do not apply to genuine hedging positions defined in CFTC rule 1.3.

g) Hot Issue Securities

The US National Association of Securities Dealers has stringent rules regarding investing in newly issued securities that immediately trade at a premium to their initial public offering price in the secondary market following public distribution. These securities are known as hot issue securities and they create a US regulatory issue that has an impact on the structuring of offshore funds. Essentially, the gains and losses from trading in these securities are only to be allocated to partners not considered to be restricted individuals. There are restrictions on the participation of certain persons in hot issue securities, including members of NASD who are not permitted to sell such securities to an account in which a member, or an affiliate to a member has an interest.

Hot issue securities should be addressed in the partnership agreement and the subscription agreement should hold the necessary information concerning the investor's connection with members of the NASD.

h) Conclusion

The American regulators provide that Hedge Funds can be exempt from regulatory conditions imposed on other types of investment vehicles. They have, however, to adhere to certain requirements to remain exempt.

Assuming that sophisticated investors need less protection, regulating by exempting Hedge Funds from certain requirements may on the face of it make sense. In the light of the fact that smaller investors are increasingly aware of the opportunities offered by Hedge Fund, established investment divisions of banks and other financial intermediaries began to offer Hedge Fund of Funds to the public with an initial investment of as low as Euro 1000, e.g. DWS XAVEX Hedge Select, this assumption may be mistaken. In a time of increasing Shareholder Capitalism[270] smaller investors can hardly be ignored by regulators. Thus, the focus on Rule 506 in Regulation D of the Securities Act 1933, the agent- and finder exemption of the Securities Exchange Act of 1934, the section 3 (c) (1) and (7) Exemption in the Investment Company Act 1940 as well as the various other provisions may be outdated. New provisions for smaller investors may have to be compromised. However, like most regulators, once they have regulatory powers at

270 See Gordon (2003), p 121.

their hand they tend to make rigorous use of it, the U.S. legislator tends to over-regulate. Thus, there is the danger of classifying smaller investors as unsophisticated investors who may need more protection. More protection could, in turn, mean increased transparency and compulsory disclosure requirements, which is not in conformity with Hedge Fund's need for secrecy.

Moreover, new legislation depends on market participants and as long as the U.S. legislator does not consider smaller investors to be insufficiently protected, there is no indication of enhanced regulation and disclosure requirements.

However, when looking at the effort and costs of regulation versus the attainments of regulation, i.e. are questions of systemic risk-, moral hazard-, and problems of information asymmetries being approached in a sensible and efficient way, one may have to question this form of regulation.

Firstly, systemic risk has not been an issue for U. S. legislators, at least not before LTCM. This may, on the one hand, be due to the fact that there was no threat to the financial system posed by Hedge Funds. Thus, there was no reason to provide regulation covering systemic risk. On the contrary, possible regulatory measures like enhanced transparency, minimum capital requirements, enhanced disclosure etc. would have had a negative effect on the Hedge Fund industry. Thus, the legislator abstained.

Secondly, by rendering Hedge Funds exempt from disclosure and registration requirements, provided that they comply with the conditions to remain exempt, information asymmetries are fostered. This provides, on the one hand, that Hedge Funds can operate in relative secrecy and, thus, attain high net returns which are beneficial for U.S. capital markets and its economy, on the other hand, investors are afforded minimum protection by requiring them to comply with the requirements to become sophisticated investors. Here the investor sacrifices his or her protection under the law voluntarily for the sake of higher net returns. Thus, information asymmetries persist under the current U.S. legislative framework.

Having seen that the investors sacrifice their protection for higher net returns, this may partly be due to the ability of high net worth individuals to afford their own protection and the independence from regulators that comes along with that. However, this situation poses in part a moral hazard problem because once the exemption requirements are fulfilled Hedge Funds are free to pursue their own interests, be it in the aforementioned fee structures or trading practices. In practice this is rarely an issue because Hedge Funds` reputation and the interests of investors are interconnected. Thus, ex post opportunism of Hedge Funds is rarely seen and in practice a system of checks and balances seems to be functioning efficiently. Moral hazard remains problematic at least in theory.

The U.S. legislator may, on the face of it, not comply with required objectives of Hedge Fund regulation but its regulation ensures the well functioning of the Hedge Fund industry, which is significant. It has to be added that those regulatory objectives are a product of the aftermath of the LTCM case and, thus, U.S.

regulators could not take them into account when drafting the legislation. Discounting this and keeping in mind that filing and registering to remain exempt from regulation requires very little administrative effort and, thus, transaction costs are minimized, thereby compensating for the high costs of implementation; there may actually be a state of equilibrium between costs and attainments of regulation.

The US legislator may have found and equilibrium between costs and attainments of regulation, he does not, however, utilize the beneficial knock-on-effects and synergies deriving from regulation of financial intermediaries. The author will point out later how this may optimize Hedge Fund regulation.

2. Regulation in the United Kingdom

A Hedge Fund manager located in the UK will be subject to mainstream UK regulation and require authorization by the Financial Services Authority (FSA)[271]. The FSA replaced the self-regulatory organization (SRO) and the Investment Management Regulatory Organization (IMRO)[272].

The Financial Services and Markets Act 2000 (FSMA) provides the legislative framework for the FSA's operations. The FSA assumed its regulatory and supervisory function when the FSMA came into force on 1st of December 2001. In essence, the new Act broadly replicates and harmonizes the financial regulatory arrangements previously established under a number of different enactments, including the Financial Services Act 1986. The FSMA bestows the FSA with a full range of statutory powers, such as the ability to authorize, regulate, investigate and discipline authorized persons and the power to impose penalties for market abuse[273]. The key elements to the relationship of the FSA with institutions are authorization[274]; base line monitoring to ensure compliance; sectoral reviews to assess risks posed by particular issues; monitoring programs to lessen specific risks in institutions where possible; and lastly, action required following the escalation of risks.

Rules and guidance in relation to Hedge Fund managers are to be found in the new FSA Handbook of Rules and Guidance, created in response to section 153 (1) FSMA under which the FSA is required to exercise its rule-making powers in writing. All rules under the previous regulators are to be harmonized into this one

---

271 The FSA is responsible for all facets of financial regulation in the United Kingdom and was created following an announcement by the UK government in 1997 of its intention to reform the regulation of financial services. Nine regulatory bodies were merged to create a single financial 'super regulator' with responsibilities ranging from covering the sale of insurance to controlling city dealers trading in derivatives.

272 Through which Hedge Fund managers were generally authorised.

273 Sections 1, 2 FSMA 2000.

274 Including initial risk assessment

Handbook and as a part of it, the Integrated Prudential Sourcebook (PSB) will set out the prudential requirements for all authorized firms[275].

The intention was to implement the proposed PSB on 1st of January 2004 following the assimilation of relevant aspects of the new Basle Accord and related EU legislation once concluded. The Basle Accord is an international standard to be agreed by members of the Basle Committee and the EU directive is also dependent on its progress. Once the EU Commission has introduced proposals, they will then be subject to the normal EU legislative processes involving EU Parliament, the EU Commission and Member states[276].

Sweden and Ireland were the first countries to establish 'super regulators' and both Germany and Austria are in the process of creating their own, however the FSA is the biggest undertaking yet. Its performance as a regulator will be under close scrutiny through the implementation process to see if it lives up to its marketed image as a flexible regulator. The rulebook currently appears to be growing in intrusiveness where not much is left to chance, however, the FSA has put forward proposals in areas, such as that of financial advice for more liberal regulation[277]. The Authority's biggest challenge, however, is to combine its financial services regime with that being developed in other European countries given that European regulators are required to adapt their regimes to EU directives. The Investment Services Directive (ISD) is one in a series of directives designed to facilitate the creation of a single market in financial services throughout the European Economic Area (EEA).[278] UK Hedge Fund managers who are authorized as ISD firms by the FSA are able to conduct business throughout the EEA provided they adhere to certain registration requirements.

---

275 Currently, five separate interim prudential sourcebooks are used by the FSA, but these will eventually be replaced by the Integrated Prudential Sourcebook. The sourcebooks provide sources for the Authority's requirements and guidance, in addition to manuals that outline the processes to be followed.

276 It should be added that the timetable delays of at least a year from 2001 for both the Basle Committee and EU Commission have created a dilemma for the FSA, which is eager to release the Sourcebook as soon as possible, but must incorporate the findings of these rulings. A reviewed timetable was issued by the FSA in November 2001 with three alternatives awaiting industry comment, the first being to implement the PSB in full in 2004 with the intention of making changes to reflect international standards at a later date. The second, to defer the whole until the outcome of the international agreements can be incorporated. The third alternative is to implement only material substantially consistent with the eventual complete PSB in 2004 and defer the residual that relies on the outcome of the Basle and EU agreements to be implemented in 2005, by which time the agreements should be completed and the findings reflected in the PSB. The candidates proposed for early implementation are systems and controls, investment firms not covered by the Investment Services Directive (ISD), operational risk, and some elements of market risk.

277 In the long term, however, the success of its policies will depend to a large extent on the quality of its staff and how well they undertake their responsibilities.

278 See Kaal (2004) (elaborating on the interconnections between the ISD and the regulatory situation in the US).

a) Rules and Regulations of the FSMA and FSA

The Investment Firms Division (IFD) regulates investment firms and many professional firms who perform mainstream investment business, such as the direct advice on investment products. In accordance with the FSA objective of wishing to maintain the competitiveness of the UK as a financial centre and encourage innovation, Hedge Funds appear to be regarded in a positive light.

When the FSMA came into force, firms and individuals that held equivalent status under the old legislation were permitted to continue to perform those functions without having to reapply for permission or approval as part of the transitional provisions made by the Treasury under the Act. Consultation documents are offered at present as a guide to the policy intentions of the FSA, but these remain provisional until the transition to the new regime is complete.

Partly due to the difficulties with taking over from the various SRO's, such as IMRO and the Securities and Futures Authority Limited (SFA), the FSA has not anticipated that many changes will be made to the content of legislation at this time. However, the FSMA has been expanded in some areas to an extent, such as the increased disciplinary powers granted to the FSA, which allow it to levy unlimited civil fines for actions against individuals or companies whether regulated or not; to deal with market abuse; disgorge profits and compensate victims; and request documentation and financial records, on demand, at any time[279]. The securities regime has been slightly liberalized through the removal of the net assets requirement and also through its extended application to partnerships and other persons in addition to corporate bodies. The recognized professional bodies regime under the FS Act 1986 will be replaced by the rule that professional firms[280] carrying on regulated activities will be authorized and regulated directly by the FSA although some categories of professional firms will benefit from an exclusion subject to arms length oversight by certain powers of the Authority. The responsibilities of senior management have also received new attention.

(1) Supervision by risk assessment

The supervision principle of the new regulator is risk-based as opposed to rule-based. The risk in question is that the FSA will not achieve its statutory objectives of market confidence, public understanding, consumer protection and reduction of financial crime. The FSA identifies three main sources of risk to these objectives and these are external environment risks, consumer and industry wide risks and risks from individual institutions[281]. Risks are prioritized through ana-

---

279 www.fsa.gov.uk

280 Such as, solicitors and accountants

281 http://www.hmso.gov.uk

lyzing the impact on the objectives of two factors. Firstly, should a particular risk materialize and secondly, the probability that the particular risk will occur. Institutions are allocated using a number of measures to identify the impact[282] and then classified under one of four impact bands, which are high, medium one, medium two and low. Part of the framework used to assess the probability that a risk might materialize and have an impact on FSA objectives involves setting up a risk profile of each institution from which an overall risk score is determined for each firm. All market participants will be assessed through this integrated risk assessment framework and consequent targeting or prioritizing by the FSA will occur according to how participants rate. Low risk institutions require just routine oversight based mainly on remote monitoring, while high impact, high risk entities will attract close attention. Each firm's risk profile is between the institution and the FSA and the FSA discourages use of the assessment for any other purpose. This approach should mean a light touch and mutual agreement on what risks are being run, ultimately putting trust into the senior management rather than prescribing hard ratios to follow.

(2) Regulated and Prohibited Activities

Section 19 FSMA contains a general prohibition on all firms or persons who are not authorized or exempt from carrying on a regulated activity in the UK and from holding themselves out as being authorized or exempt.[283] Regulated activities are those of a kind specified in the Treasury's Regulated Activities Order, which are carried on by way of business and related either to an investment or to property of any kind[284]. In specifying investment as including any asset, right or interest, article 4 of section 22 FSMA ensures full implementation of the Investment Services Directive (ISD).

Contravention of the general prohibition is a criminal offence for which a person may be liable to imprisonment and, or an unlimited fine[285] unless it can be shown that all reasonable precautions were taken and all possible due diligence practiced to avoid committing the offence. Persons who are not authorized or exempt from carrying on a regulated activity, or who hold themselves out as being authorized or exempt are subject to the same punishments. However, if the conduct constituting the offence involves a public display of any material, they will

---

282 Funds under management were used for previous IMRO institutions.

283 FSMA - PART II, Regulated and Prohibited Activities: The general prohibition. 19. - (1) No person may carry on a regulated activity in the United Kingdom, or purport to do so, unless he is (a) an authorized person; or (b) an exempt person. (2) The prohibition is referred to in this Act as the general prohibition.

284 Section 22 FSMA.

285 Section 23 FSMA.

be subject to the maximum fine[286]. A breach of the general prohibition may also mean that certain agreements made could be unenforceable[287], such as those entered into by the person who committed a breach or those entered into by an authorized person if the agreement is a result of activities by a person who committed a breach.

(3) Authorization to Carry On Regulated Activities

Authorized persons include those given permission under Part IV of FSMA[288] to carry on one or more regulated activities, certain persons or firms from other member states who are authorized in accordance with arrangements under the Treaty of Rome and additionally EEA firms that qualify under a Single Market Directive.

The requirements and standards that authorized persons must comply with in the FSA's regulatory system will depend on both the nature of the firm and the regulated activities for which a firm has permission to carry on. Applicants therefore must familiarize themselves with the rules, regulations and standards that will apply to their particular business and with which they must comply. It is also important that time is taken over the application and the appropriate legal advice is sought from a firm with the necessary expertise because the process is quicker if there is less need for additional correspondence on the part of the FSA to establish all necessary information.

(a) Authorization Requirement – The Business Test

A person or firm will need to conduct the business test to determine whether they need to be authorized and this simply involves assessing whether the person's or firm's activities are to be carried on in the way of a business. If activities are to be carried on in the way of a business a person or firm must determine whether these activities involve specified investments, will be regulated activities, will be carried on in the UK or whether the activities will be excluded. If alternatively the activities are not to be carried on in the way of a business, a person or firm must determine whether they will be exempt, able to carry on regulated activities without authorization, if there are any benefits from provisions in the Act that grant authorization without the need for permission under Part IV FSMA. Deciding whether an activity is carried on by way of business is a question of judgment that must take into account several factors, such as the degree of conti-

---

286 Section 24 FSMA - level 5 on the standard scale multiplied by the number of days during which the display continued.

287 Sections 26-29 FSMA.

288 Permission to Carry on Regulated Activities

nuity, the commercial element, the scale of the activity and what proportion the activity bears to others carried on by the same person, but which are not regulated[289].

In the situation where activities are carried on in the way of a business, two of the elements that must be present to render authorization necessary are investments that fall within the scope of regulation under the Act and activities carried on in relation to those specified investments that are regulated under the Act[290].

The last requirement for authorization to be necessary is that activities are carried on in the UK. Determining whether this is the case is generally easy to do, but the introduction of cross border elements can make the fact more difficult to establish[291]. There are also several instances under section 418 FSMA where persons who are carrying on a regulated activity that would not normally be considered as being carried on in the UK are classified as being carried in the UK. This is the case if the regulated activity is in another EEA State in exercise of rights under a Single Market Directive; if the marketing of a UK based collective investment scheme in another EEA State by the scheme's manager is one to which the UCITS Directive is applicable; where a regulated activity is carried on by a UK based person and an establishment in the UK is responsible for the day to day management of the activity; and where a regulated activity is carried on by a person not based in the UK, but from an establishment in the UK[292]. A person based outside the UK who sets up an establishment in the UK must be authorized if regulated activities are to be carried on and also if the management of day to day business of a regulated activity can be made the responsibility of a UK based establishment. If such a person is unauthorized they must ensure that they do not contravene other provisions of the Act, such as the controls on financial promotion[293].

---

289 AUTH 2.3.3G.

290 In the FSA regulations, specified investments include deposits, rights under contract of insurance, shares etc, debt instruments, warrants, certificates representing securities, units, rights under a stakeholder pension schemes, options, futures, contracts for differences and rights to or interests in specified investments. The various specified activities that can constitute regulated activities include accepting deposits, dealing with investments as a principal or agent, arranging deals in investments, managing investments, safeguarding and administering investments, sending dematerialised instructions, establishing etc. collective investment schemes, establishing etc. stakeholder pension schemes, advising on investments, effecting or carrying out contracts of insurance as principal, Lloyd's activities, activities in respect of regulated mortgage contracts, entering funeral plan contracts and agreeing to carry on a regulated activity.

291 For example if a client is based outside the UK or if an element of an activity occurs outside the UK.

292 AUTH 2.4.3G.

293 AUTH 2.4.5G.

(b) Gaining Permission to Carry on Regulated Activities

To gain permission to carry on regulated activities, an applicant must satisfy high level standards, that is, be familiar with the Threshold Conditions (COND) and Principles for Business (PRIN); satisfy Systems, Controls and internal arrangements (SYSC); be aware of prudential requirements for adequate resources applicable to all firms; and depending on the type of business of the applicant, be aware of the detailed prudential requirements in the applicable sourcebook.

The principles for business encompass honesty, competence and financial soundness. In the assessment of a person's suitability the FSA will look to matters, such as whether a person has prior criminal convictions, has been the subject of adverse findings in connection with misconduct, fraud and the like, undergone disciplinary proceedings or any dismissals[294]. In terms of competence the person must satisfy the relevant requirements of the FSA's Training and Competence sourcebook (TC) in relation to the controlled function performed by the person[295]. Lastly, the determination of financial soundness will involve looking at factors, such as whether the person has been the subject of any judgment debt in the UK or elsewhere that was not paid within a reasonable period[296], or whether the person has made any arrangements with his creditors in the UK or elsewhere, filed for bankruptcy, had assets sequestrated or been involved in proceedings relating to any of these[297].

The threshold conditions that must be satisfied include legal status, location of offices, adequate resources, close links and suitability. As an example, the 'adequate resources' threshold condition requires that resources of a person must be adequate in the view of the FSA in relation to the regulated activities the person plans to carry on or carries on. The 'location of offices'[298] as another example requires a body corporate constituted under the law of any part of the United Kingdom to have its head office and registered office[299] in the United Kingdom. Individuals who occupy 'controlled functions'[300] in firms that satisfy the threshold conditions will be considered fit and proper to carry out such functions.

Persons, such as employees and office holders who perform specified types of functions for authorized persons must also be approved by the FSA and this is done under Part V of the Act[301]. Approved persons must behave in a way that

---

294 FIT 2.1.3G - Fit and Proper Test for Approved Persons Sourcebook.

295 FIT 2.2.1G.

296 If paid at all.

297 FIT 2.3.1G.

298 Schedule 6 to the Act

299 If applicable

300 A controlled function is one relating to the carrying on of a regulated activity by a firm, which is specified, under section 59 of the Act, in the table of controlled functions.

301 The Performance of Regulated Activities.

complies with any statements of principle issued by the authority and can face disciplinary action if not adhered to. The Authority has power to prohibit persons from carrying out functions in relation to regulated activities.

(c) Exemptions

In the new legislation persons previously exempt for some, but not other activities now must be authorized for all their regulated activities. Section 38 of the Act allows for Treasury Exemption Orders excusing the need for specified persons or persons falling within a specified class from authorization when carrying on regulated activities. The section, however, does not apply to persons with a Part IV[302] permission who are not permitted to be exempt persons as a result of an exemption order. Section 39 of the Act provides an exemption from the general prohibition for appointed representatives of authorized persons.

To assist in defining boundaries of the activity to be regulated there are a number of exemptions listed in the Regulated Activities Order in addition to those listed in the Authorization sourcebook. Exclusions may be in relation to both investments and activity and thus each of these areas should be carefully checked for the possibilities to be clearly determined. Examples of a number of exemptions from regulated activities and investments are listed below, but not all. It is important for firms to be aware that certain exclusions relevant to these areas will be modified due to the ISD because persons otherwise referred to in the ISD as investment firms, who are caught by the Directive must be brought within the scope of regulation under the Act. A person must therefore consider whether he is an investment firm to which the Directive applies.

There are exclusions for most of the categories of specified investments. For example, there are exclusions from regulation for shares or stock from all open-ended investment companies and shares or stocks in the share capital of certain mutual or in equivalent EEA bodies; certain instruments from indebtedness including trade bills, specified banking documents and contracts of insurance; and any instruments that would otherwise fall within the specified investments category of units in a collective investment scheme except where the underlying investments covered by the certificate are issued by the same[303] issuer or constitute a single issue of public sector debt[304].

There are also numerous exclusions in relation to regulated activities of which just a few will be mentioned. The activity of dealing in investments as principal to specified transactions relating to any security or to any contractually based investment, for example, is cut back by several exclusions. One such exclu-

---

302 FSMA Part IV sections 42 and 43.

303 Non-public sector.

304 AUTH 2.6G.

sion is derived if an unauthorized person enters into a transaction relating to a contractually based investment in either of two sets of circumstances - in the first case, when the person with whom they deal with is an authorized or exempt person acting in the course of a business consisting of regulated activities and in the second case, when the unauthorized person enters the transaction through a non-UK office and deals with or through a person based outside the UK who carries on any of the activities relating to securities or contractually based investments that are generally treated as regulated activities[305]. Risk management activities involving options, futures and contracts for differences in the context of dealing in investments as principal will not require authorization provided specified conditions are met. These conditions are that the company's business consists mainly of unregulated activities and the main purpose of the risk management activities is to limit the impact of certain kinds of identifiable risks on that business[306].

The exclusions to both the regulated activities of arranging deals in investments[307] and making arrangements with a view to transactions in investments[308] are important when considered in terms of raising corporate finance.[309] Arrangements that do not, or would not bring about the investment to which the arrangements relate are excluded from article 25(1) Regulated Activities Order. Exclusions from article 25(2) Regulated Activities Order on its own include the provision of means by which parties in a transaction or potential transaction can communicate; making arrangements under which clients will be introduced to third parties who will provide independent services, such as advice provided the person to whom the introduction is made is of a specified standing[310]: and arrangements with the sole purpose of providing finance to enable persons to enter into investment transactions, but only if the arrangements actually bring about the transaction. Some activities that are excluded from both articles include arranging investment transactions to which the arranger is to be a party, which means a person cannot engage in both a dealing activity[311] and arranging deals for another with regard to any particular transaction; unauthorized persons who arrange investment transactions with the object of a transaction between an authorized person and a third party provided specified requirements with regard to advice and remuneration are followed; making arrangements for finance to be supplied by a third party provided the finance is given in exchange for an instrument acknowledging the debt; and a company's arrangement for issuing specified securities in itself.

305 AUTH 2.8.4(2)G.

306 AUTH 2.8.4(5)G.

307 Article 25(1) Regulated Activities Order. "the Regulated Activities Order" means the Financial Services and Markets Act 2000 (Regulated Activities) Order 2000.

308 Article 25(2) Regulated Activities Order.

309 AUTH 2.8.6G.

310 Including being an authorised person.

311 as principal or agent.

Exclusions from the regulated activities of safeguarding and administering investments include such activities carried on by a single person if a specified third party takes on the responsibility for the assets, such that the authorized person with permission to carry on the regulated activity[312] can delegate a portion or all of the activities without the need for the delegate to be authorized and without the protection to the owner of the assets being lost. Regulation with respect to arranging safeguarding and administration of assets will not apply to introductions in the course of business to an authorized person, or to an exempt person who acts within the scope of his exemption. In addition, a person who safeguards and administers assets will not be carrying out regulated activities if the only administrative activities in which he engages are currency conversion and document handling[313].

There are also a variety of further exclusions from the Regulated Activities Order that are linked to a range of circumstances that can be applied to several of the regulated activities relating to securities or contractually based investments. For example, certain exclusions apply to 'professions or business not involving regulated activities' in dealing with investments as an agent; arranging deals in investments and making arrangements or facilitating transactions in investments; safeguarding and administering investments; and advising on investments. These exclusions apply where the regulated activity is carried out in the course of a profession or business that does not otherwise consist of regulated activities. Also, to be excluded the activities must be regarded as a necessary part of the other services provided in the course of the profession or business and the exclusion will not apply if separate remuneration is received in respect of any regulated activity that is carried on[314].

(4) Financial Promotion in the UK

Section 21(1) FSMA prohibits unauthorized persons from communicating an invitation or inducement to engage in investment activity in the UK in the course of business. Engaging in an investment activity can be taken to mean entering or offering to enter into an agreement, which constitutes a 'controlled activity',[315] or alternatively to exercise rights awarded by a controlled investment, acquire, dispose of, underwrite or convert the controlled investment. The section also applies to a communication originating from outside the UK if it is capable of having an effect in the UK. Contravention of this section will amount to a crimi-

---

312 Or exempt person.

313 AUTH 2.8.8G.

314 AUTH 2.9.5G.

315 A controlled activity is i) an activity of a specified kind or one which falls within a specified class of activity, and ii) an activity that relates to an investment of a specified kind or to one which falls within a specified class of investment.

nal offence unless the promoter is an authorized person or the content of the communication is approved by an authorized person.

UK regulation previously placed restrictions on financial promotion by authorized persons through certain types of media[316], but the FSA Financial Promotion Order has removed these. Authorized persons or firms may make financial promotion communications[317] through any means of the media, such as the internet, radio or television broadcasts, newspapers, printed advertising, personal visits, telephone calls and any other electronic media.

(a) Real Time and Non-Real Time Financial Promotions

The Financial Promotion Order has introduced the concept of real or non-real time communications to allow a distinction to be made between the immediacy of particular types of promotions[318]. A real time financial promotion is defined as a financial promotion that is communicated through interactive dialogue, such as a telephone conversation or a personal visit. A solicited real time financial promotion is one made in the course of a visit or through another interactive dialogue that is either initiated by the recipient of the promotion or in response to an express request from the recipient[319]. Many solicited real time financial promotions will be exempt. A firm is not permitted to make an unsolicited real time financial promotion unless exempt or if the recipient has an established existing relationship with the firm; the financial promotion relates to a marketable packaged product, which is not a higher volatility fund or a life policy linked to a higher volatility fund; and the financial promotion relates to a controlled activity to be carried on by an authorized or exempt person with the controlled investments involved being readily realizable securities[320] and generally marketable non-geared packaged products[321].

COB rule 3.8.22 states that an individual[322] who makes a real time financial promotion[323] on a firm's behalf, must be confirmed by the firm to be doing it in a way that is clear, fair and not misleading; does not make claims that are untrue; at the initial point of communication makes clear the purpose of the financial promotion and identifies both himself and the firm he represents; check that it is fine to proceed in the instance where the method of communication was not previously

316 Advertisements and unsolicited calls.

317 Solicited and unsolicited.

318 COB 3.5.5R.

319 COB 3.10.1(2)R.

320 Excluding warrants.

321 COB 3.10.3R.

322 Including an adviser, call centre operator and introducers.

323 That is, solicited real time financial promotions that are not exempt financial promotions and unsolicited real time financial promotion that are exempt financial promotions.

agreed by the recipient, terminate the communication if the recipient does not wish to proceed, recognize the recipient's right to end the communication at any time and refuse the request for another appointment; give a contact point to any recipient with whom he arranges an appointment; does not communicate with a person at an unsocial hour unless previously agreed to, on an unlisted telephone number unless previously agreed to; and if applicable, acts in conformity with Conduct of Business (COB) rules concerning polarization and disclosure of status.

A non-real time financial promotion is a financial promotion that is not communicated in real time, but by such means as letters, emails, newspapers, journals, magazines, periodicals, websites, teletext service or television or radio. These means allow a financial promotion to be communicated to more than one person in identical terms by way of a system that creates a record of the communication for future reference and which does not require the recipient to respond immediately. Under COB rule 3.8.2, a non-real time financial promotion must contain the name of the firm and either an address or contact point from which the address may be obtained. A non-real time financial promotion must also be clear, fair and not misleading and a firm must be able to show that it has taken steps to ensure this[324]. Specific non-real time financial promotions are required to include an adequate and fair description of the nature of the investment or the service, the commitment required, the risks involved and also the contact name of a person and/or name and address of a firm or contact point if the financial promotion relates to the investment or service of person other than the firm[325].

(b) Direct Offer Financial Promotions

A direct offer financial promotion either communicated or approved by a firm is generally required to include enough information for a person to make an informed assessment of an investment or service to which the promotion relates. In particular it must contain, amongst other things, statements that the firm that has approved the promotion is authorized by the FSA, that the firm should be contacted if a person has any doubt regarding the suitability of the agreement related to the financial promotion and the full name and address of the person offering the investment or service being promoted[326]. Prohibited types of direct offer financial promotions include those relating to a broker fund, or a derivative or warrant unless the firm can show that the investment may be suitable for the recipient of the communication[327].

---

324 COB 3.8.4R.

325 COB 3.8.8R.

326 COB 3.9.6R.

327 COB 3.9.5R.

(c) Approval of Financial Promotions by a Firm

As mentioned above, section 21(1) of the Act prohibits an unauthorized person from communicating a financial promotion unless it is exempt or approved by a firm. A firm that approves a financial promotion has a similar responsibility to one that communicates it as most of the rules apply in the same way. However, an authorized person or firm must not grant approval to an unauthorized person or firm undertaking real time financial promotion[328]. If a firm approves a financial promotion relating to an unauthorized person under one or more of the possible exemptions, the approval must be limited to those circumstances. Similarly, the approval of a financial promotion for communication to market counterparties and intermediate customers must be limited to communications to such persons[329]. COB rule 3.12.6 states that a specific non-real time financial promotion, which relates to an investment or service of an overseas person must not be communicated or approved by a firm unless the promotion makes clear what firm has approved or communicated it and that there is no reason to doubt that the overseas person will deal with private customers in the UK in an honest and reliable way.

(d) Collective Investment Schemes and Financial Promotion

Sections 238[330]and 240[331] of the Act place restrictions on the communications and approval by firms of financial promotions related to unregulated collective investment schemes (CIS). Section 238(1) of the Act states that an authorized person must not communicate an invitation or inducement to participate in an unregulated CIS. Certain types of communications relating to unregulated collective investment schemes are exempt from the scheme promotion restriction through the FSMA[332]. Section 238(5) of the Act gives the FSA power to make rules that exempt certain promotions relating to an unregulated CIS from the scheme promotion restriction provided they are not made to the general public. An authorized person, under section 240, cannot approve, for the purposes of section 21 of the Act, the content of a communication relating to an unregulated CIS if they were unable to communicate it themselves given section 238(1).

---

328 COB 3.12.2R.

329 COB 3.12.3R.

330 Restrictions on promotion.

331 Restrictions on approval of promotion.

332 Order 2001 SI 2001/1060 - Promotion of Collective Investment Schemes (Exemptions).

(e) Exemptions

There are quite a few exemptions from the rules prohibiting financial promotions to unauthorized persons given that prohibition is only intended to strike at particular securities or the provision of a specific product. Of particular relevance to Hedge Funds, the definition of who is exempt is widened to include certified high net worth and sophisticated investors and to networks of such investors in a bid to facilitate the informal raising of capital for start-up businesses[333]. Those applying for the exemption, amongst other things, must sign a statement declaring that they qualify as high net worth individuals and accept that the schemes will not be regulated. A certificate must be produced, signed by their accountant or employer verifying that they had an annual income in the preceding financial year of no less than GBP 100,000 or held net assets valued at no less than GBP 250,000 throughout the same period. A financial promotion to these certified types of investors must not invite or induce the recipient to engage in investment activity with the person who has signed the certificate.

The Conduct of Business sourcebook and the Financial Promotions Order contain other exemptions, such as a financial promotion to, or directed only at recipients of confirmed market counterparties or intermediate customers[334] and a financial promotion that can be lawfully communicated by an unauthorized person without approval. 'One off' financial promotions[335] made only to a single person in a modified fashion are exempt and this extends to continued correspondence on the same basis if a client seeks further information. It does not, however extend to a promotional strategy whereby publicity material is sent to a wide range of investors, but with the appearance of being personalized for each investor. Also, financial promotions communicated from outside the UK, which are exempt under the Financial Promotion Order articles 30, 31, 32 or 33 will be exempt from section 21(1) of the Act if the office from which the financial promotion is communicated is a separate unauthorized person[336].

Financial promotions communicated to a person outside the UK will be exempt provided that certain conditions are met. These conditions include that the financial promotion be accompanied by evidence showing that it is directed only at persons outside the UK and that proper systems are in place to prevent recipients in the UK from engaging in the investment activity to which the financial promotion is related, for example, websites, journals and so on must be intended for a market outside of the UK. A financial promotion will be exempt if commu-

---

333 Financial Promotions Order articles 48 and 50 respectively.

334 The exemption for an intermediate customer when classified under COB 4.1.9R as an expert private customer will only apply for a financial promotion that relates to a designated investment or designated investment business for which he has been so classified.

335 Non-real time and solicited real time.

336 COB 3.2.5R.

nicated to, or through ISD investment firms established in other EEA states carrying on pass ported business in the UK.

Exemptions also exist for generic promotions to allow for discussion on the merits of putting money into shares, for example. Generic promotions must not identify, directly or indirectly, a person who provides the controlled investment to which the financial promotion relates and also must not directly or indirectly identify any person as a person who carries on a controlled activity in relation to that controlled investment[337]. Information services are exempt in that they may report a promotion by an authorized person without having sought authorization on the premise that the report does not substantially change the terms of the original promotion[338].

Solicited real time and non-real time financial promotions in relation to listing applications are permitted through article 70 of the Financial Promotions Order, however listing rules will apply. Similarly, financial promotions included in listing particulars and prospectuses are exempt, provided the articles contain details of the exemptions in relation to financial promotions included in the listing particulars and prospectuses for public offers of listed securities and in relation to prospectuses for public offers of unlisted securities[339].

(5) Investment Advice

Giving investment advice will be a regulated activity only if it applies to securities and contractually based investments. Giving generic advice about a specified investment is not a regulated activity and neither is providing information as opposed to advice, but in the latter case, the context of a communication may have an impact on its character[340]. Another requirement for giving investment advice is that it must be directed at someone holding specified investments or to a prospective investor, such as discretionary fund managers or trustees. The exclusion to this requirement includes advice given to a person who obtains it in another capacity, such as a tax professional to whom advice would be given to assist the practice of his profession[341].

Exclusions to regulations on investment advice include advice given in newspapers, websites, television, radio and so on, if the principal purpose of the report taken as a whole is not to give advice[342]. Exclusions will apply in specified circumstances where a person gives advice, which takes the form of regularly updated news, or information services or advice given over forms of the media, such

337 Financial Promotions Order article 17.
338 Financial Promotions Order article 38.
339 Financial Promotions Order articles 71-73.
340 AUTH 2.7.15G.
341 AUTH 2.7.16G.
342 Art. 38 - Financial Promotions Order.

as television and radio while acting as a trustee or personal representative; in connection to carrying on of business or profession not otherwise consisting of regulated activities; in connection to the sale of goods or supply of services; to a group member or participator in an joint enterprise; in connection with the sale of a body corporate and as an overseas person[343].

With the new Handbook, the FSA has proposed the abolition of the system of polarization with respect to investment advisers, which will effectively roll back regulation in that area through separating financial advisers into the independent and the company-tied. This will allow tied advisers to recommend products from more than one company and limit the use of commissions by independent advisers.

Polarization was introduced in 1988 to stop the issue of conflicting interest in the financial advice industry, but resulted in a loss of competition and of independent advice. The two types of adviser were also required under polarization to register and be policed, a practice which involved a large amount of bureaucracy. The financial system is more transparent now than in 1988 due to tougher consumer finance regulation and more prevalent disclosure of interest and thus it is believed that it should be better able to deal with conflicts of interest. One of the main questions of the new proposal is how consumers should pay for advice. The FSA has proposed a fee-paying system in which payment is agreed at the outset by adviser and client, working on the principle that people will accept that they should openly pay for financial advice. The FSA will most likely have to focus on its educational role to encourage and convince consumers of this concept. The FSA is aiming for October 2002 for implementation of the policy.

(a) Market Abuse

Part VIII FSMA bestows on the Authority the power to impose penalties for market abuse and sets out the kinds of behavior, which constitute market abuse. By definition, market abuse is considered to be behavior below that reasonably expected of a person in his or their position relative to the market, which occurs in relation to qualifying investments traded on a prescribed market[344]. Behavior will amount to market abuse if it meets any one or more of three specified conditions, which are:

---

343 AUTH 2.8.12G.

344 FSMA section 118 - The Treasury has prescribed markets and qualifying investments through the FSMA 2000 (Prescribed markets and Qualifying investments) Order 2001. All markets established under the rules of a UK Recognised Investment Exchange (RIE) and the market known as OFEX are markets to which section 118 applies, for example, the London Metal Exchange Limited and the London Stock Exchange plc (including AIM) (MAR 1.11.2G).

- The behavior must be based on information not usually available to those using the market, but which would be regarded as relevant if available to a regular user of the market when making the decision on the terms on which transactions in investments of the kind in questions should be effected:
- The behavior is likely to give a regular user of the market either a false or misleading impression in respect to the supply of, demand for, the price or value of investments of the kind in question:
- A regular user of the market would, or would be likely to regard the behavior as behavior that would, or at least would be likely to distort the market in investments of the kind in question.

The market abuse regime will only apply to the defined behavior that occurs in the United Kingdom or in relation to qualifying investments traded on a specified market situated in the UK or which is otherwise accessible electronically in the UK[345].

The Code of Market Conduct (MAR), made under section 119 of the Act is provided to assist firms in determining what type of behavior amounts to market abuse. In this respect, the Code will be a guideline of some relevance for particular Hedge Fund managers who carry on business in a way that may be on the borderline of being classified as market abuse.

(i) The Regular User Rule

A reasonable person who regularly deals on a market in investments of the kind in question a `regular user` is charged with deciding whether behavior falls below the standards expected and thus amounts to market abuse. In making this decision the regular user should take certain circumstances into account, for example, all the circumstances of the behavior including the characteristic of the market in question, the investments traded on that market and the users of the market; the rules and regulations of the market in question and applicable laws; prevailing market mechanisms, practices and codes of conduct applicable to the particular market being considered; the position of the person in questions and the standards that can be expected of that person at the time of the behavior given their experience, skill level and standard of knowledge; and finally, the need for market users to conduct their affairs in a way that does not compromise the fair and efficient operation of the market as a whole or unfairly damage the interests of investors[346].

---

345 Section 118(5) FSMA.

346 MAR 1.2.4E.

The intention to abuse the market does not have to exist for behavior to fall below the objective standards; however there are circumstances where the determination of whether behavior meets those standards will depend on a person's purpose[347]. There is liable to be some variation across markets with respect to the objective standard of behavior expected by regular users and the different standards that currently apply to the use of non-public information in different markets is an example. Additionally, the standard expected of a person by a regular user will vary with the person's level of experience, skill and standard of knowledge[348]. In many cases it may be appropriate to take the extent to which the behavior complies with other applicable rules into account including the rules of a prescribed market, the Takeover Code or FSA rules. However, compliance with such rules will not automatically render the behavior as not amounting to market abuse because many of these rules are not specifically directed at the types of behavior prohibited by the Act and similarly, failure to comply with such rules does not automatically dictate that market abuse has been committed[349].

(ii) Behavior

The reference to 'behavior' includes action and inaction, the latter in the sense that if a person is under a legal regulatory obligation to make a specific disclosure, failure to do so may amount to market abuse[350]. The types of behavior which will subject a person to the market abuse regime include such things as dealing in qualifying investments; dealing in commodities or investments which are the subject matter, or whose price or value is determined by reference to a qualifying investment; arranging deals in respect of qualifying investments; causing or procuring or advising others to deal in qualifying investments; making statements or representations or else disseminating information, which the regular user is likely to regard as relevant to determining the terms on which transactions in qualifying investments should be effected; providing corporate finance advice and conducting corporate finance activities in qualifying investments; and managing investments, which are qualifying investments belonging to another[351].

(iii) Misuse of Information

The restrictions regarding the misuse of information revolve around the idea that market users in all prescribed markets rely on timely dissemination of relevant

---

347 MAR 1.2.5E.
348 MAR 1.2.7G.
349 MAR 1.2.8G.
350 MAR 1.3.2E.
351 MAR 1.3.1E.

information as they might reasonably expect to receive. Therefore, those in possession of relevant information ahead of general dissemination should in most cases hold back from basing their behavior on that information and from requiring or encouraging others to engage in behavior until it is disseminated as this undermines the confidence of market users in the ability of the market to ensure access to such information. However, the expectations that market users have regarding access to information will vary between different markets[352].

Behavior will amount to market abuse with respect to the misuse of information if, in reference to any qualifying investment or relevant product, firstly, the dealing or arranging is based on information, which has a material influence on the decision to engage in the dealing or arranging; the information is not generally available; a regular user would likely consider the information as relevant information when deciding the terms on which transactions in the investments of the kind in questions should be effected; and the information relates to matters, which the regular user would reasonably expect to be disclosed to users of the particular prescribed market[353].

People are permitted by the Authority to use information that is obtained through research, analysis or other legitimate means, such as the observation of a public event - all of which is considered generally available[354]. An example of such legitimate information is that which may only be available overseas and has not been published or otherwise been made available to the public in the UK, or perhaps information which is only available on payment of a fee[355]. In terms of whether a regular user would regard a piece of information as relevant information depends on the circumstances, such as how specific, precise, material, current and reliable the information may be[356]. Two examples of disclose able information include information, which is required to be disclosed to a prescribed market under rules of an RIE, or information that relates to officially listed securities that is required to be disclosed under the Listing Rules[357].

There are a number of safe harbors, which set out descriptions of behavior that do not amount to market abuse because the behavior does not constitute a misuse of information. For example, dealing or arranging deals will not amount to a misuse of information if they were required in order to comply with a legal or regulatory obligation in the case where the obligation existed prior to the relevant information coming into the person's possession[358]. Another example is if rele-

---

352 MAR 1.4.3E.
353 MAR 1.4.4E.
354 MAR 1.4.6E.
355 MAR 1.4.7G.
356 MAR 1.4.9E.
357 MAR 1.4.14.
358 MAR 1.4.20C.

vant information is not generally available, but in a person's possession did not influence the decision to engage in the dealing or arranging in question[359].

(iv) False or Misleading Impressions

The concept behind the restrictions placed on improper conduct, which gives market users a false or misleading impression is that such market users will no longer be able to rely on the prices formed in markets or volumes of trading as a basis for their investment decisions thereby undermining confidence in the integrity of the prescribed market.

To be considered false or misleading, a regular user must consider the behavior engaged in to be likely to give users a false or misleading impression. The behavior will amount to market abuse if it is likely to give rise to a price, or value, or volume of trading which is materially false or misleading. To be likely, there must be a real possibility that the behavior will have such an effect, however this effect need not be more likely than not[360]. The general factors to be taken into account by regular users in making their assessment include, amongst other things, the experience and knowledge of the user of the market in question, the legal and regulatory requirements of the market concerned and accepted market practices and the identity and position of the person responsible for the behavior, which has been observed[361].

Behavior that gives rise to, or is likely to give rise, to a false and misleading impression and which will be considered market abuse is in the context of artificial transactions, disseminating such information, disseminating such information through an accepted channel and as the principal effect of engaging in a particular course of conduct[362].

There are three safe harbors specified in the Code where behavior is not considered as giving rise to false or misleading information and thereby amounting to market abuse and these are permitted transactions, required reporting or disclosure of transactions and Chinese walls[363]. Permitted transactions include those that effect the taking of a position or the unwinding of a position taken so as to obtain legitimate advantage of: firstly, differences in the taxation of income or capital returns generated by investments or commodities; secondly, differences in the prices of investments or commodities as traded in different locations; or

---

359 MAR 1.4.21C.

360 MAR 1.5.4E.

361 MAR 1.5.5E.

362 MAR 1.5.7E.

363 A Chinese wall is an arrangement that requires information held by a person in the course of carrying on one part of its business to be withheld from, or not to be used for, persons with or for whom it acts in the course of carrying on another part of its business (FSA Handbook Glossary).

thirdly, transactions, which affect the lending or borrowing of qualifying investments or commodities in order to meet an underlying demand for the investment or commodity[364]. Similarly, making a report or disclosure of transactions will be a safe harbor if it is made in accordance with the way specified by any pertinent legal or regulatory requirement; and if it was expressly required or permitted by the FSA rules or the rules of a prescribed market, Takeover Code or SARS, or by any other statute, regulation or rules of any competent statutory, governmental or regulatory authority that may apply[365]. With regard to Chinese walls, if an individual disseminates information, which is false and misleading he cannot be taken to have been aware that it was false and misleading if he had had access to information held by other individuals in the organization. However, this is provided the other information was effectively held behind a Chinese wall or was restricted through some other arrangements and that there was nothing known by the individual disseminating the information, or ought to have been known that would have led him to realize it was false and misleading[366].

(v) Distortion

A person is not permitted to engage in behavior that interferes with the proper operation of market forces and thus has a distorting effect. For behavior to be considered as causing distortion it must be such that a regular user would, or would be likely to, regard it as behavior that would, or would be likely to, distort the market in the investment in question. If the behavior interferes with the proper operation of market forces and subsequently positions prices at a distorted level it will be considered as amounting to market abuse. While positioning prices does not need to be the only purpose of entering into the transaction, it must be the trigger to the distortion[367]. Also, for behavior 'to be likely', there must be a real possibility that it will cause distortion, however this effect need not be more likely than not - the behavior, may or may be likely to give rise to more than one effect including the effect in question[368].

There are several other elements to be taken into consideration in determining which behavior results in distortion. Firstly, the efficiency of markets and liquidity is thought to be improved by the behavior of market users while trading at times and in sizes they find most favorable and seeking the maximum profit from their dealings. Such behavior in itself is therefore unlikely to amount to a distortion[369]. Similarly, in relation to a normal price trading range, high or low prices

364 MAR 1.5.24C.
365 MAR 1.5.25C.
366 MAR 1.5.27C.
367 MAR 1.6.4(1)E.
368 MAR 1.6.4(2)E.
369 MAR 1.6.5E.

will not necessarily indicate that someone has engaged in behavior with the purpose of positioning prices at a distorted level. High or low prices may simply result from the normal interaction of supply and demand[370].

Behavior that will constitute market abuse with regard to price distortion includes price positioning and abusive squeezes. In terms of price positioning, entering transactions with the purpose of positioning prices of a qualifying investment or relevant product at a distorted level will be market abuse[371]. The FSA considers that positioning prices does not have a legitimate commercial rationale and therefore trading large volumes of qualifying investments with the purpose of positioning prices is market abuse[372].

A person engaging in an abusive squeeze will usually have firstly, a significant influence over the supply, or demand for a qualifying investment or relevant product, including the delivery mechanism or secondly, a position either directly or indirectly in an investment under which quantities of the qualifying investment or relevant product in question are deliverable. It will be market abuse if such persons engage in behavior with the purpose of positioning the price at a distorted level at which others must deliver, take delivery or defer delivery to satisfy their obligations[373]. However, the normal interaction of supply and demand can relatively frequently result in squeezes that may lead to market tightness and therefore this is not in itself abusive. Also, it is not in itself abusive to have a significant influence over such things as the supply or demand, or delivery mechanisms for an investment through ownership, borrowing or reserving the investment in questions[374].

There is only one safe harbor from distortion as market abuse and this includes behavior, which complies with the London Metal Exchange's document 'Market Aberrations: The Way Forward'[375]. This document governs the behavior expected of long position holders, which will not amount to market abuse because the behavior will not amount to distortion[376].

(vi) Penalties for Market Abuse

The FSA has power under section 123(1) FSMA to either impose a penalty or to make a statement noting that a person has engaged in market abuse if the

---

370 MAR 1.6.6E.

371 MAR 1.6.9E - the purpose, however, must be an actuating purpose, not necessarily the sole purpose of entering into the transaction.

372 MAR 1.6.10E.

373 MAR 1.6.13E - this must be an actuating purpose, not necessarily the sole purpose of entering into the transaction.

374 MAR 1.6.14E.

375 London Metal Exchange's document (1988).

376 MAR 1.6.19C.

FSA believes that a person has actually engaged in market abuse or has, by taking or refraining from taking any action, encouraged or required another person to engage in behavior which would otherwise qualify as market abuse. The FSA must give a warning notice to any person it proposes to take action against. If the notice concerns a proposal to impose a penalty it must contain a statement of the amount of the proposed penalty and if it concerns a proposal to publish a statement it must state the terms of the proposed statement[377]. If the FSA decides to take action against a person it must deliver a decision notice to the person stating the amount of the penalty in the case where the decision notice regards the imposition of a penalty, or the terms of a statement in the case where a decision notice regards the publication of a statement. A person who receives a decision notice reflecting the Authority's wish to take action may refer the matter to the Tribunal[378].

A penalty cannot be imposed if there are reasonable grounds to demonstrate that the person in question either believed on reasonable grounds that his behavior did not amount to market abuse or had taken all reasonable precaution and practiced all due diligence to avoid engaging in market abuse[379]. Similarly a penalty cannot be imposed if there are reasonable grounds to demonstrate that the person in question either believed on reasonable grounds that his behavior had not required or encouraged another person to engage in behavior, which would otherwise have amounted to market abuse if engaged by the first person, or had taken all reasonable precaution and practiced all due diligence to avoid requiring or encouraging another person to engage in behavior, which would otherwise have amounted to market abuse if engaged by the first person[380].

(b) Money Laundering

Money laundering is dealt with in the Money Laundering sourcebook (ML), which applies to every relevant firm with respect to the firm's relevant regulated activities and to the money laundering reporting officer of a relevant firm[381]. Its scope is very broad with 'relevant firm' essentially meaning all firms except for those within the limited exception for firms concerned only with certain insurance activities and UCITS qualifiers. Like all FSA regulations, this sourcebook only applies to activities carried on from an establishment maintained by the firm[382] in the UK[383].

---

377 Section 126 FSMA.

378 Section 127 FSMA.

379 MAR 1.1.5G.

380 MAR 1.1.6.

381 ML 1.1.1R.

382 Or its appointed representative.

383 ML1.1.5R.

Relevant firms are required to have effective anti-money laundering systems and controls for the purpose of reducing the opportunities for money laundering in relation to relevant firms and to ensure approved persons appropriately exercise their responsibilities with respect to the systems and controls. The objective of the sourcebook is to reduce the possibilities for carrying on financial crime and one of the requirements for a relevant firm, in addition to having to set up and operate arrangements is to appoint a money laundering officer (MLRO)[384]. The MLRO is responsible for overseeing the firm's anti-money laundering activities and implementing anti-money laundering strategies and policies.

(c) Official Listing

The regime for recognized investment exchanges and clearing houses under the Financial Services Act, 1986 (FS Act 1986) will be broadly continued by the FSMA although the FSA's powers under the Act will have a wider reach. The UK Listing Authority (UKLA) of the FSA carries out the responsibility for admitting securities for official listing and ensuring that listed companies comply with their ongoing obligations under the listing rules. UKLA has the power to impose a financial penalty on a listed company or director where the listing rules have been broken.

(d) Collective Investment Schemes

Collective investment schemes are defined in section 235 FSMA as firstly, any arrangement with respect to property of any description including money, the purpose or effect of which is to enable persons taking part in the arrangements[385] to participate in or receive profits or income arising from the acquisition, holding, management or disposal of the property or sums paid out of such profits or income; and secondly, which are not excluded by the FSA Act[386].

The collective investment scheme sourcebook has been created for the purpose of consumer protection in providing a regulatory regime for investment companies with variable capital (ICVCs) and authorized unit trusts (AUTs). The sourcebook applies in large to ICVCs, directors and depositaries of ICVCs and managers and trustees of AUTs.

Open-ended investment company (OEIC) regulations created by the government under Section 262 of the Act permit the establishment of ICVCs in the UK. Authorized open-ended investment companies are authorized persons according to Schedule 5.1(3) of the Act and thus an ICVC is an authorized person. An

---

384 ML 2.1.2R.

385 As owners of the property or any part of it otherwise.

386 Order 2001 (SI 2001/1062) (Collective Investment Schemes).

ICVC is constituted by an instrument of incorporation drawn up by its directors, at least one of which is required to be an authorized corporate director (ACD). A depositary is also required for the safekeeping of the scheme and to comply with section 19 FSMA, the depositary and ACD must each be authorized persons.

An AUT is a collective investment scheme whereby the property is held on trust for the participants by the trustee under section 237 FSMA and authorization is provided by an authorization order in force under section 243 FSMA. The AUT will be constituted by a trust deed entered into by the manager and trustee. Under section 243(7) FSMA the manager and trustee must both be authorized persons and have permission to act in their respective capacities.

The regulated activities carried on in reference to a collective investment scheme are typically establishing, operating or winding up of a collective investment scheme. The activities are regulated where the actual schemes are authorized schemes for the purposes of the UK product regulation regime under Part XVII FSMA dealing with collective investment schemes as well as for unregulated schemes[387]. Additionally, the Regulated Activities Order contains the express provision to make acting as a trustee of an authorized unit trust scheme into a regulated activity. As such, with respect to authorized schemes[388], acting as a trustee of an authorized unit trust scheme will be a regulated activity; acting as a depositary of an open-ended investment company that is authorized under regulations made under section 262 FSMA will be a regulated activity; acting as a sole director of such a company will be a regulated activity; managing an authorized unit trust scheme, which amounts to operating the scheme will be a regulated activity; an open-ended investment company authorized under regulations made under section 262 FSMA will become an authorized person in its own right under Schedule 5 FSMA; as will operators, trustees or depositories of UCITS schemes constituted in other EEA states under Schedule 5 FSMA if those schemes qualify as recognized collective investment schemes for the purposes of section 264 FSMA[389].

Of the range of activities specified as being regulated in relation to collective investment schemes, there are no exemptions. Exclusions do exist in relation to the issue of whether or not what is being done relates to something that is a collective investment scheme[390].

387 AUTH 2.7.12G.

388 That is, schemes that are permitted to be promoted to the public.

389 AUTH 2.7.13G.

390 AUTH 2.8.10G.

(6) Investment Businesses

Until the introduction of a single prudential sourcebook, investment businesses[391] will be subject to the rules set out in the Interim Prudential Sourcebook for Investment Businesses (IPRU(INV)). The term 'investment businesses' refers to members' advisers, investment management firms, authorized professional firms, personal investment firms, securities and futures firms, service companies and the Society of Lloyd's. The sourcebook sets minimal capital and other risk management standards aimed at mitigating the possibility that firms will be unable to meet their liabilities and commitments to consumers and counterparties. Rules are specified for each of the different types of business and these will apply to a firm immediately prior to authorization by the FSA. When authorized, a firm must comply with the chapter that is most appropriate for its business.

Most Hedge Funds in the UK were previously regulated by IMRO. In the IPRU(INV) sourcebook, previous IMRO firms are now subject to the financial resources rules specified for investment management firms[392], which will be discussed in more detail later on in this section.

There are rules that apply as a whole to firms carrying out investment businesses such as those found in the Conduct of Business sourcebook. For example, a firm that communicates information to a customer in the course of its designated investment business must ensure that reasonable steps are taken to communicate in a way that is clear, fair and not misleading[393]. It is this rule that enables a customer to bring an action for damages under section 150 FSMA to recover loss from a firm communicating information in the course of a designated business that is not clear, fair or is misleading. All communications with customers are embraced under this rule, such as financial reports, client agreements and any correspondence that is not a financial promotion.

To ensure that a firm, which conducts investment business with or for a customer does not undertake it in a way that conflicts with its duty to the customer, the FSA has imposed restrictions, such as a prohibition on inducements, certain requirements when using a soft commission agreement[394] and disclosure requirements.

If there is likely to be, in connection to designated investment businesses, a conflict to a material extent with any duty a firm may owe to its customers, a firm must ensure that no person acting on its behalf either offers, gives, solicits or accepts an inducement, or directs or refers any actual or potential item of designated

---

391 Which includes those firms previously regulated under IMRO.

392 IPRU(INV) Sourcebook - Chapter 5.

393 COB 2.1.3.

394 A soft commission agreement is an agreement where a fund manager agrees, whether formally or informally, to provide a broker with a certain amount of commission in any one period in return for the provision of services 'free', either in-house or by third parties.

investment business to another person on its own initiative or the instruction of an associate[395].

COB rule 2.2.8 states that a firm must not, either directly or indirectly, deal in investments as agent for a customer, through any broker, under a soft commission agreement unless certain requirements are met. These requirements include that a written agreement has been entered into for the supply of goods and services, which do not take the form of, or include cash or any other direct financial benefit; the broker has agreed to provide best execution to the firm; and lastly, the firm has taken reasonable steps for transactions in which the broker acts as principal to ensure that commission paid under the agreement will be sufficient to cover the value of the goods or services received and the cost of execution[396].

Accepting goods and services supplied under a soft commission agreement will not constitute an inducement by a firm provided the goods and services are directly relevant to and used to assist in providing a firm's customers with investment management services, advice on dealing in, or on the value of any designated investment, custody services related to designated investments belonging to customers, or services relating to the valuation or performance measurement of portfolios[397]. Such goods and services that would be considered relevant include research, analysis and advisory services. Such goods and services that are not considered by the FSA to be relevant include computer hardware not associated with specialist computer software, employee's salaries and membership fees to professional organizations to name a few.

There are also certain disclosure requirements associated with soft commissions. If a firm plans to enter into a client agreement authorizing it to deal for a customer either directly or indirectly with, or through the agency of another person, under a soft commission which the firm has, or knows that another member of its group has with that other persons, the firm must disclose to the customer in writing both of the existence of the soft commission agreement and the firm's, or group's policy, if relevant, relating to soft commission agreement[398]. Unless exceptions apply, certain details must be provided through periodic disclosure to clients by a firm that has, or knows, or ought reasonably to know that another member of its group has a soft commission agreement with another person under which either the firm or that other member of its group deals for a customer[399]. Periodic disclosure is not necessary if the customer of a firm is habitually resident overseas and has requested the firm not to do so, or if a firm has information from

---

395 COB 2.2.3R.

396 COB 2.2.8R.

397 COB 2.2.12R.

398 COB 2.2.16R.

399 COB 2.2.18R.

which it is reasonable to conclude that the customer does not wish to receive this information[400].

Firms are expected to conduct business with due skill, care and diligence and in meeting this requirement they are permitted to rely on others up to an extent. In such a case a firm must show that it was reasonable for them to rely on information provided to it in writing by another person[401]. In general, firms may rely on such information from an unconnected authorized person or a professional firm unless they are aware, or ought to be reasonably aware, of any facts that would give reasonable grounds to question the accuracy of any such information[402].

Any firm that makes a written or oral communication to a customer in the course of, or in connection with, its designated investment business must pay due regard to its customers and in doing so must not exclude the duties it owes or liabilities it has to a customer under the Act or the regulatory system unless it has good reason to do so[403].

(a) Investment Management Firms

The Financial Resources component of IPRU(INV)[404] outlines the financial requirements for investment management firms[405]. The Handbook Glossary defines an investment management firm as 'a firm whose permitted activities include designated investment business, which is not an authorized professional firm, bank, building society, credit union, energy market participant, friendly society, ICVC, insurer, media firm, oil market participant, service company, incoming EEA firm[406], incoming Treaty firm[407] or UCITS qualifier[408], whose permission does not include a requirement that it comply with IPRU(INV) 3 or 10[409] or 13[410]. Investment management firms in this definition also include a firm:

a) Which was a member of IMRO immediately before commencement; and which was not, immediately before commencement, subject to the

400 COB 2.2.19R.
401 COB 2.3.3.R.
402 COB 2.3.5G.
403 COB 2.5.3R.
404 IPRU(INV) sourcebook - Chapter 5.
405 Other than European investment firms.
406 Without top-up permission.
407 Without top-up permission.
408 Without top-up permission.
409 Securities and futures firms.
410 Personal investment firms.

financial supervision requirements of the FSA[411], or PIA (Personal Investment Authority Limited) or SFA[412];

b) Whose permission includes a requirement that it comply with IPRU(INV)5[413];

c) Which was given a Part IV permission on or after commencement, or which was authorized under section 25 of the Financial Services Act 1986 immediately before commencement and was not a member of IMRO, PIA or SFA; and for which the most substantial part of its gross income, including commissions, from the regulated activities included in its Part IV permission is derived from one or more of the following activities:

   i. Managing investments other than for private customers or where the assets managed are primarily derivatives;
   ii. OPS activity;
   iii. Acting as the manager or trustee of an AUT;
   iv. Acting as the ACD or depositary of an ICVC establishing, operating or winding up a collective investment scheme[414];
   v. Safeguarding and administering investments.

A general requirement for investment management firms in the Investment Businesses sourcebook is that they possess adequate financial resources. IPRU (INV) rule 5.2.1(2) requires that a firm must have, at all times, no less than the amount and type of financial resources than its financial resources requirement. A firm's financial resources can be taken as its own funds if the firm is subject to an own funds requirement[415] under IPRU(INV) rule 5.2.3(2); its liquid capital, if the firm is subject to a liquid capital requirement under IPRU(INV) rule 5.2.3(1)(a); its own funds and its liquid capital where the firm is an ISD firm subject to an own funds requirement and a liquid capital requirement under IPRU(INV) rule 5.2.3(1)(b); or its own funds or liquid capital where the firm is an ISD firm and a trustee of an authorized unit trust scheme subject to an own funds requirement and a liquid capital requirement under IPRU(INV) rule 5.2.3(1)(c). The FSA provides

411 Section 43 of the Financial Services Act 1986.

412 Under lead regulation arrangements.

413 Investment management firms.

414 Other than an AUT or ICVC.

415 Unless otherwise stated, the own funds requirement is calculated in accordance with Table 5.2.3(3)(b) and the liquid capital requirement and total capital requirement (the sum of the expenditure based requirement, position risk requirement, counterparty risk requirement, foreign exchange requirement and other assets requirement) are calculated in accordance with Table 5.2.3(5) in Chapter 5 of the Interim Prudential Sourcebook for Investment Businesses.

a methodology by which firms must calculate their own funds and liquid capital subject to certain requirements[416].

A firm's financial resources requirement is determined, like actual financial resources, depending on the particular category a firm falls under. Under IPRU (INV) rule 5.2.3(1) the financial resources requirement of a non ISD firm comprises a liquid capital requirement greater than £5,000 and greater than its total capital requirement unless the firm falls within an exception. Exceptions to this requirement on non ISD firms includes those firm's whose permitted business includes the holding of customers' monies or assets and who executes transactions in investment for itself or its customers[417] or firms that are trustees of an authorized unit trust scheme whose permitted business consists of activities other than trustee activities and constituting specified trustee business.

A firm which is an ISD firm has a financial resources requirement of an own funds requirement and a liquid capital requirement, which is its total capital requirement unless the liquid capital requirement of an ISD firm with an expenditure based requirement consisting of 6/52 of its annual audited expenditure is greater than one quarter of its annual audited expenditure and greater than its total capital requirement.

The financial resources requirement for a firm, which is an ISD firm, but also a trustee of an authorized unit trust scheme or a depositary of an investment company with venture capital (ICVC) is the higher of an own funds requirement and liquid capital requirement. In this case the own funds requirement is either £4 million for a firm, which is a trustee of an authorized unit trust scheme, or a depositary of an ICVC, or £5,000 for any other firm. The liquid capital requirement is its total capital requirement unless the liquid capital requirement of an ISD firm with an expenditure based requirement consisting of 6/52 of its annual audited expenditure is greater than one quarter of its annual audited expenditure and greater than its total capital requirement.

(b) Rules on Large Exposures relating to ISD firms

An ISD firm must be able to monitor its individual large exposures and the total of its large exposures on a daily basis under IPRU(INV) rule 5.2.7(2). The firm must recalculate its large exposures position in a full and detailed manner before executing any transaction which may end in a breach of the limits, which are set out in IPRU(INV) rule 5.2.7(3). Unless it qualifies for an exception, an ISD firm must make certain: firstly, that each large exposure does not exceed either 25 per cent of its own funds or 20 per cent of its own funds where the expo-

416 Own funds and liquid capital are calculated in accordance with Table 5.2.2(1) in Chapter 5 of the Interim Prudential Sourcebook for Investment Businesses.

417 Unless in respect of venture capital investment for non-private customers.

sure is to an associate of the firm and secondly, that the aggregate of its large exposures does not exceed 800 per cent of its own funds. Exempt exposures may be excluded from the calculation of a firms large exposures and an appropriate amount may be deducted for partially exempt exposures[418].

(i) Record Keeping

A firm must ensure that adequate accounting records are maintained and when required by the FSA, be prepared to submit such reports in a timely manner[419]. As such, a firm's records must be - up to date and able to demonstrate the firm's financial position at any time with reasonable accuracy; demonstrate a firm's compliance with its financial resource requirements; and provide information necessary to prepare financial statements and periodical reports firstly, which may be required by the FSA and secondly, which the firm's auditor may need to form an opinion on any statements of the firm on which they may be required to report.

Proper accounting records must be kept by a firm in English to show and explain its own account transactions distinguishing between trading book and non-trading book transactions[420] and to show detailed information in relation to movements and holdings of customer's money, assets and liabilities[421]. They must be maintained for a minimum of six years and during the first two years, the accounting records must be kept either at the place where the firm carries on business or in a manner where they can be produced within 24 hours from the time they are requested[422].

(ii) Consolidated Supervision

The financial viability of a firm, which is a member of a group may suffer damage from excessive risks or financial deficiencies in other parts of the group hence certain rules are designed to watch for such weaknesses. Firms will be subject to consolidated supervision unless they qualify under either one of the exceptions stated in IPRU(INV) rules 5.7.1(2) and (3) listed below[423]. A firm that is subject to consolidated supervision is required to provide all information requested of it to enable the FSA to assess the risks to which the firm may be subject as a member of its particular group[424].

418 IPRU(INV) 5.2.7(4)R.
419 IPRU(INV) 5.3.1(1)R.
420 IPRU(INV) 5.3.1(3)R.
421 IPRU(INV) 5.3.1(4)R.
422 IPRU(INV) 5.3.1(6)R.
423 IPRU(INV) 5.7.1(1)R.
424 IPRU(INV) 5.7.1(4)R.

The first exception to the rule on consolidated supervision is through IPRU(INV) rule 5.7.1(2) for a firm that fulfils the conditions that the financial resources rules do not apply or if the firm is included in the supervision, on a consolidated basis, of the group of which it is a member by another competent authority. The second case for exception is through IPRU(INV) rule 5.7.1(3), which applies firstly, to each member of the group, which is an ISD firm or a European investment firm (a) that is subject to either a liquid capital requirement in accordance with IPRU(INV) rule 5.2.3(1) or to an equivalent capital regime; (b) complies with its financial resources requirement and large exposures requirements laid out in IPRU(INV) rules 5.2.7(2) to (5), or with the equivalent rules of its regulator; and (c) has systems to monitor and control the sources of capital and funding of all other financial institutions within the group. The rule also requires that each member of the group under FSA regulation notify the FSA of any serious risks that could undermine financial stability of the group and follow out any corrective action required by the FSA. The third requirement for exclusion under 5.7.1(3) is that the firm has applied for and obtained from the FSA a waiver from the consolidated supervision rule.

(7) Enforcement

The new legislation grants a single set of statutory investigation and enforcement powers to the FSA, which allows it to investigate and discipline authorized firms that breach the FSA rules or other FSMA Requirements[425]. Those engaged in regulated activities without authorization can be subject to criminal prosecution, such that law breakers could face imprisonment. Under FSMA, anyone who puts out misleading financial information could face unlimited fines[426]. As an example of the new broad scope of the FSA's authority, its powers include the right to name, shame and fine financial executives for transgressions at their firms. In full, the FSMA has statutory right to withdraw a firm's authorization; discipline both firms and people approved by the FSA through public censure and financial penalties; seek injunctions; impose penalties for market abuse; prosecute a variety offences; and require compensation be paid to consumers[427]. The Regulatory Decisions Committee (RDC) is the main body in the decision making process for all fundamental regulatory decisions. The approaches to transgressors will also most likely change in the future from what used to be quietly demanding corrective action to an aggressive public action on misdemeanors.

---

425 FSMA - Part XIV.

426 See FSMA - Part XIV, also FSMA – Part I sections 2-5.

427 FSMA - Part XV.

b) Conclusion

Overall, the English regulator does not provide, other than the American regulators, a general exemption opportunity for Hedge Funds. A Hedge Fund manager located in the UK will be subject to mainstream UK regulation. Thus, Hedge Funds are subject to the same supervision and regulation as any other investment vehicles.

A state of equilibrium between costs and benefits of regulation for the American regulator can be assumed. The FSMA, on the other hand, provides a single legal framework instead of the several different ones used by predecessor organizations. As a result, it combines existing law and self-regulatory requirements in many areas. This, in turn, simplifies regulatory activities significantly and decreases transaction costs. Thus, the FSA can also be assumed to provide a state of equilibrium between costs and attainments of regulation.

However, the new framework does display significant downsides. Firstly, and generally, due to its recent implementation it is not yet sure if the new framework will prevail and meet the demands of the Hedge Funds Industry. There are various indicators suggesting that Hedge Funds may be at a loss with this form of regulation.

As mentioned earlier, the supervision principle of the new regulator is risk-based as opposed to rule-based. The FSA identifies external environment risks, consumer and industry wide risks and risks from individual institutions[428]. Upon prioritization of risks FSA objectives provide a risk profile of each institution from which an overall risk score is determined for each firm. All market participants will be assessed through this integrated risk assessment framework and consequent targeting or prioritizing by the FSA will occur according to how participants rate. Since Hedge fund managers aim to achieve substantial absolute returns by engaging in aggressive trading tactics to profit from market inefficiencies and performance is measured by absolute returns, which is essentially profit as opposed to a standard benchmark with traditional funds, they are likely to be assessed as highly risky. As high impact, high-risk entities Hedge Funds will, thus, attract close attention by the FSA. This, in turn, may result in higher transparency standards, which is not in conformity with the aforementioned penchant for secrecy. This is a hypothetical scenario, which may in any given form be highly detrimental to the Hedge Fund industry.

One provision of concern is section 418 FSMA where persons who are carrying on a regulated activity that would not normally be considered as being carried on in the UK are classified as being carried in the UK. Hedge Fund operations frequently involve cross border elements and offshore transactions. Many Hedge Funds have been established offshore in tax-free jurisdictions because this

---

428 http://www.hmso.gov.uk.

essentially places the funds out of the reach of their national tax regimes. The removal of capital controls in the 1980s made this possible and spurred the rapid growth in offshore assets. High tax countries, such as the UK have been taking steps to prevent the loopholes through which tax is lost on offshore assets[429], among them the new framework and especially section 418 FSMA. By treating offshore Funds like UK national funds problems are inevitable. The offshore tax benefits are the ultimate marketing tool for Hedge Funds, besides the high performance and comparatively low risk. Curtailing these opportunities is a strong disincentive to achieve high net returns and puts Hedge Funds at a loss. Hedge Funds can still move to another jurisdiction but offshore Funds operating through the UK are at a loss. Their very existence is in danger when they loose their ability to operate offshore.

Hedge Funds must satisfy high level standards in order to gain permission to carry on regulated activities, i.e. be familiar with the Threshold Conditions (COND) and Principles for Business (PRIN); satisfy Systems, Controls and internal arrangements (SYSC); be aware of prudential requirements for adequate resources applicable to all firms; and depending on the type of business of the applicant, be aware of the detailed prudential requirements in the applicable sourcebook like the FSA's Training and Competence sourcebook (TC). These requirements precipitate transaction costs and do not equally ameliorate the aforementioned regulatory requirements. The financial system is, however, more transparent under these requirements than in 1988 due to tougher consumer finance regulation and more prevalent disclosure of interest. Thus, it is believed that it should be better able to deal with problems of information asymmetries. On the other hand firms are expected to conduct business with due skill, care and diligence and in meeting this requirement they are permitted to rely on others up to an extent. In general, firms may rely on such information from an unconnected authorized person or a professional firm unless they are aware, or ought to be reasonably aware, of any facts that would give reasonable grounds to question the accuracy of any such information. Even questioning the accuracy of such information may not be sufficient to avoid information asymmetries in the market. Without a strong market incentive for accuracy those information are not reliable and information asymmetries may be exacerbated.

[429] Other initiatives include such moves as taxing world-wide income over domestic-source income; anti-avoidance legislation to remove tax advantages of trust settlements; taxation of foreign gains, even in the form of capital, as income; and pressure on offshore jurisdictions to agree to mutual assistance treaties and come in line with international standards.

3. Germany[430]

To this date there are only very few registered Hedge Funds in Germany[431]. German and international big banks have tried for years to persuade investors in Germany of the advantages of Hedge Funds[432]. In the last five years, especially after "DWS Xavex Hedge Select" was set up, the public seems to have become aware of the Hedge Fund potential which resulted in an increased interest in Hedge Fund investing.

Normally, Hedge Funds are off-shore entities because regulation is less tight, which permits fund managers to make more flexible and short-term decisions. However, investing in Hedge Funds in Germany can be done in either of two vehicles. Investors can chose between domestic and foreign investment schemes[433].

Domestic investors i.e. domestic schemes in Germany were principally subject to investment restrictions for separate trust assets according to KAGG[434]. These restrictions had negative effects especially in a bear market. Investment companies operating under such a scheme need to be licensed by the BAFin. Domestic schemes can be close-end funds and open-end funds. Closed-end funds are possible as AGs[435], which have to be listed at a German stock exchange and need a depository bank. The situation for open-end funds is slightly more difficult. The only viable solution used to be that of assets collected in a fund without legal personality – so called "Sondervermögen" –, which is based on a contract between the capital investment company and the investors.

Usually, in case of an open-end fund, the fund assets are owned collectively by the investors and have to be kept separately with a depository bank[436].

---

430 The elaboration in this Chapter is primarily focused on the old regulatory framework for Hedge Funds, i.e. KAGG, which mostly prohibited Hedge Funds from doing business in Germany. The Chapter on Direct Regulation of Hedge Funds will elaborate on the new rules for Hedge Funds in Germany, Investmentmodernisierungsgesetz (InvG), vom 15. Dezember 2003, BGBl. 62, 19.12.2003, zuletzt geändert durch *Art.* 8 *Abs.* 8 des Gesetzes vom 04. Dezember 2004 (*BGBl.* I *S.* 3166). That chapter will also show the interplay between the old KAGG and the new InvG.

431 DWS Xavex Hedge Select: Commerzbank ADZ Fund: DRESDNER BANK AG AI GLOBAL HEDGE ZERTIFICAT.

432 See Schultz (2001), p. 1.

433 See BAKred (1998), p. 1. – as will be seen in the chapter "Regulators decide to regulate Hedge Funds directly," the German legislator has significantly updated is regulatory framework relating to Hedge Funds.

434 Gesetz über Kapitalanlagegesellschaften (Capital Investment Companies Act) of 1957 last amendment: April 1st, 1998.

435 Aktiengesellschaften (company limited by shares).

436 See BaKred (1998), p. 2 – "Apart from these two mentioned scenarios there are several types of investment policies: - securities funds (after implementation of the EU-UCITS-Directive.

The relevant law for foreign schemes is the AuslInvG[437], which is divided into three parts – distribution of NON-UCITS, distribution of UCITS and Tax Regulations. In case a German investor wants to invest in a foreign Hedge Fund, this direct investment in a foreign Hedge Fund is subject to sec.1, subsec.1AuslInvG. If this German investment is considered a capital investment in an investment company the ASTG[438]applies.

As to tax issues in Hedge Fund investing - holders of foreign investment shares are basically levied in the same way as German investment shareholders. Non-registered foreign investment schemes are treated less favorably. They may, however, appoint an authorized person to furnish certain information to avoid most of the disadvantages[439]. Generally, if a Hedge Fund qualifies as an investment fund, that is, operates under the principle of spreading risk and using specific investment instruments, and has an appointed tax representative, all income from the fund[440] will be subject to tax in the hands of the investors[441] in the calendar or financial year during which it accrues. The income from a Hedge Fund that is an investment fund without an appointed tax representative will be taxed on a standardized and approximated basis and the Hedge Fund itself is not accountable to tax. A Hedge Fund that does not qualify as an investment fund will be subject to general tax rules and how investors will be taxed depends on how the fund is legally structured - in a partnership, investors are taxed on their portion of profits accrued and in a corporation, on dividends received. The individual German investor may avoid income tax on part of his income if certain conditions hold.

Although there had been no fundamental changes in accounting or tax regulation in the aftermath of LTCM, the German legislator enacted the InvG in December 2003. The significant change in German Hedge Fund Regulation will be discussed in the Chapter on Direct Regulation.

IV. *Regulatory Proposals*

Various proposals for reviewing and improving the risk management process of banks and financial institutions have been made. The author elaborates fur-

---

All German securities funds are UCITS) – real estate funds, - money market funds, - mixed funds, - fund of funds, - participation funds. ".

437 Auslandsinvestmentgesetz (AuslInvestG), vom 28. Juli 1969 (BGBl. I 986), idF vom 11.10.1995 (BGBl. I 1250).

438 Auslands Steuer Gesetz - Foreign Tax Relations Act.

439 Care is advisable for the investor in case a non-registered investment fund licensed for sale in Germany (which is usually the case with Hedge Funds) does not appoint domestic tax representatives and does not regularly give evidence of details relevant for taxation, such as interest, dividend, profits made from sales and other profits.

440 Including realised capital gains.

441 Corporate and individual.

ther on what should have been done under a traditional legal regulatory approach in order to solve the aforementioned problems.

LTCM had become the poster child of regulators world-wide. In the aftermath of its near-collapse, regulators including the Basle Committee on Banking Supervision (Basle Committee)[442], the International Organization of Securities Commissions (IOSCO)[443], the Board of Governors of the U.S. Federal Reserve System (Board), the U.S. President's Working Group on Financial Markets (PWG)[444], the Counterparty Risk Management Policy Group (CRMPG)[445], the Multidisciplinary Working Group on Enhanced Disclosure[446] (MWGED)[447], the Committee on the Global Financial System (CGFS)[448], the International Swaps and Derivatives Association (ISDA)[449] and, summarizing the above mentioned Reports, the Financial Stability Forum[450] Working Group on Highly Leveraged Institutions (Summary Report)[451] have been reviewing ways to improve the regulatory framework relating to highly leveraged institutions (HLIs) and Hedge Funds, both of which referred herein as the "Hedge Funds". Regulators are concerned that banks and financial institutions are exposed not only to direct expo-

---

442 The Basle Committee on Banking Supervision Report of working group on banks' interaction with HLIs; The Paper on Sound Practices for Banks' interaction with HLIs, published in January 1999; and the follow up assessment, published in January 2000.

443 See IOSCO Technical Committee Report on Task Force on Hedge Funds and other HLIs, November 1999.

444 See U.S. President's Working Group Report on Hedge Funds Leverage and Long Term Capital Management, April 1999.

445 See The Counterparty Risk Management Policy Group Report Improving Counterparty Risk Management Practices, June 1999

446 The Multi-disciplinary Working Group on Enhanced Disclosure was established in June 1999 and consisted of representatives from the BCBS, DGFS, IAIS and IOSCO. The mandate of the MWG was "to assess the feasibility and utility of enhanced disclosure by financial intermediaries." It did so by organising a study of disclosure by a range of financial firms representing various financial sectors (banking, insurance, broker-dealers, mutual funds, leveraged investment funds, finance companies and pension funds). It reported to the four sponsoring Committees in February 2001.

447 MWGED is conducting a pilot study to test the efficiency of risk-based disclosures as a follow up to the proposals made by the CGFS Group on Disclosure.

448 See CGFS proposal on Disclosure.

449 See ISDA Collateral Review 1999.

450 http://www.fsforum.org/

451 The Financial Stability Forum Working Group on Highly Leveraged Institutions ("Summary Report") was founded by the G7 Finance Ministers at the inaugural meeting of the G7 Financial Stability Forum on 14th of April1999. The purpose of the group was to assess the risk to financial stability caused by highly leveraged institutions; as well as to evaluate the work that has been done by existing official committees and industry bodies on the subject. This also included the level of implementation of any recommendations, to help improve levels of co-operation between such bodies and to identify issues that have not already been covered, with the ultimate objective of encouraging a consensus on the way forward for regulators and supervisors.

sure to Hedge Funds[452] but secondary exposures to losses from liquidation of collateral and the re-balancing of portfolios under adverse market conditions. The rapid or disorderly de-leveraging of large positions in a volatile and illiquid market will lead to higher volatility and illiquidity and have knock–on effects on the portfolios of creditors as well as third parties.

Financial crises as that involving LTCM are partly traced back to a lack of transparency. But regulators also opine that improved transparency through enhanced disclosure to the public should help market participants make better, more informed judgments about market integrity and the creditworthiness of borrowers and counterparties. They are therefore reviewing the adequacy of public disclosure.

The most common approach of regulators consists of three main prongs of change to the regulatory framework relating to Hedge Funds: 1. Enhanced transparency. 2. Direct regulation, 3. Indirect regulation.

1. The Board of Governors of the U.S. Federal Reserve System

The Board of Governors of the U.S. Federal Reserve[453] issued supervisory guidance regarding counterparty credit risk management[454] on 1st February 1999. Examiners and supervisory staff at each Federal Reserve Bank and domestic and foreign banking organizations supervised by the Federal Reserve are instructed to evaluate whether banking institutions:

- Devote sufficient resources to the management of the risks involved in growing highly profitable or potentially high-risk activities and product lines;
- Have internal audit and independent risk management functions that adequately focus on growth, profitability, and risk criteria in targeting their reviews,
- Archive an appropriate balance among all elements of credit risk management including both qualitative and quantitative assessments of counterparty credit-worthiness;

---

452 I.e. measured by the unwinding cost.

453 The Federal Reserve, the central bank of the United States, was founded by the U.S. Congress in 1913 to provide the USA with a safer, more flexible, and more stable monetary and financial system. Today the Federal Reserve's duties fall into four general areas: (1) conducting the nation's monetary policy; (2) supervising and regulating banking institutions and protecting the credit rights of consumers; (3) maintaining the stability of the financial system; and (4) providing certain financial services to the U.S. government, the public, financial institutions, and foreign official institutions.

454 See U.S. Federal Reserve (1999b).

- Measurement and evaluation of both on and off-balance sheet exposures, including potential future exposure; adequate stress testing; reliance on collateral and other credit enhancements;
- Ensure that actual business practices confirm with stated policies and their intent; and are moving in a timely fashion to enhance their measurement of counterparty credit risk exposure, including the refinement of potential future exposure measures and the establishment of stress testing methodologies that incorporate the interaction of market and credit risks.

This supervisory guidance for examiners and supervisory staff supervising large, complex banking organizations[455] reiterates and expands existing supervisory materials of the Federal Reserve and other regulators and in established industry standards. Supervisors and examiners have been instructed to conduct target transactions testing on activities, business lines and products experiencing significant growth, above normal profitability or large potential future exposure. This guidance and the report on HLIs by the Working Group of the Basle Committee discussed above were formally included in the Federal Reserve's Trading and Capital Markets Activities Manual in its March 1999 update.

2. Hong Kong Regulatory Framework

After the Asian financial crisis in 1997-98, and, thus, the LTCM case, Hong Kong authorities clamped down on the ability of hedge funds to borrow securities and sell them short, making it hard for funds to execute their most basic strategy. Regulators also stepped up spot investigations of hedge-fund management companies, financial advisers and distributors in an approach some industry members called draconian. It was an effort to scout out and stop the funds that were speculating against the Hong Kong dollar and the stock market[456].

Furthermore, Hedge Funds have been criticized by the chief executive of the Hong Kong Monetary Authority (HKMA)[457], Joseph Yam[458], for contributing to

455 And distributed by them to domestic and foreign banking organisations with significant trading and derivatives credit exposure.

456 See WSJ (2001).

457 The HKMA is the government authority in Hong Kong responsible for maintaining monetary and banking stability. HKMA was established on 1 April 1993 by merging the Office of the Exchange Fund with the Office of the Commissioner of Banking. Its main functions and responsibilities are governed by the Hong Kong Exchange Fund Ordinance and the Hong Kong Banking Ordinance and it reports to the Financial Secretary. Its main functions are: -keeping the Hong Kong dollar stable, -managing the Exchange Fund - Hong Kong's official reserves in a sound and effective way, -promoting the safety of Hong Kong's banking system, -developing Hong Kong's financial infrastructure to enable money to flow smoothly, freely and without obstruction. Fur-

the Asian economic crisis. He has called for greater transparency of markets, particularly OTC[459] markets. He believes a better disclosure framework should be created. Secondly, he has called for Hedge Funds to be regulated. He supports such indirect regulation of Hedge Funds as imposing capital charges on lending to Hedge Funds and raising margin and collateral requirements. Last, to prevent regulatory arbitrage, he suggests higher risk weights for counterparty transactions for banks doing business with offshore financial entities that do not comply with Basle core principles.

The Hong Kong Securities & Futures Commission ("SFC") participates in this debate through its membership of IOSCO. The SFC has been taking industry views as to the regulatory positions of Hedge Funds. The SFC has not – at least as to date – issued any specific view on how it might seek to regulate the activities of theses funds, to the extent these activities are undertaken in Hong Kong.

This is the nub of the problem – fund managers and advisers bases in Hong Kong and undertaking the business of management or advice from Hong Kong will be subject to SFC's licensing regime and, in particular, the Fund Manager Code of Conduct (the "Code"). The Code sets out conduct requirements for persons registered with the SFC whose business involves the discretionary management of collective investments, including unit trusts and mutual funds. The Code would not apply to a "non-discretionary" Hedge Fund adviser based in Hong Kong giving "advice" to an offshore Hong Kong Fund Manager. To this extent the Code[460] is limited in its application. In addition, even if the Code were applicable, it does not place specific restrictions on a fund manager's trading activity and, in particular, the extent to which the manager can use gearing. This is, of course, a very different situation in respect of those authorized mutual funds in Hong Kong, one example of which is ED&F Man's AHL Diversified Futures Fund product.

In the authorized funds area, the SFC is able to approve certain specialized types of fund including:

---

thermore, the HKMA's policy objectives are: to maintain currency stability, within the framework of the linked exchange rate system, through sound management of the Exchange Fund, monetary policy operations and other means deemed necessary; to promote the safety and stability of the banking system through the regulation of banking business and the business of taking deposits, and the supervision of authorised institutions; and to enhance the efficiency, integrity and development of the financial system, particularly payment and settlement arrangements.

458 Joseph Yam was chief executive of the Hong Kong Monetary Authority in 1999.

459 Over-the-Counter (OTC) Transactions are transactions between parties that are not executed on an organised exchange but rather are privately negotiated on a bilateral basis between the parties. Stocks of smaller companies, as well as forward contracts and other derivatives, are traded in OTC markets.

460 This in any event, does not have the force of law.

- Unit Portfolio Management Funds;
- Money Market/Cash Management Funds;
- Warrant Funds;
- Leveraged Funds;
- Futures and Options Funds; and
- Guaranteed Funds.

However, given the abovementioned trading strategies of most Hedge Funds, they would be highly unlikely to authorization in Hong Kong – even with the fullest of disclosure and risk warning.

3. International Organization of Securities Commissions

IOSCO is an international grouping of securities market regulators. Its current membership comprises regulatory bodies from 91 countries that have day to day responsibility for securities regulation and the administration of securities laws[461]. IOSCO recognizes that sound domestic markets are necessary to the strength of a developed domestic economy and that domestic security markets are increasingly being integrated into a global market[462]. The IOSCO By-Laws[463] express the intent that securities regulators, at both the domestic and international levels, should be guided by consistently high regulatory standards which will result in not only more protected investors but also in reduced systemic risk. Therefore, the three core objectives of securities regulation are[464]:

- The protection of investors;
- Ensuring that markets are fair, efficient and transparent;
- The reduction of systemic risk.

In order to attain these objectives the Executive Committee of the organization has established two specialized working Committees[465]. For the purpose of

461 See www.iosco.org.

462 See IOSCO (1998), pp. 2-3 - the Preamble to IOSCO's By-Laws states: "Securities authorities resolve to co-operate together to ensure a better regulation of the markets, on the domestic as well as on the international level, in order to maintain just, efficient and sound markets: to exchange information on their respective experiences in order to promote the development of domestic markets; to unite their efforts to establish standards and an effective surveillance of international securities transactions; to provide mutual assistance to ensure the integrity of the markets by a vigorous application of the standards and by effective enforcement against offences.".

463 See IOSCO (1998), p. 4.

464 See id. at 6.

465 I.e. the Technical Committee and the Emerging Markets Committee. IOSCO (1998), p. 8 – "The Emerging Markets Committee, endeavours to promote the development and improvement of efficiency of emerging securities and futures markets by establishing principles and minimum

this dissertation, the focus shall remain on the Technical Committee, which is made up of sixteen agencies that regulate some of the world's more developed and internationalized markets[466]. Its objective is to review major regulatory issues related to international securities and futures transactions and to co-ordinate practical responses to these concerns[467].

The Report of the Technical Committee[468] of November 1999 suggests that more prudent practices by regulated firms that are universally applied across sectors and appropriately encouraged by diligent supervisors should have a significant effect on reducing some elements of systemic risk raised by the activities of HLIs. However, this is considered unlikely to be enough as bilateral information flows may give only a partial picture of the ability of HLIs to create market disturbances of the extent to which a particular firm's own financial position may be damaged if an HLI failed. Also, the best efforts of individual regulated firms and the incentives provided by regulators to encourage prudent risk management practices will not be sufficient to reduce the systemic risks of concern. Therefore, the Technical Committee opines that additional measures beyond enhanced risk management at regulated firms should be considered. Further reduction of systemic risk and the potential for destabilization is said to require accurate and up-to-date information about relevant activities of HLIs to be in the hands of those who can act to mitigate those risks. Therefore, additional transparency regarding HLI activities should be required.

The Technical Committee believes that information at regulated firms about HLIs should always be available to regulators because exploring greater public disclosure by HLIs and institutions with dealings with HLIs is the most promising immediate avenue to address the potential systemic risk and market destabilization concerns raised by HLIs. It may, however, be necessary to revisit the imposition of reporting requirements on HLIs directly if a sufficient level of enhanced public disclosure of information to address these concerns proves not to be achievable.

---

standards, preparing training programs for the staff of members and facilitating exchange of information and transfer of technology and expertise. It has set up Working Groups to address the following functional areas: Disclosure and Accounting; Regulation of Secondary Markets; Regulation of Market Intermediaries; Enforcement and the Exchange of Information; Investment Management.

466 See id. at 9.

467 See id. at 10-11 (elaborating that: "The work of the Technical Committee is divided into the following five major functional subject areas: Multinational Disclosure and Accounting; Regulation of Secondary Markets; Regulation of Market Intermediaries; Enforcement and the Exchange of Information; Investment Management. The Technical Committee has set up specialized Working Groups to address each of the above mentioned subject areas. The members of these Working Groups meet several times during the year and tackle, almost on a continuous basis, the mandates that they receive from the Technical Committee.").

468 See IOSCO Technical Committee (1999).

Summarizing, the Technical Committee of IOSCO made the following proposals[469]:

Overall Risk Management Framework:

- Financial intermediaries should have a clear credit risk strategy and credit risk management policy and process. Dealings with HLIs, and with all other counterparties, should follow this. This strategy, policy and process should be specified by senior management and approved by the Board[470].
- As part of this, senior management[471] should set an overall tolerance for risk, including loss potential in adverse markets. The Board of Directors should approve this[472].
- The expected contribution of individual business lines[473]to the risk reward profile should be specified by senior management.
- The risk management framework should integrate market risk and credit risk elements where appropriate[474].
- Financial intermediaries should have a credit department, independent of line management, to perform credit analysis and monitor compliance with approved credit limits[475].
- Financial intermediaries should maintain documentary evidence of critical control processes and periodically assess the firm's adherence to them.
- Policies on counterparty relations with HLIs should clearly indicate the circumstances in which exceptions may be granted and the procedure to be followed.
- Financial intermediaries should consider their approval procedures for new products capable of generating credit risk.
- Financial intermediaries should have contingency plans and procedures to be followed in the event of a dislocation to the operations of a HLI counterparty.

---

469 See id. at 6f.; FSF (2000), p. 62.

470 See also Basel Committee and CRMPG.

471 Senior Management is a group of executives or other management body with the authority and responsibility to direct and oversee a Hedge Fund Manager's day-to-day activities on behalf of a Hedge Fund. Senior management is typically responsible for risk allocation among portfolio managers, or "risk selectors".

472 See also PWG and CRMPG.

473 Including dealings with HLIs.

474 See also Basle Committee and PWG.

475 See also PWG and CRMPG.

- Financial intermediaries should have a clear policy, which includes disclosure and monitoring provisions, on investment in counterparty HLIs by employees, directors, significant shareholders or the firm itself.

Credit assessment and ongoing monitoring of HLIs[476]:

- Financial intermediaries should have effective counterparty risk rating systems.
- Before starting a relationship with a HlI, financial intermediaries should receive adequate information to inform their internal credit approval processes[477]. This should include information on:
    - Aggregate financial information[478]
    - Financial performance[479]
    - Details of risk management procedures and controls[480]
    - Results form[481] risk measurement tests[482]
    - General direction and scope of trading activities, including investment strategies[483]
    - Amount of leverage[484]
    - Liquidity and funding profile[485]
    - Details of large or concentrated positions.
    - Details of key personnel and organizational structure[486]
    - Where possible third party information such as credit registers or references form known parties should be assessed[487]
    - The legal status and investment authority of the HLI[488]
    - The connected entities of an HLI or group of HLIs[489]

---

476 See IOSCO Technical Committee (1999), pp. 9-10; FSF (2000), pp. 63-64.

477 See also PWG (albeit not specified in detail) and Basle Committee.

478 Covering both on and off-balance sheet positions. See also Basle Committee.

479 See also Basle Committee and CRMPG.

480 See also Basle Committee and CRMPG.

481 And methodology of.

482 VAR, stress tests. See also Basle Committee and CRMPG.

483 See also Basle Committee and CRMPG.

484 See also Basle Committee.

485 Including back office structure. See also Basle Committee and CRMPG.

486 Including back office structure. See also Basle Committee.

487 In all cases, financial intermediaries should be confined that they are dealing with institutions of sound reputation before starting counterparty relationships. See also Basle Committee.

488 See also Basle Committee.

- The purpose and structure of the transaction should be identified and the repayment capacity analyzed against several scenarios.
- Procedures should be in place to ensure that the information received above is updated on a timely basis[490]
- Financial intermediaries should adopt written policies governing use of proprietary information provided by counterparties.

Exposure Measurement[491]:

- More useful measures of PFE[492] need to be developed[493]
- When exposures are large or illiquid, market-to-market figures should be supplemented by an estimation of liquidation based replacement value[494].
- Better stress testing[495]/scenario analysis[496] should also be used to test exposures[497].

489 If there are connected entities: the relative size and activities of group member, the role that the lead member plays in the group as a whole and; the nature and size of any intra-group transactions.

490 See also PWG, CRMPG and Basle Committee (Basle adds – "updates should be received at least quarterly and more frequently when exposure increases significantly or there is high market volatility").

491 See IOSCO Technical Committee (1999), pp. 9 f.; FSF (2000), p. 65.

492 Potential future credit exposure.

493 See also PWG and Basle Committee.

494 PWG and Basle Committee agree with IOSCO that exposure measurement is an area in which further work needs to be undertaken.

495 Stress test is a general term for the practice of subjecting a model (e.g. a VAR model) to inputs that are adjusted to represent extreme or unusual changes in market factors. The sources of stress may be actual historical changes in market factors or hypothetical changes.

496 I.e. the practice of subjecting a model (e.g. a VAR model) to adjust inputs in order to assess the impact of a specified scenario of market events on a Hedge Fund's portfolio. A scenario could be historical (e.g. by reproducing the events of October 1997) or hypothetical (e.g. by simulating an event that would stress the market factors to which the Hedge Fund is most exposed)

497 Basle Committee and PWG as well as CRMPG agree that tests should assess concentration risk (both to a single counterparty and to groups of counterparties); correlation risk amongst both market risk factors and credit risk factors; and risk that liquidation of positions could significantly move the market. Particular analytical focus should be given to the impact of stress events on large or illiquid sources of risk.

Limit setting[498]:

- Financial intermediaries should establish firm-wide credit limits for individual counterparties. Such limits should consider exposures arising form all transactions or services exposing the firm to credit risk and should be developed in line with the overall risk policy[499]
- Consideration should also be given to the counterparty sub-limits for particular products.
- Financial intermediaries may wish to consider an aggregate credit limit for HLIs as a group based on PFE, Liquidation-based replacement value and/or other factors[500].
- Limits should be monitored at least daily with a clear procedure for bringing down exposures if they are breached.

Collateral, contractual provisions and valuation[501]:

- These should each be the subject of clear, written policy. This is the responsibility of senior management[502]
- Collateral agreements with counterparties should be clearly documented
- Collateral agreements and contractual provisions with HLI counterparties should be aligned with the financial intermediary's assessment of counterparty credit risk[503]
- Financial intermediaries should have guidelines to determine when initial margin should be requested. As a general practice, initial margin should be required form HLI counterparties[504]
- Appropriate haircuts[505] should be applied[506]
- Collateral should be valued at least daily and preferably on a more frequent basis[507]

---

498 See IOSCO Technical Committee (1999), p.32; FSF (2000), p.65.

499 Unilateral agreed by Basle Committee, PWG and CRMPG.

500 See also PWG and CRMPG (which gives four possibilities and suggests firms may want to use more than one.)

501 See FSF (2000), p. 66.

502 See also PWG and Basle Committee.

503 See also Basle Commitee.

504 See also CRMPG and Basle Committee.

505 FSF (2000), p. III-5 – i.e. "The difference between the market value of an asset posted as collateral and the value attributed to such an asset by a party in determining whether the collateral requirements of such party have been met. A haircut is intended to protect a party that receives collateral from fluctuations in the value of the instruments posted as collateral.".

506 Factors include the creditworthiness of the counterparty and the liquidity and volatility of the collateral. Also Basle Committee.

- Stress testing should be conducted on the value of collateral held. Financial intermediaries should be aware of correlation[508] between the value of collateral held and their own trading positions[509]
- Financial intermediaries should be alert to the possibility that collateral value is negatively correlated with the market value of contracts of the possibility of counterparty default[510].

Legal Risk[511]:

- Financial intermediaries need a full understanding of any counterparty HLI's[512]
- The legal basis of documentation will not necessarily have been tested in all jurisdictions. Therefore, financial intermediaries should bay particular attention to: the legal status of netting[513] and collateral terms

---

507 See also Basle Committee and PWG.

508 Correlation is a standardised measure of the relative movements between two variables, such as the prices of two different securities. The level of correlation between two variables is measured on a scale of –1 to *1. If two variables move up or down together, they are positively correlated. If they tend to move the in opposite directions, they are negatively correlated.

509 See also Basle Committee.

510 See also Basle Committee.

511 Technical Committee of IOSCO (1999), p. 16; FSF (2000), pp. 68, III-7 : "Legal Risk is the risk of loss arising from uncertainty in laws, regulations or legal actions which may affect transactions between parties. Legal risk may include issues related to the enforceability of netting agreements, the perfection of collateral, the capacity of parties, the legality of contracts etc. ".

512 I.e. legal form, legal authority to enter into transactions; legal limits on the way it may deal; legal relationships with any related entities; and which country's laws govern the entity and/or specific transaction. Also PWG.

513 Netting involves exposures on multiple transactions between the same two counterparties and reducing them down to a single net exposure amount by offsetting the positive exposure with the negative. Netting provisions are typically included in master agreements between two parties and provide that positive market-to-market values on transactions for one counterparty will be offset by negative market-to-market values for the same counterparty on other transactions for purposes of determining net payments to be made or amount of collateral to be delivered, for instance. Bilateral netting arrangements take the following forms: 1. Payment netting: This form of provision generally provides that payments to be made between parties with respect to one or more transactions governed by a master agreement may be netted to a single net payment amount where payments are scheduled to occur on the same day and in the same currency. Some provisions also permit netting of payments in different currencies. 2. Close-out netting: This form of netting becomes operative only in an event of default or an "termination event", such as the credit rating downgrade. Under a master agreement, the positive contract value for a particular counterparty are netted against the negative contract values for the same party for all transactions subject to the master agreement. (e.g. the current ISDA master agreement – ISDA (1992) – specifies, that, if a default or termination event occurs, all transactions covered by the master agreement will be terminated and the values of the various transactions will be netted to a single closeout amount). 3.

and conditions; obligations at the end of the contract; events of default; covenants and close-out provisions[514].

- Financial intermediaries should ensure that all legal documentation supporting the transaction is clear and complete[515]
- Financial intermediaries should assess the extent to which the failure of an HLI might raise problematic bankruptcy issues that would complicate the orderly liquidation of positions.

Reporting to senior management[516]:

- Senior management information should also highlight possible correlation between firms own proprietary positions and counterparty positions and/or collateral pledged by counterparties[517].

With regard to the role of regulators in individual firms' risk management[518] IOSCO finds:

- Sound practices are vulnerable to erosion by competitive pressures. Regulators should monitor, and encourage improvements in, financial intermediaries with significant HLI business[519]. This might include:
  - Assessing adequacy of risk management procedures[520].
  - Assessing compliance with both internal risk management procedures and the sound practices identified in the various reports[521].

Netting by novation: Two counterparties agree that "matched" pairs of transactions (e.g. transactions that have the same settlement date) will be deemed terminated and replaced by a single transaction requiring a payment equal to the difference between the values of the two original transactions. Netting by novation is common in foreign exchange transactions in which parties (typically banks) are likely to have a large number of offsetting payments due in the same currency on the same settlement date. 4. Cross-product netting: Bilateral netting arrangements are increasingly being extended to permit netting across products, often through the use of master-master agreements. (e.g. a party could reduce its current exposure to another party by offsetting positive mark-to-market values for its OTC swap positions under one master agreement against its foreign exchange positions which have negative mark-to-market value under a different master agreement, provided both master agreements have been executed between the same parties.

514 See also PWG.

515 IOSCO – documentation, including master agreements where appropriate, should be executed prior to a transaction being initiated. CRMPG – should be executed within 90 days of a transaction. Pending execution, firms should use long form confirmations.

516 See FSF (2000), p. 69.

517 See also CRMPG.

518 See FSF (2000), p. 72.

519 See also PWG and Basle Committee.

520 See also PWG and Basle Committee.

521 See also PWG and Basle Committee.

- Applying an appropriate supervisory response to any shortcomings[522].
- Groupings of regulators should co-operate to minimize opportunities for regulatory arbitrage[523].
- Direct regulation of HLIs is not appropriate at this stage[524]

Finally, IOSCO makes recommendations with regard to greater transparency[525] in regulatory reporting by financial intermediaries:

- IOSCO considers regular reporting, but favors enhanced public disclosure directly by the HLI. Reporting[526] should be considered if public disclosure initiatives fail. Nevertheless, in all cases information at financial intermediaries should be accessible by its regulators. When crises occur, firms must be prepared and able to provide regulators with requested information in a timely way.
- Reporting of disclosure should be by HLIs directly rather than by financial intermediaries.
- With Regard to enhanced public disclosure by HLIs IOSCO opines that HLIs should be encouraged[527] to provide enhanced public information.
- With regard to detailed specification of information, which should be disclosed, IOSCO identifies types of information, which should be considered when specifying data. Specific suggestions, however, are deferred to MWGED.

4. Basle Committee

As it is arguable that counterparties may not receive sufficient information about risk exposures through due diligence and exposure monitoring process, the Basle Committee[528] recommended in its Report on Banks' Interactions with

---

522 This might include a greater intensity of supervisory oversight or the use of formal or informal regulatory sanctions against firms that do not comply. Alternatively, some supervisors make use of variable capital ratios and/or prohibitions or restrictions on certain activities. See also Basle Committee. IOSCO- in extreme cases, regulators may consider closure of the firm.

523 See also Basle Committee.

524 See also Basle Committee. PWG states it should be reconsidered if indirect measures and greater transparency are shown not to be working in an effective manner.

525 See IOSCO Technical Committee (1999), pp. 21 f.; FSF (2000), pp. 76 f..

526 Either via financial intermediaries or direct form the HLI

527 Supported by market pressure or incentives.

528 The Basle Committee is made up or representatives form Belgium, Canada, France, Germany, Italy, Japan, Luxembourg, the Netherlands, Sweden, Switzerland, the United Kingdom and the United States. In most cases countries have two representatives, one from the central bank and

HLIs[529] dated January 1999 conducting a general review of the adequacy of public disclosure and considering whether a credit register for bank loans should be extended to HLIs. The register would collect in a centralized place information on the exposures of international financial intermediaries to single HLIs that are capable of creating systematic risk.

In its report on Banks' Interactions with HLIs[530], dated January 1999, the working group on HLIs of the Basle Committee[531] sets out three policy responses to the risk generated by HLIs. The Working Group of the Basle Committee recommends:

- That supervisors encourage banks to pursue more prudent risk management policies by formulating standards for sound practices in bank/HLI dealings; developing a more comprehensive due diligence process, formulating a more consistent process of stress testing, and

---

another form a bank supervisory agency. The committee met secretly for many years, without publishing the results of its discussions. In 1981, it issued the first of what has become an annual Report on International Developments in Banking Supervision. It has also published various studies and proposals from time to time. The major purpose of the Committee since its inception has been "to close gaps in the supervisory net and to improve supervisory understanding and the quality of banking supervision world-wide." It has pursued these objectives in three ways: by exchanging information on the operations of international banks and on national regulatory policies and practices; by developing new approaches to the supervision of international banks; and by "reviewing the desirability of setting standards" in bank capital and other areas – BIS (1989). Because the Committee was born in the crisis atmosphere of the 1974 bank failures, it naturally focused its early attention n the prudential supervision of international banks. The chief outgrowth of this concern was a document, known as "The Concordat", first published in 1975. The Concordat established two principles that have since animated the Basle Committee's work: (1) "That no foreign banking establishment should escape supervision" and (2) "That the supervision should be adequate, see BIS (1983). The significant policy implication of these phrases was that banking supervision had become a multilateral activity. By the terms of the Concordat, primary responsibility for international banking supervision was given to the parent country's authorities. Host supervisors were expected to regulate "foreign bank establishments operating in their territories as individual institutions". Thus, bank branches would be supervised by parent authorities, subsidiaries would fall under the purview of the hosts. The Concordat recognised, however, that "these responsibilities of host and parent authorities are both complementary and overlapping", See BIS (1983).

529 See BIS (1999b).

530 See id.

531 The working group on HLIs of the Basle Committee is comprised of the Commission Bancaire (Paris); Bundesaufsichtsamt für das Kreditwesen (BAKred) (Berlin); De Nederlandsche Bank (Amsterdam); Eigenössische Bankenkommission (Bern); Financial Services Authority (London); Bank of England (London); Board of Governors of the Federal Reserve System (Washington, D.C.); Federal Reserve Bank of New York; Office of the Comptroller of the Currency (Washington, D.C.); Federal Deposit Insurance Corporation (Washington, D.C.); and Secretariat of the Basle Committee, Bank of International Settlements.

implementing improved methodologies for measuring potential future exposure. In addition, the Basle Committee recommends supervisors to review existing regulatory standards including capital treatment of the credit exposures arising out of derivatives and repurchase transactions with HLIs; and relying on a differentiated supervisory treatment of individual bank (e.g. capital and reporting requirements, large exposure limits) depending on the riskiness of their particular lines of business;
- Enhancing transparency by conducting a general review of the adequacy of public disclosure and considering whether a credit register for bank loans should be extended to the HLI context; and
- More direct regulation of HLIs, including licensing requirements, fit and proper tests, and minimum standards for capital and risk management.

5. Basle Committee and IOSCO joint consultative paper

The Basle Committee and IOSCO in their joint consultative paper on public disclosure of trading and derivatives activities[532] issued in February 1999 recommended the disclosure by banks and financial institutions to financial statement users of summary information, both qualitative and quantitative, on the scope and nature of trading and derivatives activities and how these activities contribute to earnings profiles. Banks and securities firms are also encouraged to disclose information produced by their internal risk measurement and management systems on their risk exposures and their performance in managing these exposures.

6. Credit Risk Management Policy Group

The Counterparty Risk Management Policy Group (CRMPG) is a group consisting of twelve major commercial and investment banks[533] formed in January 1999 after the near collapse of LTCM[534].

The objective of the group was to redevelop standards for strengthening risk management practices at the banks, securities firms and other dealers to avoid similar events like those of LTCM in the future. Therefore, the CRMPG released

---

532 See BIS (1999a).

533 Members of the group include senior-level practitioners from the following organizations: Barclays Capital, Bear Stearns, Chase, Citigroup, Credit Suisse First Boston, Deutsche Bank, Goldman, Sachs & Co., Lehman Brothers, Merrill Lynch, J.P. Morgan, Morgan Stanley Dean Witter, and Warburg Dillon Read (UBS AG). Senior practitioners from ten other firms, including insurance companies, investment managers, Hedge Funds, law firms, and other commercial banks supported the effort by joining its working groups.

534 United State House of Representatives, Subcommittee on Capital Markets, Securities and Government Sponsored Enterprises, Committee on Banking and Financial Services (1999), p. 1.

its report and recommendations to strengthen practices related to the management of market, counterparty credit, and liquidity risk, called "Improving Counterparty Risk Management Practices"[535]. The recommendations form an integrated framework of best market practices and flexible techniques that, when implemented together, are supposed to help promote market stability[536].

The 20 specific recommendations in the report represent a comprehensive, integrated framework, and not a series of stand-alone initiatives. They are linked together through six interconnected building blocks:

- Enhanced information sharing between counterparties.
- An analytical framework for evaluating the effects of leverage on market liquidity and credit risk;
- Improved credit risk estimation techniques;
- Stronger internal limit setting, collateral margin, and other credit risk management practices;
- Improved internal risk transparency for senior management and regulators; and
- Stronger and harmonized market conventions for close-outs and other key credit documentation practices.

However, these recommendations comply, apart from slight differences, mostly with those of IOSCO[537]. Those differences and additional recommendations shall be highlighted as follows:

- With regard to the overall risk management framework, CRMPG recommends additionally that senior management not only establishes a credit department, independent of line management, but also ensures that this unit is adequately staffed with employees of appropriate skill and experience[538]. Furthermore, financial intermediaries should develop credit risk cost allocation and valuation practices that provide in-

535 See CRMPG (1999).

536 The group's co-chairs, E. Gerald Corrigan, a Managing Director at Goldman, Sachs & Co., and Stephen G. Thieke, a Managing Director at J.P. Morgan, said in a joint statement: "The report serves the universal objectives of promoting greater market discipline and, over time, reducing systemic risk. We believe that "state of the art" risk management techniques should be flexible in their day-to-day application, depending on the practices of each firm and recognize that approaches to credit terms and conditions must remain at the core of the credit decision making process of individual firms."

537 See IOSCO Technical Committee (1999), pp. 9 f.

538 See FSF (2000), p. 62.

centives for business line and risk managers to manage counterparty risk in a manner consistent with the firm's overall risk tolerance[539].

- With regard to credit assessment and ongoing monitoring of HLIs, the CRMPG recommends furthermore, that specific portfolio information may sometimes be needed to manage more credit intensive activities, larger than normal exposures or higher risk counterparties[540].
- When it comes to exposure management, not only should more useful measures of potential future credit exposure (PFE) be developed, but also, when exposures are large or illiquid, should mark-to-market figures be supplemented by an estimation of liquidation based replacement value. In order to do this, firms must[541]:
  - Measure and set limits on the degree of reliance on collateral.
  - Estimate replacement cost and collateral value at potential liquidation.
  - Use liquidity-adjusted VaR[542] estimates or judgmental stress test to reflect the potential for adverse price movement to take place before a liquidation can be conducted.
  - Review collateral and margining terms in the light of the above.
  - Establish limit structures relating to pre-collateral exposures; estimated liquidation exposures and potential exposures.

---

539 See id. at 63.

540 See id. at 64; See also Basle Committee.

541 See FSF (2000), p. 65.

542 Value-at-Risk (VAR) is an integrated measure of the market risk of a portfolio of assets and /or liabilities. At the most general level , VAR is a measure of the potential change in value of a specified portfolio over a specified time interval or holding period, resulting from potential changes in market factors (e.g. prices and volatility). The VAR measure is based on the distribution of potential changes in the value of the portfolio and is expressed in terms of a confidence level. A Hedge Fund Manager's risk monitoring function should use VAR to estimate the maximum expected amount a Hedge Fund could lose over a specified period of time horizon at a specified probability level. (e.g. the risk monitoring function could calculate the maximum expected loss for a one-day period at a 95% probability level – i.e. the level of loss that should be exceeded on only five trading days out of 100.) The challenge in calculating an accurate VAR is determining the distribution of potential value changes for market factors, which requires the risk monitoring functions to choose a methodology for modelling potential changes in market factors. Different methods are currently used to determine such distribution when calculating VAR (e.g. historical simulation method, Monte Carlo Simulation Method, Analytic Variance – Covariance Method).

With regard to collateral, contractual provisions and valuation, CRMPG suggests[543]:

- The amount of initial margin should be based on PFE[544] and/or estimates of liquidation-based replacement values.
- Financial intermediaries should develop and apply independent price verification procedures. External sources should be used whenever feasible.
- In order to provide realistic estimates of the realizable values of positions, valuations should include fair value adjustments to mid-market prices. These should reflect the bid-offer spread; illiquidity characteristics; credit valuation adjustments; operational or model risks; and servicing costs of hedging.
- Confirmations for OTC transactions should be sent out by the business day following the trade date. Firms should have written evidence of a binding agreement with the counterparty within five days.
- Financial intermediaries should track unexecuted masters, unsent confirmations and unconfirmed trades. They should develop incentives for business units to correct deficiencies in documentation. This might include trading restrictions, mandatory unwinds and reserves set aside against potential losses[545].
- Financial intermediaries should implement the recommendations of the ISDA 1999 Collateral Review[546] on best practice in the use of collateral. These include best practices on the structure of collateral functions in individual institutions[547], as well as guidance on market practices[548].

As to confidentiality of information within financial institutions CRMPG states:

- Financial intermediaries should have in place internal written procedures governing the use and access to proprietary information provided by trading counterparties as a basis for credit evaluations[549].

---

543 See FSF (2000), p. 67.

544 Potential Future Credit Exposure.

545 See FSF (2000), p. 67; See also PWG.

546 See ISDA (1999).

547 See ISDA (1999), pp. 37-40.

548 PWG notes the report but does not specifically endorse.

549 See also Basle Committee.

- Financial intermediaries should reach understanding with their counterparties regarding the use of counterparty proprietary information provided by trading counterparties as a basis of credit evaluations[550].

With regard to reporting requirements to senior management, CRMPG additionally opines[551]:

- The risk management function should design a flexible reporting framework to enable senior management to monitor risk profile relative to the stated tolerance.
- For large counterparty exposures, this should include: aggregate exposure; position and collateral replacement costs at both market and estimated liquidation value; a measure of potential exposure; and quantitative and qualitative analysis of vulnerabilities to large moves in specific market risk factors[552].
- Senior management should also receive contextual information to allow them to assess the degree of reliance on quantitative information and to highlight key assumptions used to develop such data[553].
- Senior management should be cognizant of and receive periodic updates on: model specification and limitations; data integrity questions; valuation methods and limitations; legal uncertainties; margining and collateral management policies; and status of counterparty documentation[554].

Furthermore, CRMPG makes several recommendations as to improvements in market practice at industry and firm level including documentation policies, practices and content, as well as collateral practices. Most of these recommendations, however, conform to those of ISDA[555]. Therefore, the dissertation only mentions recommendations other than ISDA´s[556]. With regard to documentation policies, practices and content, CRMPG opines in addition to ISDA´s recommendations that documentation should be revised to ensure that a non-defaulting party has the flexibility to value transactions in good faith and a commercially reasonable manner where circumstances warrant. Specified suggestions to aid this are given in the CRMPG report.

---

550 See also Basle Committee.
551 See FSF (2000), pp. 68, 69.
552 See also Basle Committee.
553 See in part also PWG.
554 See in part also PWG.
555 See ISDA (1999).
556 ISDA`s further recommendations can be found in the ISDA recommendations part of this dissertation.

Furthermore, CRMPG recommends various changes with regard to transparency i.e. reporting and disclosure[557]:

- Financial intermediaries with significant credit / market risk should meet their primary regulator periodically to discuss principal risk, as well as market conditions and trends with potential market disruption or systemic effects.
- If requested by its primary regulator, financial intermediaries should voluntarily provide reports to their regulator detailing large exposure information on a consolidated basis. Regulatory agencies requesting such information should reach clear understandings with institutions on the permissible use of such information and safeguards against its misuse. This report should, however, not be a blueprint for public disclosure.
- Financial intermediaries are encouraged to provide explanatory notes to the report, especially if there is a danger of misinterpretation of complex information.
- Suggested specification of information that should be reported to regulators.

With regard to public disclosure of exposures to HLIs by public companies, CRMPG acknowledged that this raises complex definitional and aggregation issues and might not be useful to investors[558]. Further discussion of these issues is said to be required.

Enhanced public disclosure by HLIs has also been an issue, CRMPG, however, argues in responding directly to the PWG's recommendations[559] that there are question about: the usefulness of this information; its uneven application to only Hedge Funds; and how it may reduce incentives to share more meaningful information with creditors[560].

7. Multidisciplinary Working Group on Enhanced Disclosure

The Multidisciplinary Working Group on Enhanced Disclosure (MWGED) was established in June 1999 and consisted of representatives form the Basle Committee of Banking Supervision, the Committee on the Global Financial system of the G-10 central banks (CGFS),the International Association of Insurance

557 See FSF (2000), p. 76.

558 See FSF (2000), p. 77. See also PWG.

559 PWG recommendations focused on Hedge Funds / CPOs and it opines that currently filed reports on CPOs should be enhanced and published. Legislation should be enacted to cover funds which are not CPOs.

560 See FSF (2000), p. 77.

Supervisors (IAIS) and IOSCO. The mandate of the MWGED was "to assess the feasibility and utility of enhanced disclosure by financial intermediaries."[561]. It did so by organizing a study of disclosure by a range of financial firms representing various financial sectors[562]. It reported to the four sponsoring Committees[563] in February 2001.

The MWGED has been considering a generic set of items which financial firms should disclose to permit shareholders, creditors, and counterparties better to assess levels of risk and the adequacy of control over this. These standards should form the baseline for information flows form HLIs to regulated firms. As noted in the earlier IOSCO report[564], a good case can be made for such disclosure to take place at a public level but, at the very minimum, they should be made bilaterally to market counterparties. Banks and securities firms should actively press for such information to be provided on a systematic and documented basis.

The conclusions of MWGED have three themes: first, a healthy balance is necessary between qualitative and quantitative disclosures[565]; second, intermediaries′ disclosures should be consistent with how they assess and manage their Thirdly, intra-period information is necessary for more complete view of an institution's to risk[566].

---

561 See BIS (2001c).

562 I.e. banking, insurance, broker-dealers, mutual funds, leveraged investment funds, finance companies and pension funds.

563 Basle Committee on Banking Supervision, Committee on the Global Financial System of the G-10 central banks, International Association of Insurance Supervision, International Association of Insurance Supervisors, International Organisation of Securities Commissions.

564 See IOSCO Technical Committee (1999).

565 See BIS (2001c), p. 8. "Financial intermediaries should disclose quantitative information describing their exposures to financial risks and the efficacy of their measurement and management of those risks. Qualitative discussion is also an important and necessary component of disclosure as it can contribute context and perspective that quantitative information cannot provide. However, qualitative discussion alone is not sufficiently informative, and quantitative information is an essential foundation to which the qualitative discussion can speak." Id.

566 See BIS (2001c), pp. 9-10 – " The disclosure of intra-period observations – in the form of high, median and low values – for disclosure items currently made by most financial intermediaries, as well as those recommended here, would improve understanding of the nature and level of risks being born by individual financial intermediaries. The use of intra-period information would be most useful for actively managed financial risks. At the current state of risk management, intra-period information should be provided for actively managed market-to-market exposures such as trading activity (see Chart 1 in Annex II for relevant results from the pilot study). For other risks, such as credit risk, the trading instruments and markets that might allow for more active management and modification of exposures have not yet reached a level of development that would make intra-period information useful. However, as the means to trade credit risk and liquidity of the credit markets evolve, at some point in the future the issue of intra-period information about credit exposures should be revisited."

8. Committee on the Global Financial System

The Committee on the Global Financial System (CGFS) is a central bank forum for the monitoring and examination of broad issues relating to financial markets and systems with a view to elaborating appropriate policy recommendations to support the central banks in the fulfillment of their responsibilities for monetary and financial stability. The Committee emphasizes the importance of assisting the Governors in recognizing, analyzing and responding threats to the stability of financial markets and the global financial system[567].

Also, the Committee focuses its attention on the nexus between monetary and financial stability, to the linkages between institutions, infrastructures and markets, to the actual and potential changes in financial intermediation and to the incentive structures built into markets and systems[568].

The Committee particularly seeks to co-ordinate its activities with other Basle-based committees, such as the Basle Committee on Banking Supervision and the Committee on Payment and Settlement Systems, in order to strengthen the overall effectiveness of the process.

9. International Swaps and Derivatives Association

The International Swaps and Derivatives Association[569] (ISDA) is a global trade association representing leading participants in the privately negotiated de-

---

[567] More specifically, the Committee's primary objectives are the following: "To seek to identify and assess potential sources of stress in the global financial environment through a regular and systematic monitoring of developments in financial markets and systems, including through an evaluation of macroeconomic developments; To further the understanding of the functioning and underpinnings of financial markets and systems through a close monitoring of their evolution and in-depth analyses, with particular reference to the implications for central bank operations and broader responsibilities for monetary and financial stability; to promote the development of well-functioning and stable financial markets and systems through an examination of alternative policy responses and the elaboration of corresponding policy recommendations." See id.

[568] The Committee further seeks to increase the transparency of financial markets and systems by promoting the design, production and publication of statistics and other information by central banks - including through the BIS - and by recommending the adoption of appropriate disclosure standards by both the official and private sectors. Where relevant, the Committee contributes to the development of an international consensus on sound principles and norms.

[569] ISDA was founded in 1985, and has today more than 550 member institutions from 41 countries on six continents. These members include most of the world's major institutions who deal in public and as privately negotiated derivatives, as well as associated service providers and consultants.

rivatives industry[570]. Since its foundation ISDA has pioneered efforts to find and reduce the sources of risk in the derivatives and risk management business[571].

Before the near collapse of LTCM prompted market stress in 1998, the ISDA Collateral Guideline[572] presented a baseline description of what collateralization is, how it works, and the attendant risks[573]. However, the Guideline was intended to be an introductory document and did not take account of the market stress conditions that affected different world markets and asset classes from late 1997 to late 1998[574]. This year-long series of market stress, which was at least partly solicited by LTCM, is key to understanding and improving credit management for derivatives[575]. A combination of various factors[576] was to blame for a significant increase in credit default events[577] involving collateralized transactions in 1997 and 1998. A result of the market stress was more attention regarding how collateral can mitigate the risk of credit derivatives. This is of special importance in the light of the fact that according to a survey with collateral practitioners, 20 per cent of all collateral agreements[578] are in place with Hedge Funds[579].

---

570 I.e. a business which includes interest rate, currency, commodity, credit and equity swaps, as well as related products such as caps, collars, floors and swaptions.

571 Among its most notable accomplishments are: developing the ISDA Master Agreement (which is widely used in international capital markets practices); publishing a wide range of related documentation materials and instruments covering a variety of transaction types; producing legal opinions on the enforceability of netting (available only to ISDA members); securing recognition of the risk-reducing effects of netting in determining capital requirements; promoting sound risk management practices, and advancing the understanding and treatment of derivatives and risk management from public policy and regulatory capital perspectives.

572 See ISDA (1998), p.1 – "The Guidelines for Collateral Practitioners ... grew out of the formation of the ISDA Collateral Working Groups in 1996. Concerned collateral practitioners, . . . were looking for support as they embarked on a new business activity for their firms. The Collateral Working Groups organised themselves to address the issues that members faced on a daily basis that had no precedent in the existing derivatives business."

573 See ISDA (1999), p. 4.

574 See id.

575 A tool frequently used by Hedge Funds.

576 See id. at 4-5. – "The stress conditions affected nearly every market world-wide, with a high degree of correlation across markets; the stress was sustained; privately negotiated derivatives were more widely used by participants in the affected markets than at any other time in the past; and collateral was much more extensively used in 1997 and 1998 than at any previous time."

577 As mentioned earlier.

578 Collateral agreements are those between two parties that govern the delivery and use of collateral. Key provisions of such agreements are: collateral delivery and return requirements, the rights of the secured party in the collateral, the type of instruments that can be posted as collateral, minimum transfer amounts, haircut provisions, the level of unsecured credit risk that each party is willing to assume (i.e. exposure thresholds above which the transfer of collateral is required).

579 See ISDA (1999), p. 7. – Collateral practitioners were asked in this survey to categorise their collateralised counterparties by type.

Firstly, however, a dissertation has to clarify what collateralization is. Collateral in general is a risk reduction tool, which mitigates risk by reducing credit exposure[580]. The effect of collateralization is to substitute the credit risk[581] of the issuer of the collateral for that of the counterparty to the transaction. Among the benefits of collateralization are that it lessens the credit spread that is charged to a counterparty[582], may reduce regulatory capital requirements[583], and equalizes the disparity in creditworthiness[584].

It remains unclear why collateralization has expanded as a risk management technique for Hedge Funds operations and banks' or broker dealers' interactions with Hedge Funds. This question has to be approached both from the perspective of the bank or broker dealer dealing with a Hedge Fund and a Hedge Fund itself. From the perspective of the bank or broker dealer, collateral is a necessary and prudent credit protection. On the other hand for a Hedge Fund giving collateral is a pre-requisite to obtain sufficient credit[585]. Receiving collateral against an in-the-money position is a means to the Hedge Fund of capitalizing the unrealized gain in a position while maintaining exposure to the position itself[586]. Since its introduction in the early 1990s, collateralization has been the fastest growing credit risk mitigation technique in use within the privately negotiated derivatives industry[587].

---

580 See id. at 3.

581 See id. - "Credit risk is the danger tat you will not receive an amount of money you are owed because the party that owes you the money is unable to pay you and defaults on its obligation. Credit risk exists whenever an institution has a relationship where a counterparty has an obligation to make payments in the future. This is true for derivatives transactions as well as loans, repurchase agreements, etc." Id at 4. "Credit risk increases the farther away in time the payment is expected, since every additional day increases the possibility that some event may cause an inability to pay." Id.

582 Decreasing credit spreads result in better pricing which may result in increased trade activity and revenues.

583 For institutions affected by the "old" Basle Accord, collateralised transactions may, depending upon the type of collateral used, qualify for a zero per cent risk weighting. Reducing regulatory capital requirements frees up capital for additional trading.

584 See ISDA (1998), p. 6 –"Financial institutions assign a credit tolerance to each counterparty which is dependent on creditworthiness. By collateralizing the MTM (market-to-market) exposure, a counterparty can participate in the derivatives market and maintain its market presence. An AAA rated firm can also expand its customer base by collateralising transactions with institutions outside its credit parameters. As a result of collateralisation, many firms have increased their customer base and increased revenues by collateralising lower rated credits, deteriorating credits or unrated counterparties."

585 Although their size, credit rating and performance record may enable Hedge Funds to obtain a degree of unsecured credit, their willingness for credit exceeds in most cases the level of unsecured credit available.

586 And hopefully realising further upside potential.

587 See ISDA (1999), p. 1.

Several firms reported that credit losses as a result of defaults by Hedge Funds in 1998 were significantly reduced or even eliminated because robust collateral agreements were in place[588]. However, collateralization has proved to be a highly successful credit risk mitigation tool during the credit market crisis of 1997 and 1998[589].

In order to avoid future market crisis ISDA established, in its Collateral[590] Review 1999[591], the following key objectives[592], which are suggestions for improvements in, market practice at industry and firm level:

- New industry standards should be adopted for documentation practices[593].
- Firms, industry groupings, service providers and regulators should support efforts to introduce greater automation in the documentation process for OTC contracts[594].
- Modification of existing law to improve close-out netting agreements[595] for financial contracts, including netting across different types of contract should be considered[596].
- Where possible, standard documentation should be harmonized across jurisdictions[597].

---

588 See id. at 2.

589 See id. – "Practitioners also emphasize that collateral does not solve all problems. It does introduce risks of its own – principally legal and operational risk, but also risks associated with the issuer of collateral assets, concentration in the pool of assets taken as collateral, correlation between an underlying exposure and collateral taken to mitigate that exposure, and the potential difficulty of selling collateral assets at a strong price. Experience over the past two years has also taught that problems can arise with internal data quality, the speed of market movements, and extreme conditions (such as the Russian debt moratorium and consequent disruptions in pricing transparency and market operation). Any of these potential risks can reduce the effectiveness of even the most advanced collateral management program.".

590 Collateral is property which is acceptable as security for a loan or other obligation. Collateral is also assets used as security for the expansion of a loan.

591 See id. at 1 "As the ISDA Collateral Review project progressed, the following key objectives were established for this project: 1. Document the state of collateral management practice as of early 1999; 2. Analyze the lessons learned form the experiences of collateral management practitioners during the periods of market stress in 1997 and 1998; and 3. Provide leadership in identifying and implementing possible improvements in market practice.".

592 See FSF (2000), pp. 74f.

593 See also CRMPG

594 See also CRMPG

595 I.e. an agreement whereby the transfers of funds between subsidiaries or separate companies are reduced to a net amount.

596 See also PWG and CRMPG – who gives detailed guidance on recommended changes. ISDA also recommends a more wide-ranging review for all laws and regulations that impact on the collateral function.

- ISDA and members should establish guidelines for informal dispute resolution practices[598].
- ISDA and members should consider revising credit support[599] documents to include the option of a shorter time cycle for valuation, delivery and liquidation of collateral[600].
- Institutions should consider drafting into their collateral agreements a provision that allows cash to be delivered in the event of a collateral delivery failure[601].
- Greater consideration should be given to the use of cash as potential collateral[602].
- ISDA and members should consider the simplification of the documentation structure and execution process of master agreements[603] and credit support documents[604].

10. U.S. President's Working Group on Financial Markets

The U.S. President's Working Group on Financial Markets consist of the following members - the U.S. Secretary of the Treasury, the U.S. Chairman of the Board of Governors of the Federal Reserve System, the U.S. Chairman of the Securities and Exchange Commission, and the U.S. Chairman of the Commodity Futures Trading Commission. These members set forth in the Report of the President's Working Group on Financial Markets[605] that the principal policy issue aris-

---

597 See also CRMPG.

598 See also CRMPG; FSF (2000), p. 75. "Collateral Practices: The ISDA recommendations on improvements the industry should make to market practices in collateral management should be implemented."

599 I.e. an arrangement offered by a party to reduce the credit risk related to it in a transaction between two parties. Credit support may take the form of a letter of credit, collateral, guarantee, margin requirements or any other arrangement with reduces the likelihood of a party's default or the magnitude of its counterparty's potential loss.

600 See also CRMPG.

601 See also CRMPG.

602 See also CRMPG.

603 A master agreement is an agreement that sets forth the standard terms and conditions of privately negotiated, bilateral transactions between two parties, such as the "1992 ISDA Master Agreement" form published by ISDA for OTC derivatives transaction – ISDA (1992). The agreements typically include payment netting and close-out netting provisions.

604 See also CRMPG.

605 The Working Group is comprised of members from the Treasury Department, Board of Governors of the Federal Reserve, the SEC and CFTC. The Council of Economic Advisers, the Federal Deposit Insurance Corporation, the National Economic Council, the Federal Reserve Bank of New York, the Office of the Comptroller of the Currency and the Office of Thrift Supervision also participate in the study and support its conclusions and recommendations. Through its con-

ing out of the events surrounding the near collapse of LTCM is how to constrain the use of excessive leverage. In view of its conclusive findings that excessive leverage can increase the likelihood of a general brake-down in the functioning of financial markets, the President's working Group on Financial Markets recommends generally the following measures in its report, Hedge Funds, Leverage, and the Lessons of Long-Term Capital Management, dated April 1999[606]:

- More frequent and meaningful information on Hedge Funds should be made public;
- Public companies, including financial institutions, should publicly disclose additional information about their material financial exposures to significantly leveraged institutions, including Hedge Funds;
- Financial institutions should enhance their practices for counterparty risk management[607];
- Regulators should encourage improvements in the risk-management systems of regulated entities;
- Regulators should promote the development of more risk-sensitive but prudent approaches to capital adequacy;
- Regulators need expanded risk assessment authority for the unregulated affiliates of broker–dealers and futures commission merchants;
- Congress should enact the provisions proposed by the President's Working Group to support financial contract netting[608]; and
- Regulators should consider stronger incentives to encourage offshore financial centers to comply with international standards.

---

stituent agencies, the Working Group will monitor the credit risk management policies of large commercial and investment banks and assess the effectiveness of the measures recommended.

606 See President's Working Group on Financial Markets (1999a).

607 See FSF (2000), p. 2 – "Improved counterparty risk management is critical to addressing concerns about the accumulation of excessive leverage in the financial system . . . These cover: firms' overall risk management framework; systems for counterparty credit assessment and on-going risk monitoring; exposure measurements methodologies; limit setting procedures; collateral, documentation and valuation policies and procedures; legal risks; and systems for reporting to senior management. Where those arrangements are inadequate, firms should not operate in highly risky and volatile instruments and markets, or with counterparties offering positions in such markets. Regulators and supervisors should reinforce this message".

608 I.e. Reducing transfers of funds between subsidiaries or separate companies to a net amount.

Most of these recommendations corresponds those of IOSCO[609]. However, there are some additional recommendations, which are beyond the scope of IO-SCO's that should be mentioned[610]

- With regard to the overall risk management framework PWG recommends, given the limitations of models, that there should be established guidelines for how qualitative judgment should be exercised by the credit department and line management. Furthermore, financial intermediaries should continuously review their risk management procedures[611].
- With regard to credit assessment and ongoing monitoring of HLIs, PWG recommends that Credit standards applied to HLI, and trading activities more generally, should be consistent with the overall credit standards of the financial intermediary[612].
- With regard to exposure management, PWG recommends additional that model validation processes, including back-testing should be reviewed and financial intermediaries should monitor their own exposures and the exposures of counterparties using an integrated framework that evaluates the linkages between market risk, liquidity and leverage[613].
- Concerning Collateral, contractual provisions and valuation, PWG recommends that financial intermediaries should consider the use of covenants permitting termination or other action if the counterparty undergoes significant changes in strategy, leverage, risk or other elements of credit quality[614].

As to the role of regulators in individual firm's risk management[615] PWG opines in addition to IOSCO's findings[616] that:

- Regulators should be encouraged to develop more risk sensitive approaches to capital adequacy[617].

---

609 The Technical Committee of the International Organisation of Securities Commissions (1999), pp. 6 f.
610 See FSF (2000), pp. 62 f.
611 See id. at 63.
612 See id.
613 See id. at 65.
614 See id. at 67.
615 See id. at 72.
616 See IOSCO Technical Committee (1999), pp. 6 f
617 See also Basle Committee.

- In particular, derivatives with similar risk characteristic to the underlying instruments should have the same capital charge for market risk.
- All regulators, particularly those in OFCs, need to be encouraged to adopt internationally agreed standards. Incentives could include a higher risk weighting for counterparties from jurisdictions not applying the internationally recognized regulatory core principles; ability to join Basle/IOSCO/IAIS working groups being made contingent on implementation of international standards; and pressure form G7 countries with close links to OFCs.
- In the U.S., there should be statutory changes to grant the SEC, the CFTC and the Treasury expanded risk assessment authority over broker-dealer and FCM unregulated affiliates.
- Regulators should carefully monitor the use of "double leverage".
- VaR and other risk models in financial intermediaries should be subject to validation procedure, including rigorous back-testing[618].
- Direct regulation of HLIs is not appropriate at this stage. The PWG states that is could be reconsidered if indirect measures and greater transparency are shown not to be working in an effective manner[619].

With regard to bankruptcy issues PWG opines[620]:

- Improvements to the close-out netting regime to allow counterparties to net across different types of contracts should be enacted into law.
- There should be clarifications that al U.S. Court would apply U.S. bankruptcy law to ancillary proceedings taking place in the U.S. This would prevent an offshore Hedge Fund from filing for bankruptcy abroad and then petition a U.S. Court to block the sale of collateral.
- The UN Commission on International Trade Law (UNCITRAL) should be codified to establish clear conventions to differentiate between a "main" and " non-main" insolvency. This would make it more likely that the jurisdiction of the main insolvency proceedings for an offshore fund would be determined by the fund's principal place of business than the jurisdictions in which it is incorporated.

In addition to its report "Hedge Funds, Leverage, and the Lessons of Long – Term Capital Management, April 1999"[621], the President's Working Group on Financial Markets issued another report "Over–the-Counter Derivatives Markets

---

618 This should be consistent with the Basle Committee's approach
619 See also IOSCO and Basle Committee.
620 See FSF (2000), p. 74.
621 See President's Working Group on Financial Markets (1999a).

and the Commodity Exchange Act, November 1999"[622]. Since the over the counter (OTC) derivatives market has remarkably expanded in the last 15 years and enable Hedge Funds to achieve extraordinarily leverage[623] there is some concern that there are no margins limits on OTC derivative positions[624]. Thus, the market has been reviewed by the PWG. Their OTC – Report states that these derivatives should be exempt from the Commodity Exchange Act 1974, for bilateral transactions between sophisticated counterparties[625]. This could eliminate the legal uncertainties that currently exist because the U.S. Congress has never explicitly stated whether OTC derivatives fall within the authority of the Commodity Exchange Act 1497[626]. Once the legal issues surrounding OTC derivatives are clarified it can be expected to see private initiatives to develop electronic trading systems for these derivatives[627]. This exchange is presumed to curtail a firm's exposure to Hedge Funds since the exchange will settle the daily net payments due instead of gross payments at the end of each reset or settlement date[628]. Furthermore, and more importantly, the exchange is said to reduce systemic risk since there will be mutual sharing of information[629].

11. Hedge Fund Industry Group

The Hedge Fund Industry Group ("HFIG") consists of a group of five large Hedge Fund managers[630]. The groups' paper "Sound practices for Hedge Fund Managers"[631] of February 2000 has been prepared in response to the recommendations of the PWG Report[632]. The objectives of the Hedge Fund Industry Group's paper was to respond to the PWG Report[633], strengthen Hedge Fund

---

622 See President's Working Group on Financial Markets (1999b).

623 End users, such as Hedge Funds, can leverage their portfolio through the use of derivatives such as swaps etc.

624 Commodity Exchange Act, 17 CFR 34 (1996).

625 15 C.F.R. pt. 35 - "Sophisticated counterparties" are defined as an "eligible swap participant" by the CFTC to be "financial institutions… that meet certain tests relating to total assets or net worth… and individuals with more than U.S.$10 million in assets".

626 Presidents's Working Group on Financial Markets (1999b), p. 35.

627 See Nazareth (2000); see also President's Working Group on Financial Markets (1999b), pp 13-14.

628 See President's Working Group on Financial Markets (1999b), pp. 21f.

629 I.e. price quotes.

630 I.e. Caxton Corporation, Kingdon Capital Management, LLC; Moore Capital Management, Inc. Soros Fund Managment LLC, Tudor Investment Corporation.

631 See HFIG (2000).

632 See President's Working Group on Financial Markets (1999a).

633 See HFIG (2000), p. 1 – "The sound practices recommendations that follow . . . are intended to respond to the PWG Report by contributing to a continuing evolution of Hedge Fund manager practices. Many recommended practices have already been adopted by a number of larger

Business Practices[634], to emphasize that not all Hedge Funds are the same[635], and to highlight the individualized Assessment and Application of Recommendations[636].

The Hedge Fund Industry Group makes the following recommendations[637]:

Organizational structures and Internal Controls[638]:

- Hedge Fund managers should clearly define the investment objectives and risk parameters for each fund and the trading policies and risk limits necessary to achieve these objectives.
- Hedge Fund managers should adopt an organizational structure that ensures effective monitoring of compliance with investment and valuation policies by allocating defined supervisory responsibilities and maintaining clear reporting lines.
- Hedge Fund managers should establish a risk monitoring function[639] that operates independently of portfolio management functions.
- Suitably qualified personnel should be retained and adequate systems established to produce periodic reporting that permits senior management to monitor trading activities and operations effectively.
- Internal procedures and periodic independent review processes should seek to ensure the enforcement of policies and identify deviations form those policies. Independent reviews should take place at least annually.

Hedge Fund managers in recent year, as their growth has resulted in the implementation of more formalized and sophisticated management policies and structures...".

634 See id. – "As part of this process and as markets continue to evolve, it is anticipated that the Recommendations will be further adapted and refined. It is intended that Hedge Fund managers, by evaluating the Recommendations . . , will strengthen their own business while contributing to market soundness by reducing the risk of their own default or failure".

635 See id. at 2 –"It is important to recognize in evaluating the Recommendations that the Hedge Fund industry is global and that the strategies, investment approaches and organizational structures of Hedge Fund managers vary greatly.... can be attributed partly to differences in size and partly to the different strategies used by Hedge Fund managers...".

636 See id. at 3 – "..., each Hedge Fund manager should assess the Recommendations based on the size, nature and complexity of its organization, its strategies and resources, as well as the objectives of the Funds it manages, and apply them appropriate...".

637 See id. at 8-27 - the following is a summarised version of the original recommendations.

638 See FSF (2000), p. 70.

639 I.e. a Hedge Fund employee or team of employees that is responsible for measuring and tracking the risk assumed by a Hedge Fund. In most cases the risk monitoring function provides an independent source of information about, and analysis of, a Hedge Fund's performance, current risk position, sources of risk and exposure to change in Market Factors. The risk monitoring function generally does not make decisions about how much risk or the types of risk the Hedge Fund should assume.

- Appropriate controls, reporting and review processes should apply to all managers and traders, whether internal or external to the Hedge Fund manager.
- Senior management should formally approve the allocation of capital to all portfolio managers.
- Third-party service providers that perform key business functions[640] should also be subject to appropriate controls and review processes.

Risk Management[641]:

- Hedge Fund managers should evaluate market risk for their portfolios both in aggregate and for relevant sub-components of a portfolio. Models used should be subject to back-testing. In addition, stress testing should be used.
- Hedge Fund Managers should employ appropriate liquidity measures, evaluate the stability of sources of liquidity and have a contingency liquidity plan for periods of market stress.
- Hedge Fund managers should establish policies and procedures to manage potential defaults by trading counterparties.
- Hedge Fund managers should monitor both accounting- based measures of leverage and risk-based measures of leverage, which reflect the relationship between the risks of a portfolio and the capacity of the Hedge Fund to absorb the impact of such risks. Managers should also recognize the interrelation between leverage and market, credit and liquidity risk[642] factors.
- Hedge Fund managers should establish procedures to limit exposure to possible operational risk[643].

---

640 Such as NA calculation.

641 See FSF (2000), pp. 70-71.

642 Liquidity risk is, with respect to asset liquidity, the inability to sell an asset quickly and/or in large volume at a reasonable price. With respect to funding liquidity, the risk that a party will not have or cannot obtain sufficient funds to meet its obligations.

643 Operational risk is the risk of loss due to system breakdowns, employee fraud or misconduct, errors in models or natural or man-made catastrophes, among other things. It may also include the risk of loss due to the incomplete or incorrect documentation of trades. Operational risk may be defined by what it does not include: market risk, credit risk and liquidity risk.

Legal and compliance[644]:

- The head of the legal function should be recognized as a member of senior management and granted sufficient authority to manage legal and compliance affairs independently and effectively.
- Hedge Fund managers should establish clear transaction execution and documentation management procedures. Documentation should be standardized to the extent possible with all counterparties on a bilateral basis. Where efficient, master/master or umbrella agreements should be used.
- Risk monitoring, liquidity analysis and stress testing should take account of the effects of contractual provisions[645].
- Hedge Fund managers should identify all potential regulatory filings and clearly allocate responsibility to appropriate personnel.
- All employees should attest in writing to their acceptance of a "code of conduct" or compliance manual on an annual basis.

Disclosure to credit providers and counterparties[646]:

- Hedge Fund managers should provide credit providers and trading counterparties with information that gives a view of their funds' risk and return profiles, including changes in net asset value[647], profit and loss volatility, changes in capital, market risk measures, and liquidity measures.

12. The Report of the Financial Stability Forum

The Financial Stability Forum ("FSF") was initiated by the G7 Ministers and Governors in February of 1999, based on a recommendation by Mr. Hans Tietmeyer, President of the Deutsche Bundesbank[648]. It was then convened in April 1999 to promote international financial stability through information exchange and international co-operation in financial supervision and surveillance.

---

644 See FSF (2000), p. 71.

645 Such as termination clause or requirements to post additional margin).

646 See FSF (2000), p. 71.

647 Net Asset Value (NAV) is the fair value of Hedge Fund's assets minus the fair value of its liabilities. NAV is the basis for determining the prices applicable to investor's subscription and redemptions. NAV would generally not include special adjustments that may be made to valuations for risk monitoring purposes, such as adjustments for illiquidity concerns. Under generally accepted accounting principles, NAV computations should include accrued interest, dividends and other receivables of the Hedge Fund, as well as accrued expenses and other payables.

648 http://www.fsforum.org/

The Forum is chaired by Mr. Andrew Crockett, General Manager, Bank for International Settlements. The Forum brings together on a regular basis national authorities responsible for financial stability in significant international financial centers, international financial institutions, sector-specific international groupings of regulators and supervisors, and committees of central bank experts. The FSF seeks to co-ordinate the efforts of these various bodies in order to promote international financial stability, improve the functioning of markets, and reduce systemic risk[649].

The Stability Forum Working Group on Highly Leveraged Institutions, on the other hand, was founded by the G7 Finance Ministers at the inaugural meeting of the G7 Financial Stability Forum on 14th of April1999. Mr. Howard Davies, chairman of the FSA, chaired the Group. The purpose of the group was to assess specifically the risk to financial stability caused by highly leveraged institutions; as well as to evaluate the work that has been done by existing official committees and industry bodies on the subject. This also included the level of implementation of any recommendations, to help improve levels of co-operation between such bodies and to identify issues that have not already been covered, with the ultimate objective of encouraging a consensus on the way forward for regulators and supervisors. In order to pursue the above mentioned objectives the FSF Working Group on Highly Leveraged Institutions issued a Report[650] called "Report of the Working Group on Highly Leveraged Institutions", 5. April 2000. The FSF welcomed the report and endorsed its recommendations.

The survey of existing studies is contained in Annex C[651] of the Report and includes a synthesis of all the recommendations of the various reports and a comparative table of recommendations. In Annex C, the material is divided up into five subject areas: risk management of HLI exposures in financial intermediaries;

---

649 http://www.fsforum.org/

650 See FSF Working Group (2000).

651 A survey of existing studies is contained in Annex C of the report and includes a synthesis of al the recommendations of the various reports and a comparative table of recommendations. The reports surveyed were: "The Basle Committee on Banking Supervision (Basle Committee) Report on working group on banks' interaction with HLI's and the Paper on Sound Practices for Banks' interactions with HLIs, published in January 1999 and the follow up assessment published in Jan. 2000; IOSCO Technical Committee Report of Task Force on Hedge Funds and other HLIs, Nov. 1999; U.S. President's Working Group Report on Hedge Funds Leverage and Long Term Capital Management, April 1999; Counterparty Risk Management Policy Group Report Improving Counterparty Risk Management Practices June 1999 (CRMPG); Multidisciplinary Working Group on Enhanced Disclosure (MWGED) is conducting a pilot study to test the efficiency of risk –based disclosures as a follow up to the proposals made by Committee n the Global Financial System (CGFS) Group on Disclosure; International Swaps and Derivatives Association (ISDA) Collateral Review 1999; Sound Practices for Hedge Fund Managers Report, Feb. 2000; Tiger Management LLC report on its own risk management procedures; The Synthesis of recommendations p. 51 – Tabular presentation of recommendations p. 62.

risk management in Hedge Funds; the role of the regulators in supporting sound practices; market improvements; transparency reporting and disclosure requirement. The first area of risk management was covered by PWG, Basle, IOSCO and CRMG with most groups producing similar recommendations[652]. The second area, focusing on Hedge Funds' own approach to risk management was specifically considered by the Hedge Fund Managers' Report and the Tiger Report[653]. These developments were a response to the recommendations in the PWG. Regulatory issues were dealt with in the reports by Basle, IOSCO, PWG and ISDA. In the area of market practice, IOSCO and Basle focus on the firm whereas CRMPG, PWG and ISDA also deal with industry wide approaches.

The main body of the FSF Report defines HLIs and their market functions and strategies and then considers the main problem areas associated with such organizations in the areas of systemic risk and market dynamics issues concerning the impact of Hedge Funds on small and medium – sized open economies. This latter area breaks new ground as none of the previous reports specifically ventured into this complex and controversial area. In Annex E the report assesses eventually the impact of HLIs and includes analysis of difficult issues such as market manipulation and other aggressive trading practices[654] by including the findings of a Market Dynamics Study Group.

a) The Working Group Recommendations

FSF`s Working Party addressed the problems associated with accumulation of high levels of leverage and the inevitable systemic risk associated with such an accumulation, as the two major issues arising out of the LTCM crisis. The question of how to manage a sudden and disorderly collapse in the HLI sector is a direct result of these two issues. Such a collapse may precipitate potential direct and indirect losses witch feed of each other. This, in turn, may detrimentally affect the value of collateral, drastically reduce liquidity and cause losses to market players, the financial system and the whole global economy. Six countries were selected for analysis of the market dynamics issues. These issues are concentrated on the potential effect of aggressive trading practices[655] and the potential distorting effect

---

652 See above the summaries.

653 Both are industry groups that issued their own recommendations in response to the PWG Report.

654 See FSF (2000), Annex E.

655 The Report of the G7 Financial Stability Forum´s Working Group on Highly Leveraged Institutions considered the issue of possible market manipulation, particularly in the context of currency markets, citing as examples " aggressive" trading a number of Hedge Fund market practices. These included: " Heavy selling of currencies at illiquid times to move prices and the quoting of off-market prices. Dissemination of rumours about impeding policy actions or forecasts of adverse economic outcomes that seem to correspond to positions already in place ("talking the

of large positions in small and medium-sized open economies. Among the selected countries are: Singapore, Hong Kong, Malaysia, Australia, New Zealand and South Africa. Whether manipulation was involved and their impact on market integrity could not be ascertained by the working group. The members where somewhat divided on this issue, but took this view overall because they recognized the fact that many practices and correlated positions may be subject to various interpretations and that it is very difficult to establish motive and to overcome a high burden of proof in this area.

The key recommendations in the report concern: greater risk sensitivity in bank capital adequacy regulation; Hedge Fund risk management; enhanced regulatory oversight of HLI credit providers; counterparty risk management; sustaining industry progress; building a firmer market infrastructure; enhanced public disclosure by HLIs; enhanced public disclosure practices generally and enhanced national surveillance of financial market activity[656].

The Working Group particularly approved the suggestions of earlier studies, such as Basle, IOSCO and CRMPG suggestions for improving counterparty risk management; and the regulatory oversight of HLI credit providers[657].

A revision of the Basle Accord on capital adequacy arrangements as well as industry based proposals for Hedge Funds' own risk management policies and practices are supported by the Group[658]. Furthermore it fully endorses U.S. proposals to improve public disclosure by HLIs both by statutory and regulatory means. Recommendations concerning markets dynamics issues include improved national market surveillance by enhancing FOREX and OTC derivatives markets data, and producing some good practice guidelines for FOREX trading in the light of concerns about abusive and aggressive trading practices.

b) Implementation Progress

Upon completion of the Summary Report by the FSF Working Group on HLIs, which outlined its findings and recommendations to the FSF, the FSF supported the recommendations and agreed to review progress towards implementa-

---

book"). Spreading of Information about positions and strategies at critical times. Correlated HLI position taking within markets either by coincidence or design. Position taking across markets either within single domestic systems (e.g. the Hong Kong double play) or across markets with the intention to move prices in the illiquid market and induce spillover to the liquid market"

656 See FSF (2000), Executive Summary p. 3.

657 A credit provider is either a bank, securities firm or other third party that extends credit to a Hedge Fund, either in connection with financing a Hedge Fund's purchases or securities or other instruments or through stand-alone loan facilities. A counterparty may be viewed as a credit provider when it engages in uncollatralized or partially collateralised OTC derivatives transactions with a Hedge Fund.

658 See FSF (2000), Executive Summary, p. 3.

tion in March 2001. A review of the overall effectiveness of the recommendations was agreed for March 2002. In the meantime, however, the Working Group on HLIs issued another Report on the "Progress in Implementing the Recommendations of the Working Group on HLIs" as a note to the FSF by the Chairman of the HLI Working Group[659].

In Annex 1 of the Report[660] of the Working Group, the IMF prepared an overview of developments in the Hedge Fund Industry during 1999-2000. Though constrained by the limited availability of industry data, this points to a number of interesting conclusions[661]:

- Hedge Funds recorded, on average, modest positive returns on capital under management during 1999 and 2000, outperforming most of the major market indexes.
- The number of Hedge Funds[662] has increased since 1998. The limited available information on Hedge Fund activities, including press reports, suggests that the main source of inflows to Hedge Funds were pension funds, insurance companies, and major banking institutions[663]. Investment allocation by these investors still appear to represent a very small percentage of portfolio assets.
- The average size of Hedge Funds probably decreased. Many large macro Hedge Funds either ceased operations entirely, or have been significantly scaled back. This seems to reflect two considerations: a reassessment of the risk-adjusted expected returns on large directional positions on asset prices; and the industry's′ perception that increased scrutiny of Hedge Funds investments would adversely affect potential returns.
- As expected by market observers, market discipline of Hedge Funds appears to have increased since the near collapse of LTCM.
- Partly as a result of these developments, some have observed that activities in OTC derivatives markets and some of the underlining markets have become more highly concentrated, and these markets are widely seen as less liquid than they were in the mid- to late 1990s. This applies to advanced-country markets as well as emerging debt and foreign exchange markets.
- Available data on leverage suggests that overall leverage[664] within the industry has probably fallen.

---

659 See FSF Working Group of HLIs (2001).

660 See id. at 2.

661 See id. at 3-4.

662 And to a lesser extent total capital under management.

663 Which are all regulated entities.

664 Weighted average leverage ratio for funds that choose to report to MAR/Hedge.

- There has been growth in the industry in Europe and to a lesser extent Asia.

As seen earlier, the Basle Committee and IOSCO reported similar trends[665].

13. Summary

In summary, the proposals by international bodies and regulatory authorities focused on:

- Financial intermediaries` risk management - proposals on these issues came from Basle Committee, IOSCO, PWG and CRMPG.
- Risk management in Hedge Funds - only PWG and in response to that a group of five large Hedge Funds (so called Hedge Fund Industry Report) made recommendations.
- Improving the role of regulators in individual financial intermediaries with significant Hedge Fund business esp. firms` risk management – proposals came from Basle Committee, IOSCO, PWG and CRMPG.
- Improvements in market practice at industry and firm level - whereas the IOSCO`s and Basle Committee`s reports focus primarily on firm-level improvements. The CRMPG report, the PWG and ISDA 1999 Collateral Review make a number of recommendations that will require concerted industry action as well as action by individual firms.
- Transparency: reporting and disclosure recommendations – were made by Basle Committee, IOSCO, PWG, CRMPG and MWGED.

14. Conclusion

After seeing that most of the described proposals can be summarized in five major topics, it has to be shown, by way of hypothetical effect analysis, how effective and useful implementation of various proposals could be and where shortcomings can be identified.

Firstly, regulating financial intermediaries is deemed to be a step in the right direction. Many proposals remain, however, too opaque to be seriously considered. For example, when IOSCO, CRMPG and Basle Committee propose that financial intermediaries should have a clear credit risk strategy and credit risk management policy and process, they do not provide an elaborate description on how to actually implement those proposals. They also do not take into consideration that guidelines for those measures may, due to differences in business models and specialization, apply to some and not to others and costs to either adjust these

---

665 See BIS (2001b).

guidelines or require financial intermediaries to comply with adjusting requirements may be immense. Moreover, it has been proposed for financial intermediaries to have a credit department, independent of line management, to perform credit analysis and monitor compliance with approved credit limits. Some financial intermediaries introduced these institutions and it has proved very cost intensive. Another proposal is to insist on receiving adequate information for the internal credit approval process of intermediaries before starting a relationship with an HLI. This, again, is a procedure already in existence and only the quality of information is an issue, thus, this is rather a transparency problem. It has also been suggested to focus on better stress testing, Value at Risk and Monte Carlo scenarios. However, these tests are always dealing with historic data and a good performance in running a portfolio through extreme historic market volatility can never be an indicator of high risk sensitivity for future events because not one market situation is ever like the other.

Secondly, risk management in Hedge Funds is problematic considering that asymmetric allocation of information is in part prompted by the secrecy under which Hedge Funds operate. The less information the market has about Hedge Fund's activities, the easier it is for them to steal a march on it. In other words: the greater the secrecy, the less the "market impact" of them dealing in a particular security, currency or other financial instrument. Thus, compulsory internal risk management for Hedge Funds has an impact on the very nature of conducting their business. It is questionable if it would be worth compromising the well functioning of the Hedge Fund industry for the sake of enhanced regulation. This is exemplified when looking at the costs, which would presumably far exceed the expected attainments, of implementing these suggestions.

Thirdly, improving the role of regulators in individual financial intermediaries with significant Hedge Fund business, i.e. risk management especially by reevaluation of adequacy of risk management procedures, emphasizing compliance with both internal and risk management procedures and the sound practices identified in the various reports, may be an adequate first step. Here, however, significant transaction costs are involved and the costs of setting up and implementing cannot be underestimated either. Thus, it remains to be seen if these detrimental effects could not be avoided attaining comparable results.

Fourthly, improvements in market practice at industry and firm level by, for instance, modifying the existing law to improve close-out netting agreements for financial contracts, including netting across different types of contracts, may, on the face of it, sound promising. Unfortunately markets always follow their own patterns and improvements would require market demand, which has not been indicated by those reports that recommended improvements in market practice. Accordingly, improvements can only be dictated by markets themselves. Another proposal in this line of argumentation was to harmonize standard documentation across jurisdictions. Documentation of transactions is dictated by individual jurisdictions, thus, harmonizing documentation would, at least partly, require harmonization of various jurisdictions. This form of direct regulation is, as mentioned before, unsuitable because jurisdictional arbitrage and national protectionism are inevitable. ISDA`s proposal to establish guidelines for informal dispute resolution practices seems appropriate to minimize transaction costs and find efficient albeit informal solutions. This is in part due to the fact that ISDA is a private undertaking and, thus, more adaptable to the demands of its members.

Fifthly, reporting and disclosure requirements, i.e. transparency as a prudential tool is generally suitable to address problems of information asymmetries. However, the author has pointed out earlier that secrecy is essential to Hedge Funds' success. Hence, asymmetric allocation of information is in part prompted by the secrecy under which Hedge Funds operate. In a way the penchant for secrecy is understandable because the less information the market has about Hedge Fund's activities, the easier it is for them to steal a march on it. However, the very nature of high Hedge Fund performance used to be the fact that money flow, combination of strategies and diverse financial products as well as the enormous amounts of money, leveraged or not, could barely be traced in an internationally investing Hedge Fund. Furthermore, even the CPRMPG and the Hedge Fund Group appears to recognize that disclosure may be appropriate in certain circumstances. But they suggest that this be done on an informal and confidential basis[666]. On the other hand public quarterly reporting would give financial institutions a profile of the Hedge Funds that are their counterparties. The abovementioned reports and recommendations, however, all clearly mandate more frequent interchanges of information and monitoring of credit, market and liquidity on an ongoing basis. This may be due to their assumption that publicly available quarterly information would not meet such standards. Taking this as an index of the necessary market discipline it remains questionable what would be accomplished by quarterly public reporting when the necessary market discipline seems to require a continuous process of risk evaluation. Moreover, the majority of reports and recommendations mention public disclosure of measures like VaR, stress testing etc. but non of them mentions public disclosure of portfolio structures – possibly assuming that this would have disastrous effects for the industry because it would put Hedge Funds at an unfair disadvantage to their competitors in the market place, as well as being incompatible with their aforementioned private nature. Keeping this in mind it remains questionable how meaningful public disclosure of VaR, stress testing etc. really is without knowledge of the structure of the portfolio being evaluated. In the context of requiring highly leveraged Hedge Funds to

---

666 See Roth (2001), p. 106 – "Indeed, most of the representatives of the private sector that have testified at Congressional hearings on the matter held thus far have suggested that information furnished to regulators relating to hedge funds be kept confidential, and there has been general agreement that `proprietary` information would be treated as confidential.".

report their financial information only confidentially, possible moral hazard problems have to be mentioned. In this context disputable issues like the discretion of regulators to use the information as well as supervisory responsibilities have to be underscored. Overall it cannot be ascertained if the disclosure requirements proposed by various reports are really necessary. Also, in light of the fact that other players like internationally active banks operating in these markets, which only have to file quarterly financial statements, they do not separate their "proprietary" trading desks as separately reporting entities, it is questionable why those rules should only apply to Hedge Funds.

Eventually, all these wide- ranging initiatives in the aforementioned areas are said to be inherently pro-active with details left to be filled in at a later date. Postponing regulatory initiatives can, assuming that these initiatives are effective and efficient, blur and confuse individual regulatory objectives. Thus, is should not be "policy" to introduce a particular kind of control or regulation but specific objectives should be identified. For instance disclosure requirements should be decided in terms of whether the objective is to monitor systemic risk, or market manipulation, to prevent money laundering, to enable counterparties to assess risk, to inform investors, or to some combination of theses.

It can generally be insinuated that a greater emphasize on the role and function of Hedge Funds is necessary and the process of regulatory "creep and convergence" occurs in a way which takes proper account of the Hedge Funds` distinctive features.

Moreover, there is the concern that Hedge Funds themselves may suffer if required to implement risk management-, organizational restructuring-, legal and compliance restructuring-, as well as disclosure to credit providers and counterparties proposals. Despite lacking applicable estimates it can be assumed that implementing these proposals bears tremendous transactions costs and endangers Hedge Funds to either be forced to operate off-shore entirely or file bankruptcy because their operations do not remunerate any longer. To put it differently, the aforementioned necessary equilibrium between the cost and effort of regulation and the expected attainments of regulation remains problematic. The costs for Hedge Funds to abide by rules are too high i.e. if Hedge Funds were to implement all risk management rules proposed by the aforementioned papers they would, of course, on the one hand, address various moral hazard problems, on the other hand, the costs of implementing these changes would be too high and, thus, Hedge Funds would not remunerate any more. Thus, there is no equilibrium between costs of regulation and the expected attainments of regulation.

H. Direct Hedge Fund Regulation

As discussed earlier, in the aftermath of LTCM, regulators have voiced concern, among other things, about the amount of leverage, and the increased risk exposure that hedge funds use to amplify trading strategies and increase absolute returns.[667] The LTCM experience was, arguably, an eye opening experience for many hedge funds with similar leverage and risk exposure. Addressing these con-

---

667 *See e.g.* SEC - " 17 CFR Parts 210, 228, 229, 239, 240, and 249; [Release Nos. 33-7386; 34-38223; IC-22487; FR-48; International Series No. 1047; File No. S7-35-95]; Disclosure of Accounting Policies for Derivative Financial Instruments and Derivative Commodity Instruments and Disclosure of Quantitative and Qualitative Information about Market Risk inherent in Derivative Financial Instruments; other Financial Instruments, and Derivative Commodity Instruments; *see also* Bundesaufsichtsamt für das Kreditwesen (1998): Marketing of Foreign Collective Investment Schemes in Germany – Supervisory Aspects, BAKred April 1998; Counterparty Risk Management Policy Group (1999): Improving Counterparty Risk Management Practices, January 1999; Deutsche Bundesbank (1999): Hedge-Fonds und ihre Rolle auf den Finanzmärkten, Monatsbericht / Deutsche Bundesbank, Bd. 51 (1999), 3, S. 31-44, Graph. Darst; Financial Stability Forum Working Group on HLIs (2000): "Report of the Working Group on Highly Leveraged Institutions", 5. April 2000; Financial Stability Forum Working Group of HLIs (2001): "Progress in Implementing the Recommendations of the Working Group on Highly Leveraged Institutions – Note to the FSF by the Chairman of the HLI Working Group", May 2001; Hedge Fund Industry Group (2000): Sound Practices for Hedge Fund Managers, Caxton Corporation, Kingdom Capital Management, Soros Fund Management, Tudor Investment Corporation, February 2000; International Organisation of Securities Commissions Technical Committee (1999): Report on Hedge Funds and other Highly Leveraged Institutions, November 1999; International Organisation of Securities Commissions (1998): Objectives and Principles of Securities Regulation, A Report of the International Organisation of Securities Commissions September 1998; President's Working Group on Financial Markets (1999a): Report, Hedge Funds, Leverage, and the Lessons of Long – Term Capital Management, April 1999; President's Working Group on Financial Markets (1999b): Over–the-Counter Derivatives Markets and the Commodity Exchange Act, November 1999. U.S. Federal Reserve (1999b): "Supervisory guidance regarding counterparty credit risk management", The Board of Governors of the U.S. Federal Reserve, 1st of February 1999; Uniao de Bancos de Brasileiros AA, SEC No-Action Letter; Van Grover (2001), p.50.; U.S. House of Representatives (2000): H.R. 2924—THE HEDGE FUND DISCLOSURE ACT, Subcommittee on Capital Markets, Securities and Government Sponsored Enterprises, Committee on Banking and Financial Services, Washington, DC, Hearing Thursday, March 16, 2000; U.S. House of Representatives, Subcommittee on Capital Markets, Securities and Government Sponsored Enterprises, Committee on Banking and Financial Services,(1999): Hearing on "Counterparty Risk Management Policy Group Report", Thursday, June 24th 1999, Washington, D.C.; United States Congress House Committee on Banking and Financial Services Subcommittee on Capital Markets, Securities, and Government Sponsored Enterprises (2000): H.R. 2924, the Hedge Fund Disclosure Act: hearing before the Subcommittee on Capital Markets, Securities, and Government Sponsored Enterprises of the Committee on Banking and Financial Services, U.S. House of Representatives, One Hundred Sixth Congress, second session, Washington: U.S. G.P.O.; United States Congress House Committee on Banking and Financial Services Hedge fund operations (October 1, 1998): hearing before the Committee on Banking and Financial Services, U.S. House of Representatives, One Hundred Fifth Congress, second session.; United States General Accounting Office (1999): Report to Congressional Requesters, Long-Term Capital Management – Regulators Need to Focus Greater Attention on Systemic Risk, GAO Publication, October 1999; Van Grover, Robert B. (2001): U.S. Legal and Regulatory Issues Faced by Offshore Funds and their Sponsors, in: Cullen, Ian; Perry, Helen, Hedge Funds – Law and Regulation, Sweet & Maxwell, pp. 37-61.

cerns, partly in an effort to pre-empt regulatory action, many hedge funds minimized their leverage. Therefore, arguably, today's hedge fund leverage is seemingly low. However, credit monitors and some brokerage firms, along with regulators are concerned that hedge fund managers may be using new derivative products to disguise the real level of leverage.[668]

The trend towards new derivatives products and the increased risks for investors may be among the reasons for the SEC to adopt a new rule and rule amendments under the Investment Adviser Act of 1940 ("IAA").[669] This is the first time that hedge funds have been regulated directly.[670] Securities regulators in Europe and the United States have been deliberating a more direct approach to hedge fund regulation for almost a decade. Although the German BAFin and the British FSA have been updating their regulatory schemes to address developments in the hedge fund industry, the SEC is the first regulator to directly regulate hedge funds.

In December 2004, the SEC proposed a decisive amendment to Rule 203 under the Investment Adviser Act. The new rule requires hedge fund advisers to count each investor in a fund as a client and to "look through" a hedge fund to determine whether it is eligible for the private adviser exemption. Generally, the new rule would oblige hedge funds and advisers to comply with the full gamut of registered adviser regulation, including, e.g. filing Form ADV, with the SEC. Although the rule would not change the current IAA jurisdictional thresholds, which generally permit only investment advisers with at least $25 million in assets under management to register with the SEC, it will have a substantial effect on the hedge fund industry.

Besides the SEC in the US, many jurisdictions worldwide have revisiting in recent years their regulatory frameworks for hedge funds. Although hedge fund regulation has a truly international dimension, hedge fund managers are investing in most financial markets to attain highest net returns, regulators are still regulating hedge funds according to their own agendas. Some regulators like the SEC wish to tighten their rules others may wish to liberalize. Despite this rather complex array of perspectives, there seem to be three distinct themes that prevail in hedge fund regulation. This dissertation explores in further detail all three of these themes. First, the devastating experience with Long-Term Capital Management in 1998 raised concerns about the systemic risks created by hedge funds. Second, general issues about how hedge fund managers and advisers are regulated. Third, there is the marketability issue, or "retailization" as the SEC calls it, i.e. should

668 *See* WSJ, December 21, 2004, at C1.

669 *See* Registration Under the Adviser Act of Certain Hedge Fund Advisers, Friday December 10, 2004, Final Rule - SEC Release No. IA-2333; File No. S7-3—04, RIN 3235-AJ25.

670 The SEC has traditionally regulated hedge funds indirectly by monitoring the brokerage firms and banks that deal with them.

hedge fund be marketed to the general public and what are the risks involved. To put it more bluntly, should regulation be tailored to fit the needs of the general public? The latter is a rather contentious issue in Germany revolving around the recent enactment of the Investment Act and the Investment Taxation Act.

Exploring these three themes, the dissertation analyzes in Part I recent developments in the regulatory framework of the US. Scrutinizing the supposed need for SEC action, the SEC's cost benefit analysis, as well as the effects on competition, efficiency and capital formation, the author points out weaknesses in the SEC's reasoning and its approach to hedge fund regulation.

I. *Hedge Fund Regulation in the US*

To avoid any regulatory burdens, hedge funds generally do not raise funds through public offerings, advertise broadly, or engage in general solicitation, thereby avoiding regulation of the two main US governmental agencies, i.e. the Securities Exchange Commission ("SEC")[671] and the Commodity Futures Trading Commission ("CFTC").[672] Until recently, approximately 60-70 per cent of Hedge Funds were exempt from regulation by the SEC.[673] However, hedge funds are indirectly regulated through transactions with counterparties and those funds that are structured as partnerships must also follow statutory and common law partnership principles to protect interests of the limited partners.[674]

The key statutory provision pertaining to hedge funds, sponsors, and advisers are the Securities Act of 1933,[675] the Securities Exchange Act of 1934,[676] the Investment Company Act 1940,[677] and the Investment Advisers Act of 1940[678] as

---

671 With the Securities Act of 1934 Congress created the Securities and Exchange Commission. The Act empowers the SEC with broad authority over all aspects of the securities industry. This includes the power to register, regulate, and oversee brokerage firms, transfer agents, and clearing agencies as well as the nation's securities self regulatory organizations (SROs). The various stock exchanges, such as the New York Stock Exchange, and American Stock Exchange are SROs. The National Association of Securities Dealers, which operates the NASDAQ system, is also an SRO. The Act also identifies and prohibits certain types of conduct in the markets and provides the Commission with disciplinary powers over regulated entities and persons associated with them. In this broad regulatory function, the SEC also oversees hedge funds.

672 The US CFTC was created by US Congress in 1974 as an independent agency with the mandate to regulate commodity futures and option markets in the United States. The agency protects market participants against manipulation, abusive trade practices and fraud. Through oversight and regulation, the CFTC is supposed to enable the markets to serve better their important functions in the US economy--providing a mechanism for price discovery and a means of offsetting price risk.

673 See Press (2001), p.112.

674 *See* id. at 110.

675 Hereinafter the 'Securities Act".

676 Revised 1996 - hereinafter the 'Exchange Act'.

677 Hereinafter the 'Company Act'.

well as the Commodity Exchange Act of 1974. In particular, under section 3 (c) (1) and 3(c) (7) of the Investment Company Act ("ICA"), hedge fund advisers were able to rely on the so-called 'private investment company' exemptions.[679] Thus, hedge funds in the United States are generally organized to avoid regulation under the ICA by qualifying for an exclusion, from the definition of "investment company," under Section 3 (c) (1)[680] or 3 (c) (7)[681] of that Act. Each investor in the fund must be a "qualified purchaser," which for natural persons generally means having investments of at least $5 million.[682]

For hedge fund advisers, Section 203(b) (3) of the Investment Adviser Act exempted any investment adviser who: (a) has had less than 15 clients during the preceding 12 months, (b) does not hold himself out generally to the public as an investment adviser, and (c) does not act as an investment adviser to a registered investment company or a business development company.[683] Before the SEC

---

678 Hereinafter the 'Advisers Act'.

679 *See* §§ 3 (c) (1) and 3 (c) (7) of the Investment Company Act, providing in particular in § 3 (c) (1): " [...], none of the following persons is an investment company within the meaning of this title: (1) Any issuer whose outstanding securities [...] are beneficially owned by not more than one hundred persons and which is not making and does not presently propose to make a public offering of its securities. [...] (7) (A) any issuer, the outstanding securities of which are owned exclusively by persons, who at the time of acquisition of such securities, are qualified purchasers, and which is not making and does not at that time propose to make a public offering of such securities.[...]".

680 15 U.S.C. 80a- 3(c) (1).

681 15 U.S.C. 80a- 3(c) (7).

682 *See* Section 2 (a) (51) of the Investment Company Act [15 U.S.C. 80a-2(a) (51)].

683 *See* for a complete description of the old SEC exemptions under § 203 (b) of the Adviser Act: 14A U.S. Sec. Law for Financial Trans. § 14:15. 9 EXEMPTIONS FROM SEC REGISTRATION, Section 203(b) of the Advisers Act provides five narrow exemptions from registration. (This is in addition to Section 203A of the Advisers Act, which generally prohibits SEC registration for investment advisers with under $25 million in assets under management, Section 206A of the Act, which permits the SEC to exempt any person or class of persons from any provision of the Advisers Act or any rule thereunder where appropriate, and Section 202(b) of the Act, which provides that no provision of the Advisers Act will apply to the United States, the states, and their agencies, agents, and employees unless the provision specifically refers to them.) The exemptions under Section 203(b) of the Advisers Act are as follows. First, Section 203(b)(1) exempts any intrastate adviser, which is any investment adviser: (a) all of whose clients reside within the state in which the adviser maintains its principal office and place of business, and (b) who does not provide advice or issue analyses or reports concerning securities listed or admitted for unlisted trading on any U.S. exchange. Second, Section 203(b)(2) exempts "any investment adviser whose only clients are insurance companies." Third, [...] Fourth, Section 203(b)(4) exempts any investment adviser that is a "charitable organization" (as defined in Section 3(c)(10)(D) of the Investment Company Act), or is a trustee, director, officer, employee, or volunteer of a charitable organization acting within the scope of his employment or duties, whose advice, analyses, or reports are provided only to one or more of the following: (a) a charitable organization, (b) a fund operated for charitable purposes (i.e., one excluded from the definition of "investment company" under Section 3(c)(10)(B) of the Investment Company Act), or (c) a charitable trust or other donative instrument

adopted the safe harbor in 1985, it had been issuing a long line of no-action letters[684] requiring an investment adviser to look through an entity and count each individual advisee or member as a separate client. Reliance on SEC no-action letters alone led to significant ambiguity. This ambiguity was further exacerbated by the continuing change of the position of the Second Circuit. The Second Circuit from 1976 to 1977 had characterized the individual limited partners as the "clients" of the general partner.[685] Later the Second Circuit withdrew that characterization in *Abrahamson v. Fletscher*,[686] holding that general partners of limited partnerships investing in securities were investment advisers, leaving unanswered the question whether the partnership, or each of the partners, should be counted as clients,[687] which was later overruled on other grounds by *TransAmerica Mortgage Advisors, Inc. v. Lewis.*[688]

Despite the establishment of a "looking through rule" through various SEC no-action letters, there was no registration requirement under the Adviser Act before the safe harbor was enacted in1985, nor was there any registration requirement under the safe harbor rule after its enactment. Accordingly, the safe harbor permitted advisers to manage large amounts of securities indirectly through several hedge funds that would collectively have had hundreds of investors. More

---

described in Section 3(c)(10)(B) of the Investment Company Act, or a trustee, administrator, settlor (or potential settlor), or beneficiary of any such trust or other instrument. Last, Section 203(b)(5) exempts church employee benefit plans [...], any person eligible to establish and maintain such a plan, or any trustee, director, officer, or employee of or volunteer for any such plan or person, if that person, acting in that capacity, provides investment advice only to, or concerning, church plans and related accounts or funds meeting certain requirements (i.e., those excluded from the definition of "investment company" under Section 3(c)(14) of the Investment Company Act). Any person that meets the definition of investment adviser in the Advisers Act and qualifies for one of the above exemptions from registration provided by Section 203(b) of the Advisers Act is not subject to most of the provisions of that Act. However, as an investment adviser exempt from SEC registration it remains subject to certain antifraud provisions included in Section 206 of the Advisers Act.).

684 *See* B.J. Smith, SEC Staff No-Action Letter (Dec. 25, 1975); Wofsey, Rosen Kweskin & Kuriansky, SEC Staff No-Action letter (Apr. 25, 1974); David Shillling, SEC Staff No-Action Letter (Apr. 3, 1976); Ruth Levine, SEC Staff No-Action Letter (Dec. 15, 1976); S.S. Program Limited, SEC Staff No-Action Letter (Oct. 17, 1974), Hawkeye Bancorporation, SEC Staff No-Action Letter (June 11, 1971).

685 Fed. Sec. L. Rep. (CCH) 95, 889, at 91, 282 n. 16.

686 568 F.2d 862, 872 n. 16 (2d Cir. 1977), cert. denied, 436 U.S. 913 (1978) (Circuit Judge Timbers, holding: " [. . .] that general partners of investment partnership were "investment advisers" within meaning of Advisers Act.").

687 For an extensive and enlightening discussion see Robert Hacker and Ronald Rotunda, SEC Registration of Private Investment Partnerships after Abrahamson v. Fletschner, 78 Colum. L. Rev. 1471, 1477 (1978).

688 444 U.S. 11 (1979) (the Supreme Court, Mr. Justice Stewart, holding on certiorari, that there exists a limited private remedy under the Investment Advisers Act of 1940 to void an investment advisers contract, but Act confers no other private causes of action, legal or equitable.).

precisely, section 12 of the Exchange Act[689] in combination with Rule 12g-1[690] requires registration of any issue with 500 holders of record of a class of equity securities and assets in excess of $10 million. Practically speaking this meant that a single hedge fund could have up to 499 investors. Moreover, under Rule 203 (b) (3) –1 (a),[691] an investment adviser may count a legal organization as a single client so long as the investment advice is provided based on the objectives of the legal organization rather than the individual investment objectives of any owners of the legal organization.[692] Until the SEC adopted the new rule, discussed below, there was considerable uncertainty whether advisers to unregistered investment pools were required to look through the pools to count each investor as a client, or could count each pool as a single client.[693] In the absence of a particular rule on the issue, rule 203 (b) (3) –1 was interpreted to generally allow an adviser to count each hedge fund as one client. Accordingly, combining the limits of Section 12 of the Exchange Act and Rule 12g-1 with Rule 203 (b) (3) –1, a hedge fund adviser used to be able to have 14 funds with 499 investors in each. This is a total of 6,986 investors.

Given the number of investors, among other considerations, the SEC decided, after long deliberation and despite significant opposition among the own ranks, to consider regulating the hedge funds industry in a more direct fashion.

1. SEC Requires Registration of Hedge Fund Advisers

Utilizing its Rule making authority under the Advisers Act,[694] the SEC, in December 2004, has issued a rule proposal to require hedge fund advisers to register under the Investment Adviser Act ("IAA").[695] However, the vote of the commissioners was a rather narrow one and the rule was eventually issued only by a by a three to two vote.

---

689 15 U.S.C. 78h.

690 17 C.F.R. 240.12g-1.

691 17 C.F.R. 275.203 (b) (3) –1 (a) (2)(i).

692 *Id.* (stating that:"[a] limited partnership is a client of any general partner or other person acting as investment adviser to the partnership.").

693 *See* SEC Release No. IA-2333; File No. S7-3—04, RIN 3235-AJ25, at 72055.

694 The SEC has broad rulemaking authority under Section 211 (a) [15 U.S.C. 80b-11(a) of the Investment Adviser Act. Section 211 (a) asserts that the Commission may adopt rules "necessary or appropriate to the exercise of the functions and powers conferred upon the Commission elsewhere in this title" and "May classify persons and matters within its jurisdiction and prescribe different requirements for different classes of persons and matters.". *See also* Section 202 (a) (17) of the Act [15 U.S.C. 80 (b) –2 (a) (17)] (stating that: "The Commission may by rules and regulations classify, for the purposes of any portion or portions of this title, persons, including employees controlled by an investment adviser.").

695 *See id.*

a) The SEC's Rationale for Regulation

The SEC cites the growth of the hedge fund industry, the broadening exposure of investors to hedge fund risk, as well as the growing number of instances of malfeasance by hedge fund advisers as the main reasons why the previous regulatory scheme for hedge fund advisers was inadequate.[696] As a result of such insufficient regulation, the SEC, in its efforts to remedy the alleged increase of hedge fund fraud[697] and other alleged illegal market activities conducted primarily by hedge funds,[698] claims to have lacked basic information about hedge fund advis-

---

[696] *See* SEC Release No. IA-2333; File No. S7-3—04, RIN 3235-AJ25, at 72059.

[697] The SEC claims that: "The growth in hedge funds has been accompanied by a substantial and troubling growth in the number of our hedge fund fraud enforcement cases." *See* id. at 72056.

[698] The SEC claims to have charged persons with late trading of mutual fund shares on behalf of groups of hedge funds, and mutual fund advisers or principals for permitting hedge funds' market timing. In its final rule release, the SEC cites for this proposition, among others: SEC v. Security Trust Co., N.A., Litigation Release No. 18653 (Apr. 1, 2004) (consent to judgment by trust company charged with facilitating late trades and market timing by affiliated hedge funds over at least a three-year period); In the Matter of Stephen B. Markovitz, Administrative Proceedings Release No. 33-8298 (Oct. 2, 2003) (Commission found that Markovitz engaged in late trading on behalf of hedge funds). See also In the Matter of Alliance Capital Management, L.P., Investment Advisers Act Release No. 2205 (Dec. 18, 2003) (Commission found that investment adviser permitted known market timers, including Canary hedge funds, to market time its mutual funds, in exchange for the timers' investments in Alliance's investment vehicles); In the Matter of James Patrick Connelly, Jr., Investment Advisers Act Release No. 2183 (Oct. 16, 2003) (Commission found that vice chairman of mutual fund adviser permitted market timing by known market timer, including at least one hedge fund). We have also sanctioned mutual fund advisers for permitting certain investors to engage in undisclosed market timing of their funds; hedge funds were among the market timers in these cases. In the Matter of RS Investment Management, Investment Advisers Act Release No. 2310 (Oct. 6, 2004); In the Matter of Janus Capital Management, LLC, Investment Advisers Act Release No. 2277 (Aug. 18, 2004) SEC v. PIMCO Advisors Fund Management, LLC, Investment Advisers Act Release No. 2292 (Sept. 13, 2004) (Commission found that mutual fund adviser entered into a market timing arrangement permitting over 100 mutual fund market timing transactions by hedge funds in exchange for hedge funds' investment in adviser's other investment vehicles; mutual fund adviser also provided hedge funds with material nonpublic portfolio information concerning four of the adviser's mutual funds); In the Matter of Banc One Investment Advisors Corporation and Mark A. Beeson, Investment Advisers Act Release No. 2254 (June 29, 2004) (Commission found that investment adviser permitted Canary hedge fund manager Edward Stern to time the adviser's mutual funds, contrary to the funds' prospectuses; helped arrange financing for the timing trades; failed to disclose the timing arrangements; and provided Stern with nonpublic portfolio information); In the Matter of Pilgrim Baxter & Associates, Ltd., Investment Advisers Act Release No. 2251 (June 21, 2004) (Commission found that mutual fund adviser permitted a hedge fund, in which one of its executives had a substantial financial interest, to engage in repeated and prolonged short-term trading of several mutual funds and that one of its executives provided material nonpublic portfolio information to a broker-dealer, which passed it on to its hedge fund customers); In the Matter of Strong Capital Management, Inc., et al., Investment Advisers Act Release No. 2239 (May 20, 2004) (Commission found

ers, was relying to much on enforcement actions[699] and third party data.[700] Even though the SEC recognizes that the lack of "regulatory constrains," has been "a factor" in the growth and amazing success of hedge funds and the important role that hedge funds play in the worlds financial markets, it still concludes that "requiring hedge fund advisers to register under the Advisers Act will give us the ability to oversee hedge fund advisers without imposing burdens on the legitimate investment activities of hedge funds."[701] This conclusion is partly supported by the supposed evidence exemplified in a few studies, which found that there were no significant differences between performance of hedge funds managed by registered advisers and those managed by unregistered advisers.[702] However, these studies were inconclusive. Also, the extent of cross-sectional variability in hedge

---

that investment adviser disclosed material nonpublic information about mutual fund portfolio holdings to Canary hedge funds, and permitted Canary and the adviser's own chairman to engage in undisclosed market timing of mutual funds managed by adviser).

699 Hedge fund advisers were and remain subject to the antifraud provisions of the old regulatory regime. More precisely, the antifraud prohibitions of section 206 IAA [15 U.S.C. 80b-6], including provisions restricting an adviser's ability to engage in principal trades and agency cross-transactions with clients, apply to any investment adviser that makes use of the mails or any means of interstate commerce.

700 The SEC cites among others, the following articles for its proposition that third party data is unreliable: Hedge-matics: How Many Funds Exist? Wall St. J., May 22, 2003, at C5 (enquiring: "Just how big is the hedge-fund industry? This simple question has been debated because the data on hedge funds are spotty."); William Fung and David Hsieh, Measuring the Market Impact of Hedge Funds, 7 J. of Empirical Fin. 1 (2000) ("There are varying estimates of the size of the hedge fund industry."); Harry M. Kat, 10 Things That Investors Should Know About Hedge Funds, Institutional Investor (Spring 2003) (noting that hedge fund databases are of low quality, that each database covers only a subset of the hedge fund universe, that all present survivorship bias, and that researchers attempting to analyze the hedge fund industry or fund performance may perceive matters very differently depending on the database or index they use); Letter from Craig S. Tyle, General Counsel of the Investment Company Institute, to Jonathan G. Katz, Secretary, U.S. Securities and Exchange Commission, July 2, 2003, available at http://www.ici.org (visited on Oct. 10, 2004) ("There is currently no universal database that contains records of all hedge funds, both those currently operating and those that have ceased operating."); Gaurav S. Amin and Harry M. Kat, Hedge Fund Performance 1990-2000: Do the "Money Machines" Really Add Value?, 38 Journal of Financial and Quantitative Analysis 2 (2003) ("Due to its private nature, it is difficult to estimate the current size of the hedge fund industry."). See also Bing Liang, Hedge Funds: The Living and the Dead, 35 Journal of Financial and Quantitative Analysis 309-326 (2000) (study of statistical inconsistencies in two major hedge fund databases, noting hedge funds "are basically not regulated. They report their fund information only on a voluntary basis. Therefore, the reliability of hedge fund data is an open question and is critical for hedge fund research and the investment community.").

701 *See* SEC Release No. IA-2333; File No. S7-3—04, RIN 3235-AJ25, at 72059.

702 The SEC refers specifically to one study by Hedge Fund Research, Inc., an alternative research and consulting firm, which examined the performance of approximately 2,200 single strategy hedge funds. See id. at 72059, citing Bids and Offers, Wall St. J. July 23, 2004 at C4.

fund returns makes it extremely difficult, if not impossible, to ascertain differences in hedge fund performance statistically.

In light of these preliminary considerations, the SEC seems to present a rather one-sided rationale for regulation, thereby justifying its somewhat hasty and unbalanced regulatory action.[703] In the chapter "A Strongly Worded Dissent," the author dissects the main reasons for the two dissenting commissioners to disagree with the here presented reasoning of the majority of SEC commissioners.

b) Rule 203 (b) (3) –2

Upon the adoption of the safe harbor in 1985, the SEC did not consider it inconsistent with the legislative objectives embedded in the statutory provision exempting advisers from registration, provided they fulfilled the requirements of the safe harbor.[704] Referring to an earlier statement when the SEC proposed the safe harbor, "a different approach could be followed in counting clients,"[705] and in light of the recent developments regarding hedge funds and their advisers, the SEC is now taking a different approach.

Thus, for purposes of determining the availability of the private adviser exemption of section 203 (b) (3) of the Act, Rule 203 (b) (3) –2 now requires an investment adviser to count each owner of a "private fund" towards the threshold of 14 clients.[706] The new rule implements significant changes. Thus, an adviser, to a "private fund,"[707] used to be able to rely on the private adviser exemption. This has been changed insofar as an adviser, who has advised private funds that had more than 14 investors during the course of the preceding 12 months, can no longer rely on the private adviser exemption.[708] Moreover, for purposes of the 14 client limit of Section 203 (b)(3), an adviser who advises individual clients directly, must count those clients together with the investors in any private fund it advises.[709] The new rule does not amend the general rule (subject to some exceptions) that a hedge fund adviser who is located in the US cannot register with the

703 It is also questionable if it is mere coincidence that the comment period was placed at such an inopportune time during the vacation month of August 2004 (the comments were due by September 15, 2004). It also seems unusual that the SEC would not grant an extension on the commenting period to get more of a broad array of opinions on the matter.

704 *See* SEC Release No. IA-2333; File No. S7-3—04, RIN 3235-AJ25, at 72068.

705 *See* SEC Investment Adviser Act.

706 *See* SEC Release No. IA-2333; File No. S7-3—04, RIN 3235-AJ25, at. 72069.

707 Defined in Rule 203 (b) (3) –1.

708 *See* SEC Release No. IA-2333; File No. S7-3—04, RIN 3235-AJ25, at 72070.

709 *Id.* (The SEC has, however, clarified that an adviser does not have to count itself as a client regardless of the form of ownership the adviser takes. Rule 203(b) (3) –2(a). Whereas advisers can exclude knowledgeable advisory personnel who are "qualified clients," i.e. insiders, that may be charged a performance fee. Id.).

SEC unless he or she manages at least $25million,[710] whereas an offshore adviser must look through each private fund it advises, whether or not those funds are located offshore, and count each US investor as a client and has, accordingly, to register with the SEC if it has more than 14 clients in the US, regardless of the amount of assets the adviser has under management.[711] As for funds of hedge funds, the new rule requires that a Hedge Fund adviser, who has among its investors a fund of funds that is a "private fund", is, in accordance with the general requirements of the rule, required to count the investors of the top tier fund as clients for purposes of the private adviser exemption. If the fund of funds is a registered investment company, the risks are exacerbated because an adviser may just count its top tier funds and thereby indirectly manage the assets of hundreds or thousands of investors without oversight or registration. Accordingly, the SEC requires the adviser to look through the investment company and to count its investors as clients for purposes of the exemption.[712]

In order to identify those legal organizations that advisers are required to look through, the SEC has also defined "private funds." The basis of the SEC definition is three essential characteristics shared by most hedge funds. The definition is, thus, one of differentiation. The SEC differentiates hedge funds from other pooled investment vehicles such as private equity funds[713] or venture capital funds.[714] First, for purposes of the definition of "private funds" a fund will not be considered "private" unless it is a company that would be subject to regulation under the Investment Company Act but for the exception from the definition of "investment company,"[715] as provided in sections 3 (c) (1) or 3 (c) (7) of the In-

710 Section 203A (a) (1) (A) [15 U.S.C. 80b-31(a) (1) (A)].

711 The SEC has provided that the new rule 203 (b) (3) –2 and Rule 203 (b)(3) – 1 are designed to work together. Once the offshore adviser looks through the private fund as required under Rule 203 (b) (3) –2, Rule 203 (b) (3) – 1 (b) (5) provides that only US clients must be counted for purposes of the private adviser exemption. *See* SEC Release No. IA-2333; File No. S7-3—04, RIN 3235-AJ25, at 72071.

712 Rule 203 (b) (3) – 2(b).

713 Private equity funds concentrate their investments in unregistered and typically illiquid securities, are long-term investments providing for liquidation at the end of a term specified in the fund's governing documents. Private equity investors typically commit to invest a certain amount of money with the fund over the life of the fund. They make their contributions to the fund subject to "capital calls" from the fund's general partner. One downside of private equity funds is that they rarely offer opportunities for their investors to redeem their investments. *See* SEC Release No. IA-2333; File No. S7-3—04, RIN 3235-AJ25, at 72073.

714 Venture capital funds are generally organized to invest in the start up or early stages of a company and but share most of the features that distinguish private equity funds from hedge funds, such as capital contributions over the life of the fund and the long-term nature of the investment. Typically, a venture capital fund will seek to liquidate its investment once the value of the company increases above the value of the investment. *Id.*

715 *Id.*

vestment Company Act.[716] Second, only if the fund permits investors to redeem their interests in the fund within two years of purchase, the fund will be considered a "private fund."[717] Finally, if the interest in a fund is offered based on the investment advisory skills, ability or expertise of the investment adviser, the fund is a "private fund."[718] Accordingly, if these three criteria are fulfilled, all advisers to the fund, including sub-advisers, must look through the fund and count owners as clients for the purposes of the private adviser exemption.[719]

c) Supplemental Rule Changes and SEC Reasoning

As seen, the decisive addition to the Adviser Act Rules is Rule 203 (b) (3) – 2. Overall, the SEC made amendments to Rule 203 (b) (3)-1, Rule 204-2, Rule 205-3, Rule 206 (4)-2, Rule 222-2 and Rule 203A-3, as well as Form ADV.[720]

Rule 203 (b) (3) –1 has been amended insofar as advisers may not count hedge funds as single clients under the safe harbor,[721] whereas an adviser to a private fund must look through the fund but can still rely on the Rule 203(b) (3) –1 safe harbor to determine whether each investor must count as a separate client or whether a single client may include more than one investor. The recordkeeping rules in Rule 204-2 have been amended as pertains to permitting hedge fund advisers to market their performance from periods prior to their registration with the SEC, even if they have not kept documentation that would otherwise be required by the SEC, and access of SEC examiners to records of a registered hedge fund adviser who acts as general partner, managing member or in a similar capacity.[722] To avoid disruption of existing arrangements between newly-registered hedge fund advisers and their current pool investors or separate account clients, the SEC added a grandfathering provision to rule 205-3 under the Adviser Act.[723] The adviser custody rule in Rule 206 (4) –2[724] has also been amended to allow additional

716 Section 3 (c) (1) excepts from the definition of investment company, an issuer the securities of which are beneficially owned by no more than 100 persons and who is not making or proposing to make a public offering of its securities. Section 3 (c) (7) excepts from the definition of investment company, an issuer the outstanding securities of which are owned exclusively by persons who, at the time of acquisition of such securities, are qualified purchasers and that is not making or proposing to make a public offering of its securities.

717 Rule 203 (b) (3) –1 (d) (1) (ii).

718 *See* SEC Release No. IA-2333; File No. S7-3—04, RIN 3235-AJ25, at 72075.

719 It should be emphasized that advisers and sub-advisers may not circumvent the rule by delegating the advisory function to sub-advisers or sub-sub-advisers.

720 *See id.* at 72054.

721 Rule 203 (b) (3) – 1 (b) (6).

722 *See* SEC Release No. IA-2333; File No. S7-3—04, RIN 3235-AJ25, at 72075, 76.

723 *Id.* at 76.

724 Under Rule 206 (4)-2 (c) (1) (iii), an adviser acting as general partner to a pooled investment vehicle it manages, including a hedge fund, has custody of the pool's assets. The adviser may

time for completion of audit work on behalf of advisers to funds of hedge funds that choose to distribute audited fund financial statements to investors under the custody rule.[725] Lastly, Rule 222, Rule 203A-3, and Form ADV have been changed to fit Rule 203(b) (3) –2 within the overall regulatory framework under the Adviser Act. This rulemaking is designed to alter the method of counting clients and identifying hedge fund advisers in determining adviser registration with the SEC.[726]

2. Cost-Benefit Analysis Revisited

The SEC made clear that it is "sensitive" to the costs and benefits that result form its rules.[727] Therefore, the SEC added a section on cost benefits analysis to justify its rulemaking in Rule 203(b) (3)-2. Among others, the SEC identifies benefits to hedge fund investors by deterring fraud and curtailing losses, providing basic information about hedge fund advisers, and improve compliance controls.[728] The SEC also sees benefits to mutual fund investors, other investors and markets, regulatory policy, and hedge fund advisers.

In and unusual move, Commissioners Cyntia A. Glassman and Paul S. Aktins who opposed releasing the proposal the final rule, have published a strongly worded dissent.[729] Their dissent shows that while the growth of the industry might support a call for more information, mandatory rulemaking is inappropriate as a response to the concerns underlying the rulemaking. The dissent among the SEC's own ranks exemplifies the flawed approach to hedge fund regulation precipitated by the significant risks for some of the important players in the US financial markets. A different, less direct, form of regulation might have attained the same, if not preferable, effects.

a) Regulation to Prevent Investor losses from Hedge Fund Fraud

Among the most obvious arguments for its regulation, the SEC refers to possible prevention or diminishment of losses that hedge fund investors may otherwise experience as a result of hedge fund advisers' fraud.[730] To support its rea-

---

satisfy its obligations to deliver custody account information to investors by distributing the pool's audited financial statements to investors. Rule 206(4)-2(b)(3). The current rule gives advisers 120 days from the pool's fiscal year-end to distribute the financial statements. *Id.*

725 *See* SEC Release No. IA-2333; File No. S7-3—04, RIN 3235-AJ25, at 72076.

726 *Id.* at 72077.

727 *Id.* at 72078.

728 *Id.* at *72078-79.*

729 *See* Cyntia A. Glassman and Paul S. Atkins [FR Doc. 04-26879, Filed 12-9-04; 8:45am], billing code 9010-01-p, 69 FR 72054-01, 2004 WL 2825810 (F.R.).

730 *Id.* at 72078.

soning, the SEC refers to several studies that seem to suggest that hedge fund fraud is on the rise.[731] However, the SEC fails to provide a detailed analysis of the data, which may have been necessary to justify its regulatory engagements. The SEC also refers to the increased exposure of small investors as a result of the decrease in minimum investment requirements[732] and the additional dangers that are associated with this phenomenon.[733] Even though the author does not purport to provide more accurate data, it is questionable if the data provided by the SEC may be called accurate or independent. It appears to be more or less based on hearsay, experience with enforcement actions, and anecdotal evidence. If the SEC had provided a detailed econometric analysis, the regulatory action might have had less opposition. However, a detailed independent statistical analysis of the low volume of available data may, at this point, not be possible. Given this lack of data, it seems premature for the SEC to regulate the hedge fund industry through investor counting by advisers in Rule 203 (b)(3) –2.

The SEC's reasoning includes avoiding losses for hedge fund investors. However, the new registration requirements will be costly to affected advisers. These costs will undoubtedly be passed on to investors. Net profits for investors will depreciate and such regulation does not result in fewer losses but more net losses for investors, assuming all other factors are constant. The SEC also does not appreciate the aggregated net initial direct costs associated with registration and did not estimate ongoing costs of compliance.

Apart from direct costs of registration and compliance with the new rule, there may be indirect costs that are not taken into account. Among the indirect costs could be the potential abandoning of complex investment strategies that hedge fund advisers employed before the registration requirement. Complex in-

---

[731] Bank of New York, Restoring Broken Trust (July 2004) (50% of respondents in study identified hedge funds as "most likely to be at the centre of an investment controversy" in the next five years); the SEC has brought 51 cases in which it has asserted that hedge fund advisers have defrauded hedge fund investors or used the fund to defraud others in amounts the SEC staff estimates to exceed $1.1 billion. *See* Investment Adviser Act Release No. 2266 (July 20, 2004) [69FR 45171 (July 28, 2004)].

[732] *See* SEC 2003 Staff Hedge Fund Report, at 81.

[733] *See* SEC Release No. IA-2333; File No. S7-3—04, RIN 3235-AJ25. at 72057 (citing in particular: Harriet, Johnson Brackley, new Class of Hedge Funds Reaches Beyond the Wealthy, San Jose Mercury News, Mar. 23, 2003; Pam Black, Going Mainstream, Registered Rep. , Mar. 1, 2004; Hanna Shaw Grove and Russ Alan Prince, The Street's Last Lure: Some One Going to Mint Money With the New Hedge Funds For Smaller Investors, Newsweek, May 26, 2003. And referring also to hedge fund articles in publications for physicians, i.e. John J. Grande, Alternative Investment Strategies Can offer Significant ROI, Ophthalmology Times, May 15, 2002; Leslie Kane, Where to Put Your Money: Four Experts Tell Whether You Should put Your Money, Medical Economics, Jan. 9, 2004; Also in Jenna Gottlieb, Hedge Fund Deal Raises Product's Bank Profile, American Banker, Oct. 14, 2004 (stating that fund of hedge funds are becoming mainstream and are marketed to the mass affluent).

vestment strategies distinguish hedge funds from other funds and are at the core of hedge fund industries' success story. Since this form of investment requires intuition and a highly analytical mind as well as the ability to react instantly to new information, it may be extremely difficult if not impossible to explain the exact strategy and its effects on the portfolio and the markets to SEC examiners. By instituting these highly complex investment strategies hedge fund advisers were able to utilize market inefficiencies and attain higher net returns for the fund and their clients. Distinguishing themselves with higher net returns, in turn, precipitated wealthy clients to continue to invest more in the hedge fund. This dichotomy of factors created an upward surge for the hedge fund industry, with complex investment strategies at its core. The new rule undermines the incentive to employ complex strategies as an adviser will have to make a trade-off between explaining a complex investment strategy to an examiner that may be damaging to his reputation and personal career versus the net profits that made the fund successful and create incentives for clients to invest more. Depending on the extend of SEC examination and scrutiny of strategies and their effects, the advisers may be disinclined to sacrifice his career plans, most hedge fund advisers do not put up with the stress of hedge fund investing for more than a decade and move on to other employment opportunities, and will be less aggressive in his investing. At a minimum, an adviser will spend more time explaining his strategies and less time exploring market inefficiencies and monitoring his investments.[734]

It seems difficult for the SEC to justify regulating advisers to protect investors when in other areas of regulation the SEC relegates to the individual investor to fend for him or herself as in Rule 506 and Rule 505 of the 33 Act. The counterargument would probably be that smaller investors are investing in hedge funds as well and cannot fend for themselves because they are less likely to be able to afford the advice of financial advisers, and therefore "need" SEC supervision and protection. Assuming that the SEC's analysis of the fraud data is correct, one still has to point out that it tends to be a problem among smaller funds that accept smaller investors rather than investors with more assets who are assumed to be able to fend for them. Given this fact, the SEC's approach to regulate all hedge fund advisers in Rule 203 (b) (3) –2 may be mistaken.

---

734 *See also* Alan Greenspan, Chairman, Federal Reserve Board, Testimony before the Senate Banking, Housing and Urban Affairs Committee (July 20, 2004) (elaborating on the larger effects on the economy: "Hedge fund arbitrageurs are required to move flexibly and expeditiously if they are to succeed. If placed under increasing restrictions, many will leave the industry, to the significant detriment of our economy.").

b) Improved Information and Compliance Controls?

Among the benefits of its regulation, the SEC cites providing basic information about hedge fund advisers, and improved compliance controls.[735] As indicated earlier, the SEC in updating Form ADV, which requires hedge fund advisers to file and disclose information about their business, affiliates and owners, as well as disciplinary history, provides additional information to hedge fund investors. The SEC acknowledged that the information provided in Form ADV cannot substitute investor due diligence but is only intended to provide investors with a publicly accessible foundation of basic information.[736] Proper investor due diligence, in turn, requires background checks and most likely hiring a firm for additional information. These are significant costs, which are rather unlikely to be afforded by small retail investors.

Given that one of the main arguments for hedge fund regulation was the protection of smaller "retail" investors, who cannot afford proper investor due diligence, it is at least questionable if the additional information in Form ADV justifies the transaction costs of the proposed new rule, i.e. registration costs, cost of establishing a compliance infrastructure, and ongoing costs of compliance and examination cost of compliance.

Compliance controls, as provided for in the new rule, in particular, are a matter of concern. Under the new rule, hedge fund advisers who had to register are required to have comprehensive compliance procedures in place and have to designate a chief compliance officer,[737] specify procedures governing proxy voting,[738] and need to implement a code of ethics[739] including requirements for personal securities reporting. The SEC "estimates" rather liberally those advisory firms facing the cost of establishing a compliance infrastructure will "face little cost to modify their current compliance practices to comply with the Adviser Act rules."[740] The SEC continues to "estimate" the cost for hedge fund advisers to establish the required compliance infrastructure to be on average, $20,000 in professional fees and $25,000 in internal costs including staff time.[741] The compensation costs for hiring a chief compliance officer (CCO), however, are expected to

735 *See* SEC Release No. IA-2333; File No. S7-3—04, RIN 3235-AJ25. at 72078-79.

736 *Id.* at 72079.

737 Rule 206 (4) –7.

738 Rule 206 (4) –6.

739 Rule 204A –1.

740 *See* SEC Release No. IA-2333; File No. S7-3—04, RIN 3235-AJ25. at 72081.

741 *Id.* (acknowledging that between 690 and 1,260 hedge fund advisers "would be new Adviser Act registrants under the new rule and rule amendments. [...] Aggregate start-up costs to establish required compliance infrastructure for all new registrants are therefore estimated to range from $31 to $57 million."). *Id.* at n. 333.

range from $234,000 to $300,000.[742] These and the costs of ongoing compliance and examination have, alas, not been squared with the alleged benefits of the regulation. The SEC merely "estimates" and discusses what some commenter have suggested, dismissing most critical considerations. There is no substantive discussion as to how these rules may affect competition, efficiency or capital formation. The SEC merely states that: "We do not anticipate that the new rule will introduce any competitive disadvantages. The new rule may provide a level playing field with respect to advisers' compliance infrastructure."[743]

As the new rules have not been tested and there is no comparison with other legal regimes, it is, at this point, difficult to opine whether there would be any competitive disadvantages. It remains true, however, that the SEC is the only regulator so far that has attempted to regulate hedge funds directly. Admittedly, many advisers may already be registered with the SEC in one form or another. However, the new rule is likely to have unintended effects on the hedge fund industry. These effects may be noticeable not only in the US, but also in international securities markets in which the US is a dominant player. What these effects will be and how they will affect efficiency, competition and capital formation remains to be seen. The new Rule reflects a potential shift in the philosophy underlying the SEC rulemaking under US securities law from a mere reliance on disclosure to substantive regulation of the hedge fund industry. This shift creates disincentives for US hedge fund advisers to remain subject to the US laws and may lead them to conclude that focusing on international clients may ultimately be a better long-term strategy, thereby evading the US jurisdiction. It may also deter foreign hedge fund advisers from soliciting clients in the US, or otherwise becoming subject to US law. This is significant because the US hedge fund industry was for the last 25 years a role model for other business centers and their national hedge funds. Although the legal forms and structures of hedge funds may have been different in other jurisdictions, the US style and aggressiveness of hedge fund investing was unique. Some foreign firms in effect adopted the US hedge fund approach, be it in investing or structuring hedge funds, in order to overcome deficiencies in their home country law[744] and management style. The new Rule may reduce the demand for US law, US hedge funds, and make it more problematic to solicit US investors, blocking non-US hedge funds advisors from moving toward more efficient governance and impeding the internationalization of securities markets and laws. Alternatively, the SEC and perhaps Congress may forestall such flight by re-evaluating a less direct approach to hedge fund regulation. As

---

742 The SIA Report on Management and Professional Earnings in the Securities Industry in 2003, adjusted by the SEC ($234,000) conflicts with private party estimates of $300,000. *Id.* at n. 335.

743 *Id.* at 72085.

744 Umbrella structures allowed in some instances to market American hedge funds in other countries.

will be demonstrated later, an indirect approach to hedge fund regulation via banking supervision, i.e. the Basle II Accord addresses most of the concerns and benefits hedge, funds, the regulators, as well as financial intermediaries.

c) Cost of Regulatory Arbitrage

Moreover, the SEC's cost benefit analysis may be flawed if regulatory arbitrage is taken into account. As discussed earlier, if an offshore hedge fund adviser wants to be eligible for the private adviser exemption, it must look through each private fund it advises, whether or not those funds are also located offshore, and count each investor that is a US resident as a client. Here, the decisive interconnection of new Rule 203 (b) (3) –2 and Rule 203 (b) (3) –1 is clearly visible, i.e. once the offshore adviser looks through the private fund as required under Rule 203 (b) (3)-2, Rule 203 (b) (3)-1 (b) (5) provides that only US client must be counted towards the private adviser exemption.[745] Given that the new rule creates a situation where an offshore adviser may be better of without US clients, which would enable him to escape SEC supervision altogether, the SEC's Cost – Benefit Analysis may have to take into account the problem of regulatory arbitrage.[746] Admittedly, access to the US markets and US investors is very attractive. However, in the light of recent developments in the hedge fund industry in Europe, European investors may become a welcome alternative for hedge fund advisers and would enable them to escape SEC supervision altogether.

3. A Strongly Worded Dissent

In an unusual move, Commissioners Cynthia A. Glassman and Paul S. Aktins[747] who opposed releasing the final rule, have published a strongly worded dissent.[748] Their dissent shows that while the growth of the industry might support a call for more information, mandatory rulemaking is questionable as a response to the concerns underlying the rulemaking. The dissent among the SEC's own ranks exemplifies the flawed approach to hedge fund regulation.

Broadly speaking, the two Commissioners raised as their primary concerns with the Commission's rulemaking the availability of alternatives that have not

---

[745] *Id.* at 72071.

[746] For a comprehensive analysis of developments in regulatory arbitrage in terms of corporate law, especially in Europe after the decision Inspire Art, see Kaal, Kirchner, Painter (2005) (elaborating that arbitration may be able to provide a temporary solution until regulatory competition in EU corporate law is more fully developed).

[747] Both of whom are Republicans, which somewhat illustrates the political dimension of hedge fund regulation in the US.

[748] *See* Cyntia A. Glassman and Paul S. Atkins [FR Doc. 04-26879, Filed 12-9-04; 8:45am], billing code 9010-01-p, 69 FR 72054-01, 2004 WL 2825810 (F.R.).

been considered, the pretextual nature of the rulemaking, as well as the division of the SEC's limited resources.[749]

As for viable alternatives, the dissenting Commissioners agree with the majority insofar as the importance of the quality of information is concerned. But, pooling of information from already registered entities, self-regulatory organizations, other government agencies, enhanced oversight of existing registrants, and a census of all hedge funds would have been another alternative as opposed to mandatory registration.[750] The lack of coordination with other regulators to aggregate the available information has also been criticized.[751]

Apart from the SEC's ignorance in terms of viable regulatory alternatives, the dissent refers primarily to the pretextual nature of the rulemaking as a reason for dissent, citing the SEC's reference to the need for regulatory action as a result of a combination of hedge fund growth, fraud, and retailization. These reasons are pretextual and cannot justify the majority's action.[752] More specifically, it appears as if the majority's reasoning for regulation is partly motivated by the simple fact that the hedge fund industry has grown. The dissent points out that "[T]he Commission should not assume that a greater level of regulation is needed in a flourishing industry with a wealthy and sophisticated investor base."[753] Registration would also not have prevented the violations in the enforcement cases cited by the majority. The dissent refers to the 2003 Staff Hedge Fund Report,[754] finding no disproportionate involvement of hedge funds or their advisers in fraud, inferring that the majority overstates the relative significance of hedge fund fraud.[755] From a more ideological perspective it could be argued that the SEC's information assembling in its new rule is trying to emulate and replace a function that is now handled by the market. This is a task that the Commission is not equipped to perform.

Another pretextual argument of the majority is the so-called "retailization" of hedge funds, i.e. the increasing accessibility of hedge fund to smaller and unsophisticated investors investing in pension funds and funds of funds. The dissent again points to the 2003 Staff Report, which found no retailization.[756] Given the inflow that is already so rapid that hedge fund advisers have more to invest than they can handle, they are in no need to solicit retail investors. To the extent re-

---

749 *See* SEC Release No. IA-2333; File No. S7-3—04, RIN 3235-AJ25. at 72089-98.

750 *Id.* at 72089.

751 The CFTC and the NFA both offered the sharing of information. *See* Comment Letter of the NFA (Sept. 14, 2004), and Comment Letter of the CFTC (Oct.22, 2004).

752 *See* SEC Release No. IA-2333; File No. S7-3—04, RIN 3235-AJ25 at 72091.

753 *Id.*

754 *See* 2003 Staff Hedge Fund Report, at 73.

755 *See* SEC Release No. IA-2333; File No. S7-3—04, RIN 3235-AJ25. at 720892 (citing the 2003 Staff Report).

756 *Id.* at 72093 (citing the 2003 Staff Report).

tailization takes place through incoming funds from pension funds and funds of funds, hedge fund advisers are instituting measures to pre-empt that form of retailization.[757] As pension funds limit hedge fund investments to those with registered advisers and will have a broader array of registered hedge fund advisers, "the majority's proposal ironically may stimulatc rctailization,"[758] and may ultimately have the effect of admitting retail investors.

Lastly, the dissent takes issue with the fact that the majority has departed from regulatory and statutory precedent.[759] The SEC traditionally has determined who an adviser is by looking at whether the adviser is tailoring the advice to objectives of the individual investor or if the adviser is providing advice to an entity in which individuals share profits. The majority speculates that Congress did not intend for the legal entity to be treated as the client in the hedge fund context as it is in the investment company context and therefore "awkwardly depart[s] from the established approach for identifying an adviser's clients."[760] The majority assumed that removing the adviser exemption would simply effect Congress's "unspoken" intent that an adviser who manages a significantly large asset pool must be registered. This was, according to the dissent, a fallacy as "the fact that many advisers to such pools were not registered under the Advisers Act was certainly known to Congress and allowing them to continue in their unregistered state was entirely consistent with Congress's objective of minimizing regulatory restrictions on such pools of assets."[761] Accordingly, the majority's rulemaking was contrary to Congress's intend and lacked statutory authority.

4. Another Avenue of Regulation?

The SEC in the new rule chose one particular way of regulating hedge funds in order to limit direct investments. As mentioned before, the SEC argues that this form of regulation was economically the optimal form of regulation. However, there would have been other ways available to regulate hedge funds within the legal authority of the SEC under certain federal laws.

For instance, the SEC could also have raises the "accredited investor" standards applicable to private offerings pursuant to Regulation D.[762] Such regulatory measures would, arguably, have had a similar regulatory effect on limiting direct investments in hedge funds. However, the SEC argued that leaving eligibility re-

---

757 *Id.*

758 *Id.* at 72095.

759 *Id.* at 72096-98.

760 *Id.* at 72097.

761 *Id.* at 72098.

762 Regulation D [17 C.F.R. 230.501 through 508] exempts from registration under the Securities Act of 1933 offerings and sales securities that satisfy certain conditions, including certain sales to "accredited investors." A

quirements for accredited investors unchanged also allows small businesses to continue to seek capital from historical sources,[763] and raising accredited investor standards would not address the problem of indirect exposure to hedge funds and their risks by an increasingly large number of persons who are beneficiaries of pension plans or invest through other intermediaries that are likely to meet any high standards.[764]

Another avenue of regulation could have been the gathering of information about hedge funds and their advisers from the already existing databases and research made available by hedge funds themselves, their advisers, and broker – dealers and other financial intermediaries who deal with hedge funds. The SEC has dismissed this approach with reference to its need of "information that is reliable, current, complete and in a format reasonably susceptible to analysis by our staff," too high costs of extraction of the information, and a low degree of content regarding adviser's fulfilment of their fiduciary duties.[765] As the use of Form ADV and other documents that have to be filed with the SEC under its new rule only yields very little and, conceded by the SEC, "basic information," there is little reason to belief that it would be any more complete or reliable compared with the already available information. Incurring costs for qualitatively equal or inferior information is inefficient. This is exacerbated considering that the SEC does not only impose costs of supplying the information on Hedge Fund advisers, it also incurs substantial costs itself for supervising and analyzing this new data. It also seems questionable if the SEC has opted for the efficient alternative in terms of the costs of setting up the registration requirements, administrating the assembling of new information as opposed to the costs of extracting a composite of already existing information. In order to be the efficient alternative, the efficiency concerns would have to be outweighed by the increased susceptibility to analysis of the new data.

Market surveillance, an effective tool that has been used by the SEC in insider cases, is a targeted way of finding fraud and would allow the SEC to leverage the knowledge and expertise of other regulators. More specifically, monitoring transactions through existing registrants could have alleviated some of the concerns that led the SEC to regulate directly. For instance, the oversight of prime brokers could have assisted in detecting and deterring fraud of prime brokers' hedge fund clients and obtain more information about hedge fund advisers.[766] The Federal Reserve Chairman, Alan Greenspan opined in this context: "If there was a public policy reason to monitor hedge fund activity, the best method of do-

---

763 *See* Implications of the Growth of Hedge Funds, Staff Report to the United States Securities and Exchange Commission, available at http://www.sec.gov./spotlight/hedgefunds.htm.

764 *See* SEC Release No. IA-2333; File No. S7-3—04, RIN 3235-AJ25, at 72064.

765 *Id.* at 72067.

766 *Id.* at 72091.

ing so without raising liquidity concerns would be indirectly through oversight of those broker-dealers that clear, settle, and finance trades of hedge funds."[767]

Given these concerns, and assuming that regulation would be justified, one could imagine opting into some of the old and proven regulatory schemes. Following the example of regulation in Rule 505 or 506 of the 33 Act, the SEC could simply have required hedge fund advisers to register if they cater to smaller investors, i.e. investors that invest less than $25,000. Accordingly, another avenue of regulation could have been a two-prong scheme of regulation and exception under the adviser exception. Investors with a lower volume of investment, i.e. for the sake of argument less than $ 25,000, would fall under prong one for purposes of adviser's counting of investors. Investors with more than $25,000 will be deemed to be able to fend for themselves and are exempt for purposes of counting investors under Rule 203(b)(3)-2. With this cut off, the SEC would ensure that smaller investors are protected; the SEC could uphold its public image and serve the functions given to it by the legislator. On the other hand, the secrecy and market optimization potential of hedge funds with larger investors and larger fund under management would be less tempted to opt into other jurisdictions to evade SEC supervision.

Admittedly, evading regulation via a cut-off amount of invested funds seems arbitrary. This is, however, a general problem of regulation and the line has to be drawn somewhere to preserve the benefits of exemption for the Hedge Fund industry. Another problem with this form of regulation would be the disincentive for Hedge Fund advisers to cater to smaller investors, i.e. if they count smaller investors for purposes of the adviser exemption they will have less money under management and will have more investors quicker, requiring them to register with the SEC and an early stage of raising funds to, for instance, set up a new fund. On the other hand, this form of regulation would ensure that Hedge Fund advisers would have less of an incentive to evade regulation altogether by going offshore and abstaining from soliciting American investors.

II. *Hedge Fund Regulation in the EU*

Although the hedge fund industry in the EU is still in its infancy, several initiatives have been aimed at regulating hedge funds. These initiatives were primarily EU Directives as well as implementation of these Directives in the individual Member States. For instance, the UCITS Directives may, depending on the form of implementation, directly or indirectly affect hedge fund managers who are

767 Alan Greenspan, written response to questions from Chairman Shelby in Connection with Testimony before the Senate Banking, Housing and Urban Affairs Committee, (July 20, 2004). This proposal is one step closer to direct regulation rather than relying on the Basle Accord, which determines the risk that banks can take and the calibration of their leverage with hedge funds.

regulated as investment managers under the general framework that is being changed by the directives. This was the case, as shall be seen in more detail in part D.II., in Germany where the German legislature enacted the Investment Modernization Act,[768] which significantly overhauled Germany's investment fund industry and regulation and relaxed its rigid tax regime. The Investment Modernization Act implemented the UCITS III Directive of the Council of the European Union, and, for the first time, allowed the organization and sale of domestic hedge funds in Germany. Other jurisdictions like the UK with a more developed financial market framework, the FSA regulation of financial markets and indirectly of hedge funds is among the most developed in the EU, did not implement all the aspects of the UCTIS III Directive. In the case of the UK, implementation was either not necessary because similar provision were already in place or had a far less visible impact on financial regulation in the UK.

On the face of it, the UCTIS Directives do not directly address hedge fund regulation. However, as the significance of the hedge fund industry is highlighted by the immense growth potential, European regulators have started an initiative to address regulatory concerns precipitated by hedge fund on a European level.[769] Although the European Parliament may, as a matter of law, not have the right of initiative to regulate hedge funds,[770] such initiative would have a political dimension as it fits well into the framework of the EU Commission's Action Plan for Financial Services[771] to integrate European financial markets.

1. EU Directives

In the coming years, financial market regulation in the EU will be updated and significantly changed. The coming changes are a reflection of the EU's realization that its regulatory framework has to be more harmonized to integrate all of its Member States and make it more competitive in international financial markets. In that collective investment undertakings[772] constitute a major market sector, with assets of around EUR 3.5 trillion, harmonization in this sector seemed inevitable. Accordingly, the EU has proposed several new directives. Among those are the Market Abuse Directive (MAD),[773] the Markets in Financial Instru-

---

768 Investmentmodernisierungsgesetz, vom 15. Dezember 2003, Bundesgesetzblatt No. 62, 19.12.2003, http://217.160.60.235/BGBL/bgbl1f/bgbl103s2676.pdf.

769 *See* Börsen Zeitung, EU- Pass für Hedge Fonds, 01.16, 2004; Börsen Zeitung, Neue Hedgefonds-Allianz bildet sich, 01.12.2004; Börsen Zeitung, EU Pass für Hedgefonds – Parlament eröffnet Debatte, 08.26.2003.

770 *See* Lang (2004), p. 4.

771 *See* European Commission Action Plan for Financial Services, at http://europa.eu.int/comm/internal_market/en/finances/actionplan/index.htm#plans.

772 Such as unit trusts and SICAVs.

773 Commission Directive 2004/72/EC (*Official Journal L 162, 30/04/2004 P. 0070 – 0075)* of

ments Directive (MIFID),[774] the Capital Requirements Directive (CRD),[775] and the UCITS Directive. As the UCITS Directives directly addresses and changed some regulatory aspects pertaining to hedge funds, the discussion in this paper will emphasize the Undertakings for Collective Investment in Transferable Securities ("UCITS"), so called "UCITS Directive.

The original UCITS Directive[776] came into effect in 1989, setting out certain minimum conditions that a collective investment scheme ("CIS") needed to meet to be sold on a cross-border basis. However, its scope was limited to schemes invested in shares and bonds, and whilst the manager of the scheme could market that scheme in other member States, it could not carry out other investment services. Since then, other directives such as the Capital Requirements Directive (formerly ISD) have been developed, where the passport is available to those undertaking investment businesses. So, the European Commission proposed two amending directives. These are the so-called Management Directive[777] and the Product Directive,[778] both of which were formally adopted on 21 January 2002.[779]

---

29 April 2004 implementing Directive 2003/6/EC of the European Parliament and of the Council as regards accepted market practices, the definition of inside information in relation to derivatives on commodities, the drawing up of lists of insiders, the notification of managers' transactions and the notification of suspicious transactions (Text with EEA relevance).

[774] Previously called the Investment Service Directive. MIFID is due to be implemented by the end of April 2007. Directive 2004/39/EC (*Official Journal L 145, 30/04/2004 P. 0001 – 0044)* of the European Parliament and of the Council of 21 April 2004 on markets in financial instruments amending Council Directives 85/611/EEC and 93/6/EEC and Directive 2000/12/EC of the European Parliament and of the Council and repealing Council Directive 93/22/EEC.

[775] Also called Basle II or Capital Requirements Directive / Market Risk Directive. Council Directive 93/6/EEC (*Official Journal L 141, 11/06/1993 P. 0001 – 0026)* of 15 March 1993 on the capital adequacy of investments firms and credit institutions.

[776] Directive 85/611/EEC on the co-ordination of laws, regulations and administrative provisions relating to undertakings for collective investment in transferable securities (UCITS).

[777] Directive 2001/107/EC (Official Journal L 041, 13/02/2002 P. 0020 – 0034) of the European Parliament and of the Council of 21 January 2002 amending Council Directive 85/611/EEC on the coordination of laws, regulations and administrative provisions relating to undertakings for collective investment in transferable securities (UCITS) with a view to regulating management companies and simplified prospectuses.

[778] Directive 2001/108/EC (Official Journal L 041, 13/02/2002 P. 0035 – 0042) of the European Parliament and of the Council of 21 January 2002 amending Council Directive 85/611/EEC on the coordination of laws, regulations and administrative provisions relating to undertakings for collective investment in transferable securities (UCITS), with regard to investments of UCITS.

[779] EU Press Release IP/01/1728, Financial Services: Commission welcomes adoption of two new Directives on investment funds (UCITS), Brussels, 4th December 2001 (citing internal market Commissioner Frits Bolkestein: "The final adoption of these two UCITS Directives is a fillip to the €3.5 trillion investment fund business and a real confidence boost towards accomplishing our goal of an integrated capital and financial services market by 2005. Funds will now be able to use modern investment techniques, and stimulate the cross-border growth potential with the passport regime, whilst investors will be able to rely on enhanced investor protection standards. I urge the

The Management Directive introduces a passport, similar to that available in the ISD, for the management company of a UCITS, thereby allowing such firms to carry out additional investment business on a cross-border basis, widening the activities which they are allowed to undertake as non-core services. The Management Directive also imposes new financial resource requirements and conduct of business rules, similar to the ISD on the UCITS management company. It also provides for a simplified prospectus to be used as a marketing document throughout the EEA. Moreover, the Management Directive aims to set a level playing field with "self-managed investment companies" which have not designated a management company. By introducing the concept of a simplified prospectus the Directive will provide more accessible, comprehensive information to strengthen investor protection.

The Product Directive, on the other hand, removes barriers to cross-border marketing of units of collective investment funds by widening the scope of assets in which they can invest. The Product Directive also extends the range of products in which a UCITS scheme may invest beyond merely shares and bonds. Under the new rules, although certain limitations apply, investment is now permitted in money market instruments, derivatives, deposits and in other collective investment schemes. Additionally, there are special rules for funds that replicate certain indices like tracker funds. It extends the range of financial assets in which collective investment undertakings benefiting from the single license may invest. In the future, UCITS will be permitted to invest not only in listed shares and bonds, but also in bank deposits (cash funds), money market instruments, financial derivatives (i.e. standardised option and futures contracts dealt on regulated exchanges and over-the-counter derivatives) and in other units of other collective investment undertakings (so-called "fund of funds"). The new rules also recognise investment management techniques widely and successfully employed such as "tracking" an index (i.e. investment in securities of different issuers provided for in a given index). On the face of it, it does not appear as if the UCITS Directives have a direct impact on hedge funds as they are, from a regulatory perspective, not covered by the directives. However, UCITS regulations are leading most financial intermediaries to increase compliance functions in order to better address risk management and implement corporate governance principles. Upon the realization that the EU, like the US, is trying to regulate more asset management activities, the UCITS requirements, such as risk management, compliance etc, may be said to also impacts investors' behavior. Moreover, upon implementation in the individual Member States, the UCITS Directives may, depending on the form of implementation, directly affect hedge fund managers who are regulated as investment managers under the general framework that is being changed by the directives.

Council and the European Parliament to show the same determination and co-operation as on this legislation so that we can forge ahead and build a European capital market on time."

2. Hedge Fund Regulation in the United Kingdom

Despite the world dominance of US hedge funds,[780] the UK is the leading European canter for hedge funds and their advisers. The UK hedge fund industry has an estimated 70% market share of hedge funds under management by European based advisers.[781] In global terms, it is estimated that UK registered hedge fund advisers manage around 15% to 20 % of global hedge fund funds.[782] Reflecting the market share of hedge funds, the FSA regulation of financial markets and indirectly of hedge funds is among the most developed in the EU and the implementation of UCTIS III Directive was either not necessary because similar provision were already in place or had a far less visible impact on financial regulation in the UK.

Starting with conceding that there is no accepted definition of hedge funds, the FSA defines the term by what hedge funds are not, [783] whereas most other regulators take the opposite approach trying to force a definition of the term hedge fund. It is also important to recognize that the approach of the FSA is different insofar as the entity hedge fund is not directly regulated as it is mostly not domiciled in the UK. Whilst the hedge fund manager may be located in the UK, the FSA does not have jurisdiction over an entity established and governed by another jurisdiction.[784] This approach also distinguishes the FSA approach to regulating hedge funds from other than most other regulators.

As mentioned earlier, there are three central themes in hedge fund regulation. First, the devastating experience with Long-Term Capital Management in 1998 raised concerns about the systemic risks created by hedge funds. Second, general issues about how hedge fund managers and advisers are regulated. Third, there is the marketability issue, or "retailization" as the SEC calls it, i.e. should hedge fund be marketed to the general public and what are the risks involved. These issues are reflected in the way in which the UK regulator the Financial Services Authority ("FSA") addresses regulatory issues.

---

780 The US is by far the largest hedge fund centre worldwide with an estimated pool of funds under management of US hedge fund advisers in the vicinity of 70%. *See* TASS Report.

781 See Eurohedge.

782 Due to fluctuations this is a rough estimate.

783 *See* Ashley Kovas, Developments in Hedge Fund Regulation – A UK Perspective, BAI at 20 (2003).

784 *Id.*

a) Minimizing Systemic Risk

In the aftermath of the LTCM debacle, the U.K. Financial Services Authority ("FSA") proposed a new ruling to monitor counterparty risk.[785] Under the ruling, banks acting as agents for undisclosed principals are required to disclose who their clients are when transacting business with fund management groups. It was the lack of such disclosure that left counterparties and lenders quite unable to develop a realistic view of counterparty risk. They had no picture of the overall risk in spite of the fact that most of their individual trades with the fund were adequately collateralized. The ruling was applied to banks in March 1999 and has been extended to securities firms in June 1999. The FSA also expressed concern that regulators should demand more information from banks and regulated firms on their dealings with and exposure to hedge funds.[786] Their conclusion, however, emphasized that there was no case for direct regulation of hedge funds for the sake of the investors.[787] The FSA opines that investors who have the monetary possibility to invest in hedge funds are, on the one hand, mostly aware of their risks and wealthy enough to find solutions for their own protection, on the other hand regulatory protection does not make sense if those who are to be protected, as in the case of hedge funds investors, do not demand to be protected. However, they state that the one imaginable justification of direct regulation was the promotion of systemic safety.[788]

---

785 Financial Services Authority (1998): Memorandum to the Treasury Select Committee, 28th of October 1998.

786 *See* id.

787 FSA (1998), p. 29.

788 *See* Perry/Grant: Plumbers, Gurus and Global Markets: The Financial Services Authority and the Regulation of Hedge Funs, in: Cullen/ Parry (2001), pp. 131-132, (detailing that "[a]ny such measures addressing such issues would only be applicable to a few funds whose sheer size and levels of leverage meant that they were in a position, either alone or acting with others, threaten such safety. Even direct regulation of such funds raises difficult problems, such as the inevitable attractive option of offshore regulatory arbitrage, and the fact that many regulated institutions display similar characteristics and would, therefore, also potentially be in the frame. Most reports on the LTCM crisis, including the Treasury Second Report on the World Economy have endorsed the FSA view that investor protection would not be an appropriate basis on which to regulate Hedge Funds. Current thinking favours the approach of leaving the question of general direct regulation in abeyance for the time being to allow time for industry based voluntary measures to work through. There is a general recognition that such direct regulation with authorisation requirements and prudential controls, may eventually become necessary but only on systemic and not consumer protection grounds.")

b) Regulation of Hedge Fund Managers

As mentioned earlier, the entity hedge fund is not directly regulated as it is mostly not domiciled in the UK and does not fall under FSA jurisdiction. Therefore, the FSA opted for regulating hedge fund managers, as they may be located in the UK and therefore subject FSA jurisdiction.

The FSA also does not provide special regulation for hedge fund managers. They are regulated as any other investment manager as most hedge fund managers are investment managers. Investment management requires authorization by the FSA when pursued in the UK. Without authorization the person may be criminally liable. After deliberation and consultation, the FSA has concluded that it is not necessary to provide special rules for hedge fund managers, since the existing "conduct of business rules," which are applied to investment managers generally are sufficient for hedge fund managers[789].

c) Retailization of Hedge Funds in the UK?

In its consultation with the public, the FSA asked if retailization of hedge funds should be allowed.[790] This sparked a lively debate in the UK.[791] As hedge funds can be "investment companies" and can have a corporate structure in the UK, they are publicly marketable once they are listed. Alternatively hedge funds could be structured as limited partnerships or trusts and would be regulated as "collective investment schemes," and are, as such, marketable to certain "sophisticated" investors. As such, hedge funds are marketable to institutional investors and, to a considerably more limited extent, to retail investors. The FSA also extended the scope of authorized collective investment schemes.[792] Thereby allowing hedge fund, to be more broadly marketed but still providing some limitations. Hedge Funds of Fund were also authorized for the first time.

However, it is noteworthy that the FSA decided not to liberalize the retail market further than described above. It also did not allow the retailization of hedge funds of funds. This may be a result of a lacking demand for such retailization.[793] Existing hedge funds still prefer to a have a small number of very sophis-

---

789 FSA Discussion Paper 16, "Hedge Funds and the FSA" (questioning if hedge fund managers should be subject to special rules). The Feedback Statement to DP16, of March 2003, concluded that this is not necessary as the existing "conduct of business rule" was considered generally appropriate for hedge fund managers.

790 *See* DP 16.

791 *See* Kovas (2003), p 21.

792 *See* FSA Consultation paper "The CIS Sourcebook – A new Approach" of May 2003.

793 *See* Kovas (2003), p. 22.

ticated investors who understand the nature of the funds and will leave their investments in the fund for a reasonable period of time.[794]

Despite these limits to retailization, hedge funds in the UK are undoubtedly becoming more mainstream investment products than this has historically been the case. The FSA stated in this context: "[W]e recognize that the regulatory status of presently unregulated schemes needs to be kept under review. We will continue to discuss the possibility of a new approach with market participants. This new approach would allow for a broader range of funds to be brought into the regime for investment products."[795] Accordingly, the FSA's position on hedge fund regulation and retailization is likely to further change over time.

d) The Impact of the SEC Rule on UK Hedge Fund Regulation

So far, the new SEC rule, introducing mandatory registration of hedge fund investment advisers under the IAA depending on the number of clients (more than 14) and an asset size threshold ($30mil.), has not been emulated by the UK's FSA. Under the existing UK framework, the requirement for authorization is based on the activity of fund management and location of the manager. However, Dan Waters, Asset Management Sector Leader of the FSA, opined in a speech called "Regulation and the Hedge Fund Industry: An Ongoing Dialogue," presented at the Hedge Fund Blueprint Europe Conference on February 8, 2005, that the change in SEC rules will "capture a number of UK based hedge fund managers in US regulation for the first time."[796] More specifically, the UK offshore adviser may be subject to a number of SEC Rule requirements, such as compliance with IAA record keeping requirements, providing such documents upon request by the SEC, as well as making staff available for testimony before or questioning by the SEC.[797] As some changes may have to be implemented in the FSA regulatory framework, before the compliance date of February 2006, the FSA is in discussion with the SEC on how to "arrange sensible supervisory co-operation to minimize the impact of these changes on UK fund managers."[798] Despite increasing concerns of the UK hedge fund industry and pressure from asset managers, the FSA has ruled out the direct regulation of hedge funds.[799] The first realistic measure of a regulator would be to define what exactly constituted a hedge fund.[800]

---

794 *Id.*

795 *See* Feedback Statement to DP16, at § 4.15.

796 *See* FSA, Asset Management Sector Leader Dan Waters, speech "Regulation and the Hedge Fund Industry: An Ongoing Dialogue," Hedge Fund Blueprint Europe Conference, February 8, 2005, Transcript at 10-11.

797 *Id.* at 11.

798 *Id.*

799 7/19/04 INVESTADV (citing Callum McCarthy, chairman of the FSA: "[F]or the time being hedge funds would remain unregulated" and '"We must be realistic about what we could do

3. Hedge Fund Regulation in Germany

Other than the UK, the German regulatory framework for financial market was less developed and the UCTIS III Directives did have a more fundamental effect on German financial market regulation. Implementing the UCTIS III Directive, the German legislature enacted the Investment Modernization Act,[801] in December 2003. The new Act significantly overhauls Germany's antiquated investment fund industry and regulation and relaxed its rigid tax regime, turning one of the most conservative hedge fund investment regulation schemes in to one of the most liberal. The major achievement of the Investment Modernization Act, was to allow, for the first time, the organization and sale of domestic hedge funds in Germany. More specifically, single hedge funds are now permitted to be sold to individual investors as well as to institutions. However, in both cases, hedge funds can only be sold through private placements.

The new Act is the result of significant lobbying efforts by German fund sponsors.[802] The resulting liberalization of the German investment regulations and discriminatory tax rules is reason to believe, according to some industry estimates, that significant opportunities will open up in German especially for EEA domiciled funds.[803] According to some estimates, if German investors follow the international pattern and invest up to two percent of their assets in hedge funds, the market for hedge funds in Germany will be worth around $120bn in the next five to ten years.[804] Other reports show, that those estimates are overly optimistic

---

with regulation. We can influence banks giving hedge funds credit and the brokers that sell them."').

800 *Id.*

801 Investmentmodernisierungsgesetz, of 15 December 2003, Bundesgesetzblatt No. 62, 19.12.2003, http://217.160.60.235/BGBL/bgbl11f/bgb1103s2676.pdf.

802 *See* Patricia Volhard, Christian Doerre, Out with the Old: Germany Rings in the New Year With Investment Fund Legislation, Debevoise & Plimpton Publication, December 8, 2003 (clarifying that: "As a result of significant pressure exerted by the investment fund industry, the obligation of the investment sponsor (Kapitalanlagegesellschaft or KAG) to report the assets of each of its funds to the German supervisory authority (Bundesanstalt für Finanzdienstleistungsaufsicht or BAFin) on each trading day was deleted from the final bill. As enacted, reports will need to be transmitted to the BAFin on a "regular basis." The meaning of "regular basis" will be interpreted by executive order.").

803 *See* Steffen Gnutzmann, Jeannette Platzer, Robert Welzel, Germany Looses its Hedge Fund straightjacket even further – New Rules Look set to Remodel Germany's Investment Landscape for Hedge Funds in Wake of 1 January Implementation, Hedge Funds (Special Report: Germany), April 16, 2004.

804 Id.

and had to be revised in the face of overwhelming data showing that the growth potential is not nearly as significant as previously thought.[805]

a) Overlapping Regulatory Regimes or Pre-emption?

Implementing EU Directives, addressing national concerns and keeping up with international trends in hedge fund regulation has resulted in a kaleidoscopic array of demands and approaches to hedge fund regulation. Trying to fulfil all those demands, the German legislator implemented the German Investment Act on January 1st, 2004. This act was intended to make the German hedge fund regulation regime internationally competitive whilst keeping it aligned with the national demands of the old regulation, i.e. the Investment Companies Act ("Kapitalanlagegesellschaftsgesetz" – "KAGG"). Given these sometimes diametrically opposed interests that have been accommodated in the Investment Act, an analysis of German hedge fund regulation has to address three different and partly overlapping regimes.[806]

(1) The Old but still Valid Regime

An analysis of the new developments in hedge fund regulation in Germany cannot dispense with the old regime of hedge fund regulation through the Investment Companies Act and the Foreign Investment Act. Even after the enactment of the new Investment Act, the legal connection between the old and the new regime persists.[807] Utilizing a collective investment scheme by means of a Kapitalanlagegesellschaft ("KAG") or by buying shares of an Investmentaktiengesellschaft to institute a collective investment with diversified risk, is an inevitable link to the old regime under the KAGG.[808] The link derives from the fact that only collective

---

805 *See* Financial times UK, Hedge Funds Fall short of German goals, 1/24/05 FTI 26 (reporting that: "There was a net funds inflow of just Euros 706m (Dollars 918m) to the sector following the launch of onshore hedge funds last April, compared with initial forecasts of up to Euros 10bn. Barely Euros 100m flowed into the sector in the second half of the year [. . .] BAFin, the chief regulator, took until April to prepare its guidelines for the market and give its first approval of a fund [. . .] Some asset management groups blame investors' slack take up on the regulator's slowness in approving new products. BAFin said this month that 16 funds were now approved, with a further dozen in the pipeline. The pace of approval should accelerate from an average of three months to only a few weeks in the future [. . .] investment advisers argue that the market will only develop slowly even when these teething troubles have been resolved. The sales expectations for hedge funds were probably optimistic in the first place, they say, and ignored the fact that many retail investors already put vast sums into offshore hedge funds indirectly through so-called "certificates.").

806 For a summary of the three approaches see Lang (2004).

807 *Id.* at 4.

808 *Id.*

investment schemes that comply with certain definitions could be registered with the BAFin and then distributed. All other forms of collective investments that were not defined, were also not regulated and could and still cannot be registered or distributed under the InvG.[809] In sum, the old investment law is still applicable under the InvG. Allegedly, the legislator retained this link intentionally.[810]

(a) The Investment Companies Act (KAGG)

Before the enactment of the Investment Act, hedge funds in Germany came under the purview of Investment Companies or KAGG. Due to the rather narrow definition of the KAGG, the Act was primarily applicable to investment banks, which were in full compliance with the definitions of investment companies doing business in accordance with the KAGG.[811]

The KAGG technically applies to hedge funds, as they were considered investment companies under the KAGG. However, it was almost impossible to do business as a hedge fund under the KAGG in Germany. There are several other reasons for this phenomenon: First, the KAGG was and still is not tailored to deal with the demands of complex investment strategies that hedge funds employ. More specifically, the use of derivatives and leverage strategies, typically employed by hedge funds, was prohibited for German investment companies.[812] Also, leveraging hedge fund positions, i.e. collective investment schemes (Sondervermögen under the KAGG), was restricted to 10 per cent of the value of the collective investment scheme.[813] Hedge Funds usually employ leverage strategies such as short selling to attain higher net returns. This limitation of leverage to 10 % accordingly curtailed the flexibility and potential to succeed in Germany significantly, especially considering the availability of significantly more leverage to foreign hedge funds that were in direct competition with German hedge funds.

---

809 *See* Koendgen (2001), § 113, margin-no. 34, *see also* Lang (2004), at 4.

810 *Id.*

811 § 7 (1) KAGG. (defining investment company as: "(1) Die Bezeichnung "Kapitalanlagegesellschaft" oder "Investmentfonds" oder "Investmentgesellschaft" oder eine Bezeichnung, in der diese Begriffe allein oder in Zusammensetzungen mit anderen Worten vorkommen, dürfen in der Firma, als Zusatz zur Firma, zur Bezeichnung des Geschäftszweckes oder zu Werbezwecken nur von Kapitalanlagegesellschaften und von ausländischen Investmentgesellschaften, Verwaltungsgesellschaften und Vertriebsgesellschaften (§ 2 Abs. 1 Nr. 1, § 3 Abs. 2 Nr. 1 und § 15 des Auslandinvestment-Gesetzes) geführt werden. Die Bezeichnung "Investmentfonds" darf nach Maßgabe des Satzes 1 auch von sonstigen Vertriebsgesellschaften geführt werden, die Anteile gemäß § 1 Abs. 1 oder Aktien einer Investmentaktiengesellschaft gemäß § 51 Abs. 2 vertreiben oder die ausländische Investmentanteile vertreiben, die nach dem Auslandinvestment-Gesetz im Inland öffentlich vertrieben werden dürfen. § 54 bleibt unberührt.").

812 § 9 (5) KAGG.

813 § 9 (4) KAGG.

The limitation of leverage may have been among the most important reasons to render the German hedge fund industry insignificant in international comparison.

Aside from the abovementioned limitations, the KAGG also limits the amount of assets that may be invested in foreign investment shares to five per cent.[814] The five per cent limit only applies if the assets are invested in securities.[815] Additionally, the 5% limit not only applies to the special fund in question, but also to all the investment funds managed by the respective investment company. The KAGG also restricts the acquisition of shares of foreign origin, providing that these shares cannot be acquired if they are not listed in Germany.[816] Generally, sector or theme funds, as those securities investment companies have been launching for years, would be just as suitable for an investment fund in non-regulated shares. This could have helped circumventing the KAGG restrictions. However, the German market in this sector is not liquid enough, nor is there a sufficient free float at the individual companies, and there would be no or only a very small market for such products. In turn, a fund of this kind could only be marketable if it included foreign property shares. As indicated earlier, these cannot be acquired. Thus, under the old KAGG, hedge funds in Germany were dealing with insurmountable regulatory difficulties.

---

814 § 8b KAGG (providing in pertinent part: (1) Für ein Sondervermögen darf die Kapitalanlagegesellschaft Anteile eines anderen Sondervermögens und ausländische Investmentanteile (§ 1 Abs. 1, § 15 des Auslandinvestment-Gesetzes) nicht erwerben. Abweichend von Satz 1 dürfen bis zu 5 vom Hundert des Wertes des Sondervermögens in Anteilen eines anderen Wertpapier-Sondervermögens oder in ausländischen Investmentanteilen an einem Vermögen aus Wertpapieren angelegt werden, sofern die Anteile dem Publikum ohne eine Begrenzung der Zahl der Anteile angeboten werden und die Anteilinhaber das Recht zur Rückgabe der Anteile haben. Bei einem Erwerb von Anteilen, die nicht zum amtlichen Markt an einer Börse zugelassen oder in einen organisierten Markt einbezogen sind, ist die in § 8 Abs. 2 Nr. 1 bestimmte Grenze zu beachten. Es dürfen nicht mehr als 10 vom Hundert der ausgegebenen Anteile eines anderen Sondervermögens oder Vermögens aus Wertpapieren erworben werden. (2) Der Erwerb gemäß Absatz 1 von Anteilen eines anderen Wertpapier-Sondervermögens, das von derselben Kapitalanlagegesellschaft oder einer Gesellschaft verwaltet wird, mit der die Kapitalanlagegesellschaft durch eine wesentliche unmittelbare oder mittelbare Beteiligung verbunden ist, ist nur zulässig, wenn das andere Sondervermögen gemäß den Vertragsbedingungen auf die Anlage in einem bestimmten geographischen oder wirtschaftlichen Bereich spezialisiert und der Erwerb der Anteile, sofern es sich nicht um einen Spezialfonds handelt, von der Bankaufsichtsbehörde genehmigt ist. Die Bankaufsichtsbehörde erteilt die Genehmigung nur, wenn die Kapitalanlagegesellschaft die Absicht zum Erwerb derartiger Anteile angekündigt hat und diese Möglichkeit in den Vertragsbedingungen vorgesehen ist. Die Kapitalanlagegesellschaft darf keine Gebühren oder Kosten berechnen, soweit Teile des Sondervermögens in Anteilen eines anderen Wertpapier-Sondervermögens angelegt werden. (3) Absatz 2 ist sinngemäß auf den Erwerb von Anteilen einer ausländischen Investmentgesellschaft anzuwenden, mit der die Kapitalanlagegesellschaft im Sinne des Absatzes 2 Satz 1 verbunden ist.).

815 *Id.* at (1).

816 *Id.*

(b) The Foreign Investment Act (AuslInvestG)

As a significant number of hedge funds are still incorporated in offshore jurisdictions, the Foreign Investment Act (Auslandsinvestmentgesetz – "AuslInvestG") is also applicable to those hedge funds that operate offshore and want to sell hedge fund shares in Germany. The scope of the Act entails so-called foreign investment units, i.e. funds governed by foreign law and investing in securities and other financial products according to principles of risk diversification.[818] Foreign investment units could be offered to investors in public offerings or in similar ways. However, hedge fund advisers could opt out of the AuslInvestG by deciding to offer the foreign investment units in a private placement. This was, however, only a limited safe harbor as the tax regime imposed by the third section of the AuslInvestG applied in both public and private placements,[819] and punitive taxation could be imposed if a fund was neither registered for public sale nor listed on a stock exchange.[820]

As a foreign investment company was bound to inform the German Federal Authority for Financial Services (Bundesanstalt für Finanzdienstleistungen – ("BAFin")) of its intention to sell funds in Germany,[821] whilst having to comply with the restrictions of the AuslInvestG, which were similar to those under the KAGG, it was practically impossible for foreign investment companies to sell hedge funds in Germany.

More specifically, shares in foreign investment companies, i.e. hedge funds, could only be sold in Germany if the vendor had first properly registered with BAFin. The registration was a lengthy procedure and required the vendor to submits a notification of its intend to register a fund and make certain disclosures.[822] To ensure smooth compliance with BAFin, the old regime required that the foreign investment company appoint a representative in Germany. This alone involved significant costs, let alone the lengthy and time-consuming negotiations with BAFin. As BAFin has legal authority to prohibit hedge funds from selling foreign investment shares if the requirements for public sale have not been met, or if the notification was not properly submitted, registration of a hedge fund was overburdened with uncertainty. This was exacerbated by BAFin's frequent utilization of its discretion to prohibit the public distribution of a fund if the specific requirements of the AuslInvestG or the KAGG were not fulfilled,[823] The uncer-

818 §§ 1-7 AuslInvestG. First Chapter of the AuslInvestG covers these so called foreign investment units. These include hedge funds.

819 See Lang (2004), p. 2.

820 § 18 (3) AuslInvestG.

821 § 7 (1) AuslInvestG.

822 § 7 AuslInvG.

823 *See* Lang (2004), p. 2.

tainty as to whether registration would be successful and the prohibitive taxes were insurmountable disincentives to register hedge funds under the old regime.

(c) Strategies to Overcome Regulatory Inflexibility

The deficiencies of the two acts prompted hedge fund managers to consider alternative structures to avoid the application of the old regime. Among those were the possibility of creating a Private Limited Company (Gesellschaft mit beschränkter Haftung – "GmbH"), that allowed the utilization of complex hedge fund investment strategies and participation of investors as securities holder.[824] Other strategies to avoid the AuslInvestG and the KAGG involved index certificates[825] and performance linked notes.[826]

Index Certificates are securities with or without maturity. The value of an index certificates is determined by an artificially composed reference asset.[827] The issuer is usually a German bank. The issuer pays the amount stated in the respective reference asset to the investor at a specifically prearranged time. A so-called fund sponsor, who is normally a foreign investor, then invests the amount into different hedge funds. The return is paid back to the issuer, who then divides the whole investment into certificates. These "index certificates" are distributed to individual investors. In case of maturity or cashing the amount corresponding the actual value of the index is paid back.[828] Performance linked notes work pretty much like index certificates, i.e. a German bank working as the issuer divides an investment into certificates which are distributed to investors. The crucial difference is, however, that the certificate is not linked to a defined index but directly to a hedge fund or a fund of hedge funds.[829]

Employing these strategies allowed German investors to invest in hedge funds or hedge funds of funds without being subject to most legal restrictions and punitive taxes.[830]

---

824 *Id.*

825 *Id.* (elaborating on how index certificates worked in the old regulatory framework).

826 *Id.* (citing Kayser/Steinmueller, FR 2002, 1270, 1276 et sqq.) (elaborating on performance linked notes).

827 *Id.*

828 *Id.*

829 *Id.*

830 For a complete analysis see Steck (2001), pp. 366-373(8) (elaborating on the direct marketing and distribution of hedge funds in Germany. Arguing they face regulatory and tax legal difficulties. As a result, alternative repackaging structures were developed by German banks. The author explains how repackaging structures lead to reduced selling restrictions and an optimized tax treatment of the product. The paper goes on to describe how hedge fund repackaging can be used in order to make hedge funds an eligible investment for restricted institutional investors).

(2) The Impact of the New Regime: Investment Modernization Act

(a) The Primary Objective of the Act

The single most significant innovation of the Investment Modernization Act ("InvG")[830] is that single hedge funds cannot be sold to individual investors as well as to institutions. More specifically, under the Investment Act, hedge funds have been authorized as added-risk investment funds managed by an investment company.[831] It should be noted that this authorization was a result of significant lobbying efforts by the German investment fund industry.[832] The primary objective of the German legislator when enacting the InvG was to establish a German hedge fund industry.[833] Most of the provisions are, therefore, a reflection of what the legislator deemed appropriate and politically opportune to create more incentives for hedge fund managers and the financial intermediaries who work for hedge fund managers, to use Germany as an operational base.

With the enactment of the Investment Modernization Act, the German legislature also implements the UCITS III Directives of the Council of the European Union. The significant innovation of the Investment Act include the reporting of Fund Holdings, investing in derivatives, as well as taxation of funds of funds and taxation of foreign investment funds.

(b) Modernizing Hedge Fund Regulation in Germany

It has traditionally been a problem to define hedge funds and fine-tune hedge fund regulation according to that definition. The new InvG remedies that situation only to a limited extent. Hedge funds are considered institutional investors whose managers can choose investment markets, instruments, and strategies freely and may invest with not significant statutory restrictions. For the first time, hedge funds are also defined,[834] even though the InvG does not use the term hedge fund because of the difficulties of defining exactly what a hedge fund is. The term used to define hedge fund in German is "investment scheme with additional risk"

---

830 Investment Gesetz vom 15. Dezember 2003 (*BGBl.* I *S.* 2676), zuletzt geändert durch *Art.* 8 *Abs.* 8 des Gesetzes vom 04. Dezember 2004 (*BGBl.* I *S.* 3166).

831 §§ 112, 120 *InvG.*

832 The initial draft forced the investment sponsor (Kapitalanlagegesellschaft or KAG) to report the assets of each of its fund to BAFin on each trading day. This provision was cancelled from the act as a result of significant lobbying efforts by the German Investment Fund industry. The act was amended before the enactment to only require report to be transmitted to the BAFin on a "regular basis." What "regular basis" means will be subject to interpretation by executive orders.

833 Legislative history of the act, statement of the reasons of the draft bill, p. 153, http://www.bvi.de/downldoads/invmodG_gesetzentw_200803.pdf.

834 § 112 InvG.

(Sondervermögen mit zusätzlichen Risiken).[835] The definition uses distinguishing features of hedge fund investment strategies such as the use of leverage or short selling or both to determine what a hedge fund is. A hedge fund is not restricted in the use of such strategies. The only remaining significant restriction is that they cannot be marketed by public placement but only in a private placement. As a result of the lack of a legal definition for public placement a continuing debate ensued.[836] Although it is not allowed to distribute hedge funds to a multitude of investors via private placement, the applicable legal framework to determine if placements are to be considered as private is still uncertain. The InvG has, alas, not remedied this uncertainty either.

Under the InvG, a prospectus is required regardless of whether the placement is considered private or public. The prospectus serves the particular purpose to warn the investor regarding losses and even a total loss of the investment in a hedge fund.[837] Additional information that has to be furnished in the prospectus includes: the extent of utilization of leverage or short selling strategies, information on the fee structure of he chosen hedge funds as well as information concerning the total of fees the investor has to carry, the criteria determining what hedge funds are chosen by a funds of hedge funds, and restrictions on disinvestment possibilities compared to mutual funds.[838] The InvG also requires that hedge fund of

---

835 § 112 InvG: Sondervermögen mit zusätzlichen Risiken (1) Sondervermögen mit zusätzlichen Risiken sind Investmentvermögen, die den Grundsatz der Risikomischung beachten und im Übrigen im Rahmen ihrer Anlagestrategien keinen Beschränkungen bei der Auswahl der Vermögensgegenstände nach § 2 *Abs.* 4 *Nr.* 1 bis 4 und *Nr.* 7 bis 9 unterworfen sind. Die Vertragsbedingungen des Sondervermögens gemäß Satz 1 müssen zudem mindestens eine der folgenden Bedingungen vorsehen:

836 *See* Lang (2004), p. 3 (elaborating that: "The difficulty is even greater when trying to define the term private placement under the new InvestG. Whereas under the VerkProspG the need of a prospectus is necessary for providing adequate information about the placement to the investor, this argument is not possible for the hedge fund regime of the new InvestG, since there a prospectus is considered necessary even in cases of private placements of hedge fund units. According to the VerkProspG there is a need to create a prospectus in order to provide the necessary information about placements to the investor. Therefore, it can be argued that a prospectus is not needed if the investor is well informed or has the possibility to inform himself without protection by law. This does not make sense under the new InvestG. Under the InvestG a prospectus is required even in cases of private placement and therefore the difference of private and public placement cannot be defined by criteria of information of the investor. The InvestG is assumed to prevent private investors from investing in hedge funds. The reason for distinguishing between private and public placements in the VerkProspG is to ensure sufficient information for investors. The reason in the InvestG is to protect or exclude private investors from investing in single hedge funds. Even in the legislation materials of the InvestG it is said that the interdiction of public placements of single hedge funds is to ensure that not all private investors are able to invest in hedge funds.").

837 § 117 (2) InvG.

838 Id.

funds managers/advisers have professional experience and practical knowledge about investments in hedge funds.[839]

Another key innovation of the InvG are the admission of typical features frequently employed by hedge funds, such as borrowing or the use of derivatives to increase the level of investment (leverage) and the sale of assets, which are not owned by the fund at the time they are sold (short selling).[840] More specifically, it significantly expands of the ability of German investment funds to use derivatives. German investment funds are now permitted to invest, "pursuant to their investment objectives," in derivatives based on securities, money market instruments, certain fund interests,[841] financial indices, interest rates, foreign exchange rates and currencies.[842] Alas, the new law does still not allow the investment in derivatives based on commodities, metals or hedge funds. Here are also still some restrictions with regard to the ability to invest in derivatives. Such investments are allowed as long as the fund's organizational documents provide for a direct investment in the underlying asset. However, § 51 InvG has to be interpreted to provide that a fund may only invest in financial indices, interest rates, and other assets in which the fund may not invest directly, as long as they "relate" to assets in which the fund could invest directly pursuant to its investment objectives.[843] Although the provision particularly remedies the inflexibility of the KAGG,

---

839 §120 InvG.

840 §112 InvG. (1) 1. eine Steigerung des Investitionsgrades des Sondervermögens über grundsätzlich unbeschränkte Aufnahme von Krediten für gemeinschaftliche Rechnung der Anleger oder über den Einsatz von Derivaten (Leverage), 2. den Verkauf von Vermögensgegenständen für gemeinschaftliche Rechnung der Anleger, die im Zeitpunkt des Geschäftsabschlusses nicht zum Sondervermögen gehören (Leerverkauf). Ferner müssen die Vertragsbedingungen vorsehen, dass die Anlage in Beteiligungen an Unternehmen, die nicht an einer Börse zugelassen oder in einen organisierten Markt einbezogen sind, auf 30 Prozent des Wertes des Sondervermögens beschränkt ist. Das Recht der Anleger auf Rückgabe der Anteile am Sondervermögen kann nach Maßgabe des § 116 eingeschränkt sein. (2) Sondervermögen nach Absatz 1 dürfen nicht öffentlich vertrieben werden. (3) Abweichend von § 20 *Abs.* 1 können einzelne Aufgaben der Depotbank auch von einer anderen vergleichbaren Einrichtung wahrgenommen werden, wenn vertraglich sichergestellt ist, dass die Depotbank für ein Verschulden der von ihr unmittelbar eingeschalteten Einrichtung wie für eigenes Verschulden haftet.(4) Das Bundesministerium der Finanzen wird ermächtigt, nach Anhörung der Deutschen Bundesbank eine Rechtsverordnung mit Voraussetzungen und Kriterien für eine Beschränkung von Leverage und von Leerverkäufen nach Absatz 1 zu erlassen, soweit dies zur Abwendung von Missbrauch und zur Wahrung der Integrität des Marktes erforderlich ist. Die Rechtsverordnung bedarf nicht der Zustimmung des Bundesrates.

841 But not including hedge funds.

842 §51 InvG.

843 *See* I Volhard/Doerre (2003), p. 2 (citing as an example: "[A] German fund may invest in a derivative based on a financial index comprised of U.S. stocks, if the fund's investment objective permits direct investments in U.S. stocks. As another example, a derivative based on a foreign currency will only be permitted if the fund can invest directly in securities, money market instruments or other assets denominated in such foreign currency.").

adopting regulatory means of providing for leverage and thereby enabling the utilization of short strategies, which many hedge funds depend on, the interpretation of § 51 InvG corresponds with other provisions of the old KAGG.[844] This again shows the link between the old and the new law that was intentionally installed by the German legislator.

(3) The new Investment Ordinance

The Ordinance on the Investment of the Restricted Assets of Insurance Undertakings (the Investment Ordinance)[845] has been amended to take account of the change in investment law requirements. Pursuant to *AnlV sec.* 1 (1), *no.* 15, investments in single hedge funds and funds of hedge funds within the meaning of *InvG secs.* 112 and 113 (hereinafter referred to as *investment companies*) and, pursuant to *AnlV sec.* 1 (1), *no.* 16, investments in units in investment companies with variable capital whose investment meets the requirements of *no.* 15 (hereinafter referred to as *open-ended investment companies*) are suitable for restricted assets under the terms set out in the present BAFin circular. In addition, *AnlV sec.* 1 (1), *no.* 17, permits investment in foreign investment fund units as defined by *InvG sec.* 2 (9), provided that they are issued by an investment company having its registered office in another signatory state of the *EEA* which is subject to public supervision for investor protection purposes and provided that the investment funds (*InvG sec.* 2 (8)) are subject to requirements regarding their investment policy which are comparable to those applying to added-risk investment funds under the Investment Act and provided that investors may demand payment of that part of the fund's assets corresponding to their share.

In addition to these direct investments, mixed funds, which also fall within the definition of *AnlV sec.* 1 (1), *no.* 15, may include among their investments hedge funds in the form of added-risk investment funds and units in *open-ended investment companies* up to 10% of the value of the mixed fund (*InvG secs.* 83 85; hereinafter referred to as *mixed funds*).

Furthermore, insurance undertakings can also invest in hedge funds outside the purview of investment law via structured products the debtors (issuers) of which have their registered office in the *EEA* and the earnings, repayment, market price or value of which are linked to hedge funds and by means of other forms of investment issued by companies having their registered office in the *EEA*, such as shares or profit participation rights of companies which for their part invest primarily in hedge funds (hereinafter referred to as *structured products*). Up to now

---

844 *Id.*

845 Verordnung über die Anlage des gebundenen Vermögens von Versicherungsunternehmen (Anlageverordnung - *AnlV*) vom 20. Dezember 2001 (*BGBl.* I *S.* 3913), zuletzt geändert durch Artikel 1 der Verordnung vom 12. August 2004 (*BGBl.* I *S.* 2176).

these investments could be allocated to restricted assets only via the opening clause (*AnlV sec.* 1 (2)), even if the asset could be allocated to any of the investments listed in *AnlV sec.* 1 (1) and the earnings or repayment were linked to hedge funds. For risk reasons, though, such investments should be included in the asset mix and diversification provisions of the Investment Ordinance applying to hedge funds.

b) Deficits of German Hedge Fund Regulation

The achievements of the InvG, i.e. to define hedge funds and to allow for the first time the private placement of these investment vehicles, are commendable. However, the German legislator has, alas, decided not to do away with the old approach to hedge fund regulation manifested in the KAGG and AuslInvestG. Also a more economically viable definition of hedge funds, as for instance provided by the Swiss Anlagefondsgesetz,[846] would have been preferable. As hedge funds of funds are still the only form of investment for individual retail investors in Germany, the German legislator still does not seem to trust the investment skills of the investing German public. This seems fair enough as long as the trade off is one between retailization versus full disclosure of all trades and strategies, i.e. a full disclosure of complex trading strategies would most likely be required by the legislator to protect individual investors. The author would suggest an investment cap of approximately $25.000, to determine who will be eligible to invest in hedge funds. This would provide the German legislator with enough protection for individual retail investors, who may not be able to invest such amounts. Alternatively, it is imaginable to opt for a regulatory framework under which hedge funds offering investments of less than $25.000 will disclose all of their complex strategies, whereas hedge funds that limit their offers only to investors who will invest more than $25.000, and are thus assumed to be "sophisticated" and able to fend for themselves, would not be required to disclose their trading strategies. The trade off here is – more control and protection for smaller "unsophisticated" investors coupled with less risk and lower net returns, versus less control, higher risk and correlative higher net returns for "sophisticated" investors. The argument that unsophisticated investors should have access to the same funds as sophisticated investors does not make sense as unsophisticated investors would rarely accept paying up to thirty per cent incentive and performance fees. The proposal would accommodate most of the interests represented in the debate over hedge fund regulation. The legislator would fulfil its role of protecting the investing public, hedge fund managers could keep their high net returns for sophisticated investors and exploit market inefficiencies being able to invest

---

846 Swiss Investmentfunds Act (Bundesgesezt über Analagefonds vom 18.03.1994, Anlagefondsgesetz – "AFG"), http: www.gesetze.ch/sr/951.31/951.31_000.htm.

with no direct supervision or regulatory control, the investing public or "unsophisticated" investors would still have access to hedge fund only under a different more restrictive regulatory regime. An example underscoring that such a regime could work is the significant pressure that had to be exerted by the investment fund industry to do away with the obligation of the investment sponsor (Kapitalanlagegesellschaft or KAG) to report the assets of each of its funds to the BAFin on each trading day. This exemplifies the diverging interests of the legislator and the German hedge fund industry.

Under the InvG trading reports will need to be transmitted to the BAFin on a "regular basis." The meaning of "regular basis" will be interpreted by executive order. It is the interpretation of regular basis that could make or break the hedge fund industry in Germany. An interpretation requiring close scrutiny of the data by the BAFin could create disincentives to engage in complex investment strategies that could later turn out to be rather difficult to explain and/or to justify upon examination with BAFin. Also, hedge fund managers would spend more time justifying their investments then actually investing.

Hopefully, the concerns about an interpretation of "regular basis" will be irrelevant in light of European initiatives to directly regulate hedge funds via a passport regime. The implementation of such a directive would hopefully address most of the concerns raised in this paper. Only time will tell.

c) Conclusion

Although one might say that the UCITS Directives has nothing to do with hedge funds as they are, from a regulatory perspective, hedge funds are not covered by the directives. However, UCITS III regulations are leading most financial intermediaries to increase compliance functions in order to better address risk management and implement corporate governance principles. Upon the realization that the EU, like the US, is trying to regulate more asset management activities, the UCITS III requirements, such as risk management, compliance etc, also impacts investors' behavior. If it creates more trust in hedge funds and ultimately leads to a retailization of hedge funds remains to be seen. European initiatives to create a passport regime for hedge funds via a EU directive are first warning signs that the EU may follow the path taken by the American SEC to require more direct regulation of hedge funds. The impact of such regulation raises concerns as it may create the wrong incentive structure for hedge fund managers. A regulatory framework that distinguishes between sophisticated and unsophisticated investors by means of minimum investments would address the problems with the incentive structure and would accommodate most of the parties' interests. It remains to be seen if EU and national regulators see the benefits of such a form of regulation, which would be specifically tailored to the demands of the highly sensitive hedge fund industry.

I. Normative Analysis

Having demonstrated that most regulatory approaches do not comply with the required criteria for Hedge Fund regulation, preferable scenarios shall be underscored. The hypothesis of the dissertation - Hedge Fund regulation via banking supervision is the preferable alternative to regulation - will be tested here. Before addressing these issues, the dissertation will proceed with a summary why regulation other than indirectly via Basle II is suboptimal.

I. *Analysis of Model Approaches to Hedge Fund Regulation*

1. Co-coordinated International Co-operation

As seen earlier, one model approach to Hedge Fund regulation is the setting up of an international body to control worldwide Hedge Fund investment strategies and actual investing. The problem of establishing jurisdiction over Hedge Funds, a significant number operate through offshore financial centres[847] and the fact that imposing national direct regulatory requirements may drive more Hedge Funds offshore[848] prompted regulators to suggest this approach. Thus, regulators have called for co-operation and the adoption of international regulatory standards[849] at least by the key jurisdictions[850].

Proponents of this international authority have claimed that this initiation of a co-operative and comprehensive international co-coordinated action would ensure proper standards and timely international surveillance[851]. It is, however, questionable if co-coordinated international co-operation will ever realistically be an option. It is to be expected that the administrative costs, the immense transaction costs as well as the costs of setting up such a venture and, most importantly, the differing interests especially of offshore heavens and, hence, jurisdictional arbitrage will ultimately hinder such actions. Furthermore, proponents of this regulatory approach do not seem to reflect on the question what effects such an approach would have on the Hedge Fund industry and world wide financial markets. Hedge Funds may afford to relocate offshore with all its detrimental repercussions, i.e. costs, client losses etc. but a national economy will inevitably suffer when all its Hedge Funds are forced out. Also, the inevitable restructuring of investment strategies by various Hedge Funds may result in a significant loss of for-

847 See Eichel (2002).
848 So called jurisdictional arbitrage.
849 See Eichel (2002).
850 I.e. Europe: England, Germany; Asia: Hong Kong, Tokyo
851 The Economist (2002b), p. 12.

eign direct investment (FDI) for various countries participating in the co-coordinated international co-operation.

2. National direct Regulation

National regulators are also considering direct approaches to reduce creditor and systematic risk associated with investment in Hedge Funds. As mentioned earlier, the objective of direct regulation would be to prevent the excessive expansion in the size and risk-taking by Hedge Funds that could lead to disruption in financial stability. Licensing requirements, fit and proper tests and minimum standards for capital and risk management have been proposed. And, all but the smallest Hedge Funds may be required to file quarterly reports.

However, there are various obstacles that have to be faced by regulators. They do not want to over-regulate the industry and are, thus, concerned with limiting the regulation to entities that actually engage in activities that give rise to potential systematic risks. There is concern that the imposition of additional limitations on Hedge Funds may also impose unwarranted burdens on other types of private investment pools, such as venture capital funds and structured financings that do not raise the same concerns as Hedge Funds. Thus, national regulators try to focus on loss regulation.

But, the purpose of regulation is to protect investors from excessive risk-taking and loss regulation does not apply to Hedge Funds, which are invested precisely for their risk strategy outside the regulated sector. It has, furthermore, to be pointed out that the average long/short equity Hedge Fund is less risky than a long-only portfolio in the current market environment and that the use of leverage is at an all-time low[852]. Also, assuming that national regulation serves its purposes, competition among regulators has knock on effects on transparency. Information is already flowing more freely between different national regulators. Multinational institutions like the IMF, BIS and FSF all play useful part in this, but it is bilateral communication between national regulators that matters most for transparency. Co-coordinated international co-operation, i.e. a global regulator, would negate this competition between national regulators. Even if, hypothetically, a global regulator could replace national regulators it would require a global consensus on what exactly should be regulated. Given national incoherent political interests and the problem of uniting them to set up an international body, the idea of a single global regulator is not on any serious agenda. Thus, direct national

---

852 Meropi on Friday 15. Feb. 2002, from Reuters – "The Hedge Fund industry says it is being made a scapegoat for problems in financial markets, following recent comments by Hans Eichel, German finance minister, reports Reuters. Mr. Eichel had called for international supervision of Hedge Funds and for a temporary ban on the short selling of shares, as a means to reduce threats to the world financial system. Hedge Fund executives at a conference organised by the Alternative Investment Management Association, said that Mr Eichel misunderstood the industry...".

regulation has significant downsides and the aforementioned equilibrium between attainments and costs of regulation cannot be accomplished.

3. Indirect Regulation

In most jurisdictions regulators do not have regulatory authority over Hedge Funds. However, they can use the regulatory authority over their respective regulated entities[853] in order to regulate Hedge Funds indirectly. Regulators can use a number of regulatory tools including capital, margin and reporting requirements to regulate Hedge Funds. The author has identified indirect regulation to be the most beneficial form of regulation for all involved parties. Firstly, relying on private sector practices by counterparties and creditors minimizes regulatory expenses significantly, thus, a state of equilibrium between costs and attainments of regulatory initiatives may be granted. By approaching Hedge Fund's counterparties as potential regulatory targets the necessary opaqueness of the activities of Hedge Funds is preserved, which ensures that Hedge Funds can continue to operate world-wide and, thus, expose market inefficiencies. Which form of indirect regulation is the most awarding shall remain to be seen.

4. Prudential Hedge Fund Regulation

Prudential control measures include improved supervision and regulation of HLI credit providers, a firmer market infrastructure, increased HLI disclosure, enhanced national market surveillance and good practice guidelines for foreign exchange trading.

As mentioned earlier, there are at present no precise formulas for devising an effective integrated prudential Hedge Fund regulation. Prudential Hedge Fund regulation as a combination of indirect and direct measures lacks precision because it combines too many measures. This combination of measures precipitates the danger of one measure indirectly leveling, exacerbating or annulling others. A balanced set of measures, however, may take years to assemble. It is, furthermore, the model's assumption that, in order to be effective, supervisors should adopt a multi-dimensional assessment of risks of their intermediaries and supervise its intermediaries, where possible, on a group basis rather than as a stand alone registered entity. On the face of it, this seems a viable solution. However, assessment on a group basis is more complex, thus, more transaction costs will be generated. Those costs could be avoidable.

---

[853] E.g. securities regulators over broker-dealers, prime brokers, material affiliates of broker dealers.

II. *Hedge Fund Regulation by Banking Supervision*

Banking supervision seems to be a rather advantageous form of addressing the concerns of regulating hedge funds. As demonstrated earlier in this dissertation, information asymmetries and thus moral hazard are the major concerns demanding Hedge Fund regulation. The asymmetric information framework and, thus, the prominent role played by banking institutions and other financial intermediaries that make private loans, is an important feature of financial systems. These institutions play such an important role because they are well suited to reduce adverse selection and moral hazard problems in financial markets[854]. Banks have particular advantages over other financial intermediaries in solving asymmetric information problems[855]. They have advantages in preventing risk taking by borrowers because they can use the threat of cutting off future lending to improve a borrower's behavior[856]. Banks also have advantages in reducing moral hazard because they can engage in lower cost monitoring than can individuals[857]. Banks also have advantages in contracting, i.e. specifying interest rates, collateral requirements, and other contractual terms that help sort borrowers into risk pools that reduce adverse selection and moral hazard incentives for borrowers to engage in risky activities. Furthermore, banks` advantages in information collection activities are enhanced by their ability to engage in long-term customer relationships and to issue loans using lines of credit arrangements[858]. Moreover, banks` ability to scrutinize their borrowers` checking account balances may provide them with an additional advantage in monitoring the borrowers` behavior[859].

In summary, banks seem superior in addressing asymmetric information- and moral hazard problems. Thus, banks and banking supervision should be the starting point and basis when trying to regulate Hedge Funds.

1. The Core Principles for Effective Banking Supervision

The Core Principles for Effective Banking Supervision[860] represent a global standard for prudential regulation and supervision of banks. It presents a comprehensive set of twenty-five Core Principles that have been developed by the Basle

---

854 As pointed out by Edwards and Mishkin (1995), the traditional financial intermediation role of banking has been in decline in both the United States and other industrialized countries because of improved information technology that makes issuing securities easier. Nonetheless, banks continue to be important in the financial system.

855 See Mishkin (2001), p. 4.

856 See Stiglitz/Weiss (1983).

857 See Diamond (1984).

858 See Berger/Udell (1995).

859 See Nakamura (1993).

860 See BIS (1997).

Committee as a basic reference for effective banking supervision. The Principles are designed to be applied by all countries in the supervision of the banks in their jurisdictions. The vast majority of countries has endorsed the Core Principles and have declared their intention to implement them. The Committee sees the formulation of the Core Principles Methodology as an iterative process, with refinements made as experience is gained[861]. Developments of regulatory and supervisory standards and procedures will lead to additions and revisions. Thus, Basle II is being updated periodically. The Core Principles may be the groundwork of effective banking supervision and there may be various overlaps with the New Capital Adequacy Framework, i.e. various principles in the New Framework are closely linked to criteria for assessment of compliance with the Core Principles in the area of Capital Adequacy. It is, however, the New Framework, which, expected to be adopted by more than one hundred countries, is of paramount importance when discussing Hedge Fund regulation.

2. The New Capital Adequacy Framework

The Basle Committee on Banking Supervision issued on 16th January 2001 a proposal for a New Basle Capital Accord dubbed Basle II[862] that, once finalized, will replace the 1988 Accord ("Accord"). Basle II outlines a series of measures which, taken collectively, amount to a fundamental revision to the Committee's 1988 Accord[863]. The New Basle Capital Accord is more extensive and complex than the 1988 Accord. But the complexity of the new framework could be perceived as a natural reflection of the advancement and innovations in the financial marketplace and the need for a more risk-sensitive framework[864]. Intended only to apply to internationally active banks, and representing an informal agreement between the central banks and bank supervisory agencies of the G –10 countries, the 1988 Accord has since become accepted as the de facto universal standard for assessing banks′ capital adequacy[865]. Thus, a proposal to revise the Accord is a matter of immense significance for the international financial system. The new framework, however, is intended to align regulatory capital requirements more closely with underlying risks, and to provide banks and their supervisors with several options for the assessment of capital adequacy. The Committee's objective was to lay the groundwork for a flexible capital adequacy framework that has the capacity to adapt to changes in the financial system and will enhance safety and soundness[866].

---

861 See id. at 4ff.
862 See BIS (2001a).
863 See BIS (1999b), p. 4.
864 See id. at 4.
865 See Cornford (2000), vii.
866 See BIS (1999b), p. 4.

The proposal is based on three mutually reinforcing pillars that allow banks and supervisors to evaluate properly the various risks that banks face[867]. The New Basle Capital Accord focuses on: minimum capital requirements, which seek to refine the measurement framework set out in the Accord; supervisory review of an institution's capital adequacy and internal assessment process; and market discipline, through effective disclosure to encourage safe and sound banking practices[868].

The New Accord is supposed to meet the following supervisory objectives[869]:

- It should continue to promote safety and soundness in the financial system and, as such, the New Framework should at least maintain the current overall level of capital in the system;
- It should continue to enhance competitive equality;
- Constitute a more comprehensive approach to addressing risk; and
- Should focus on internationally active banks, albeit its underlying principles should be suitable for application to banks of varying levels of complexity and sophistication.

However, when discussing the New Capital Adequacy Framework[870], dubbed "Basle II", from the perspective of Hedge Fund regulation, it is important to understand the historical events and pressures under which they were developed. The final stages of the New Framework's preparation began in the aftermath of the rescue operation for LTCM and the turbulence in financial markets, which followed the Russian government's forced restructuring of its own short-term debt and its moratorium on the servicing of a wide range of private-sector external obligations in August 1998[871]. Thus, it may be conjectured that Basle II was, at least partly, motivated by the events surrounding LTCM and, therefore, by the same concerns and problems.

867 See Cornford (2000), p. 11.
868 See BIS (1999b). pp. 5-7.
869 See id. at 5.
870 See BIS (1999b).
871 See Fleming (1999), pp. 33ff.

a) Key aspects of Basle II

The key aspects of the proposals are highlighted below[872]:

(1) Pillar 1 - minimum capital requirements[873]

In the proposals for Pillar 1 - minimum capital requirements - the Committee intends to replace the one-size-fits-all framework set out in the 1988 Accord with a variety of options[874]. The New Basle Capital Accord sets out those options from which banks, with the authorization of their supervisor, can choose depending on the complexity of their business, as well as the quality of their risk management. This framework is said to motivate banks to improve continuously their risk management capabilities so as to make use of the more risk-sensitive options and, thus, produce more accurate capital requirements. The Committee also is placing greater emphasis on banks' own assessment of the risks to which they are exposed in the calculation of regulatory capital charges.

For credit risk, a standardized approach building upon the 1988 Accord and introducing the use of external credit assessments will be available for less complex banks. Banks with more advanced risk management capabilities, which can meet rigorous supervisory standards, can make use of an internal ratings-based approach. Under this approach, some of the key elements of credit risk, such as the probability of default of the borrower, will be estimated internally by a bank. These changes are considered to be major improvements over the existing system[875]. The Committee is also proposing an explicit capital charge for operational risk. A number of possible options for this calculation are elaborated on in the consultative package. With respect to the overall level of capital, the primary goal is to deliver a more risk-sensitive methodology that on average neither raises nor lowers regulatory capital for banks, after including the new operational risk capital charge. Naturally, capital requirements may increase or decrease for an individual bank depending on its risk profile.

(2) Pillar 2 – supervisory review process[876]

Under Basle II, the supervisory review will become an integral part of capital standards and an essential complement to the first pillar. Supervisory review is assigned the task of ensuring banks operate above minimum regulatory capital

872 See BIS (1999b), pp. 26-62.

873 See id. at 26-51.

874 See Karacadag/Taylor (2000), p. 27.

875 See id.

876 See BIS (1999b), pp. 53-58.

rations and maintain adequate internal risk control and capital allocation processes. The New Basle Capital Accord proposes procedures through which supervisors ensure that each bank has sound internal processes in place to assess the adequacy of its capital and set targets for capital that are commensurate with the bank's specific risk profile and control environment. This internal process would then be subject to supervisory review and intervention where appropriate. The critical role of supervisory review in Basle II as a whole, especially if a process-oriented approach to bank capital is adopted, means that supervisory capacities will have to be upgraded in both developed and emerging economies.

(3) Pillar 3 – market discipline[877]

The third pillar consists of disclosure requirements and recommendations set out in the package that will allow market participants to assess critical information describing the risk profile and capital adequacy of banks. The proposals provide more detailed guidance on the disclosure of capital structure, risk exposures and capital adequacy.

For the first time, market discipline is assigned an explicit and essential role in capital standards and its importance as a vital complement to the first two pillars in Basle II cannot be overstated. As capital requirements shift towards a process-oriented approach, banks′ capital adequacy will be less clear-cut and more difficult to evaluate. Involving market participants as "third-party" reviewers of banks′ risk management and capital allocation systems thus becomes a necessary complement to the supervisory review of capital adequacy. The "third-party" review both enhances the overall evaluation of capital adequacy and provides banks added incentives to maintain capital commensurate with their risk profiles.

Market discipline could play an equally important role in capital standards by serving the purpose of reviewing the reviewers. Supervisors not only face a technically more challenging task, but in the exercise of discretion and judgment over subjective and qualitative matters, they are likely to come under political pressure from banks and other interested parties. Market discipline could act to counter such forces and provide supervisors with incentives to conduct their responsibilities rigorously and even handedly. Bank disclosure is the principal instrument through which market discipline is envisaged to operate in Basle II. To this end, the Committee has issued a separate paper, outlining guidelines on the disclosure for banks′ capital structures, risk exposures, and the bases of their capital ratios[878]. Beyond disclosure, however, Basle II offers little guidance on specific instruments and ways of enhancing market discipline.

---

877 See id. at 60-62.

878 See BIS (2000).

b) Implementation

It is envisioned that the New Accord will be implemented in member jurisdictions in 2004. This timetable is said to accommodate national rulemaking procedures and allow adaptation of banks' internal systems, supervisory processes and regulatory reporting. However, the Basle committee bank supervisors have learned not to make rash promises about its timetable for setting the new capital regime for banks. Originally planned for 2004, Basel II was postponed a year last June and has now slipped even further. Without an official announcement, members of the committee talk about a starting date of 2006.

The political negotiations surrounding the implementation of Basel II has heightened awareness of risk among banks. It has prompted them to overhaul their credit-scoring methods and to tighten up their operations. It has also forced them to get to grips with a hitherto unregulated area of risk: Basel II requires capital as a buffer for operational risk—losses from events such as business interruptions, bomb attacks and rogue trading.

III. *Conclusion*

Having seen that banks are generally superior in addressing asymmetric information- and moral hazard problems, the author infers that regulating financial intermediaries may be superior to all other forms of Hedge Fund regulation. Hence, Hedge Fund regulation has to start with banking supervision. Having also seen how Basle II is sets out to regulate and address the remaining problems, the hypothesis of this dissertation that the new capital adequacy framework called Basle II will have an indirect but beneficial regulatory effect on Hedge Funds can be confirmed.

As mentioned earlier, the model of the relational or incomplete contract provides that parties do not attempt to find an answer to all contingencies at the time the relation commences[879], a governance structure shall be built that will allow the parties to solve problems when, and if, they arise and concord and collaboration become embedded standards of the association. The ultimate goal of incomplete contracts is to reinforce the relation itself. An optimal regulation will comply with these demands. As a regulatory minimum standard Basle II attains the desired incomplete regulation. Moreover, the new Framework provides a voluntary standard. Investor and creditor relations are significantly improved by enhanced transparency and reliability. Thus, participating banks reinforce the relation with its creditors and, hence, Hedge Funds. Applying Basle II to Hedge Fund regulation is, thus, in conformity with the requirements of incomplete contract theory.

---

879 See O`Kelley/Thompson (1999), p. 10.

The three pillars of Basle II constitute a set of rules applicable to financial intermediaries i.e. banks which indirectly regulate Hedge Funds. Indirect regulation via Basle II extinguishes problems of lacking jurisdictional authority and, thus, jurisdictional arbitrage because Basle II will be a Framework for banks worldwide. Also, Basle II would be a single unilateral Framework that enhances transparency and lowers transaction costs by replacing various national frameworks that would otherwise be necessary. Furthermore, indirect regulation provides that the Hedge Fund industry will not incur costs by implementing their own risk monitoring systems and measurements and there is, thus, no danger that Hedge Funds might not remunerate any more. Systemic risk problems are addressed because Basle II will not only regulate and alter credit standards of banks but also Hedge Fund's level of leverage. Hence, credit markets are saver. Moral hazard problems are addressed because the three pillars guarantee, by introducing market discipline, internal ratings and supervisory review, a change in lending practice and disclosure. This, in turn, will further decrease the capital – leverage ratio of Hedge Funds. Hence, moral hazard problems comparable to the LTCM case are less likely to occur. This could possibly have a knock on effect on the fee structure of Hedge Funds and the associated milder moral hazard problems. Moral hazard is also addressed because banks under Basle II calibrate, at least partly, their own risk with their own risk measurement tools and ex post opportunism of Hedge Funds is increasingly unlikely considering that not only Hedge Funds but also their financial intermediaries are endangered to loose their reputation and market position in case it transpired that their risk evaluation of a counterparty Hedge Fund is insufficient. The three pillars provide adequate protection against opportunism by enhancing banks` review of counterparty risk.

Problems of asymmetric allocation of information are addressed by the third pillar, which provides that disclosure requirements and recommendations are set out, which will allow market participants to assess critical information describing the risk profile and capital adequacy of banks. Those risk profiles will obviously cover Hedge Fund exposures and their credit lines. Thus, Hedge Fund's dependency on banks and other financial intermediaries will enable banks to negotiate terms in a more favorable way when faced with critical financial scenarios. Negotiations, in turn, are likely to decrease information asymmetries. Furthermore, the New Framework acknowledges considerable advantages in the internal ratings-based approach, under which capital requirements would be set on the basis of a bank's own quantitative and qualitative assessment of its credit risk. This is especially effective in terms of addressing problems of asymmetric information. For instance, internal ratings may incorporate supplementary information about borrowers that is usually beyond the reach of institutions providing external credit assessments, and may cover a much broader range of borrowers. This information, in turn, may be made accessible to other financial intermediaries and investors. Information asymmetries are, thus, minimized. Moreover, the existence of the regulatory option of the internal rating-based approach with the flexibility it provides could offer banks the incentive to undertake further development of their internal techniques for managing and measuring credit risk which would have knock-on effects on Hedge Funds. On the other hand, however, the dissertation has demonstrated at length that Hedge Funds need to remain in secrecy because the less information the market has about Hedge Fund's activities, the easier it is for them to steal a march on it. Hence, a perfect regulatory solution will provide for Hedge Funds to remain in secrecy whilst addressing information asymmetries. Here, indirect Hedge Fund regulation via Basle II provides, on the one hand, as seen above, that information asymmetries are addressed. Indirect regulation allows, on the other hand, for Hedge Funds to remain exempt from disclosure and transparency requirements because only financial intermediaries are required to unveil that information. Thus, the regulatory approach via the New Framework is, again, preferable.

As demonstrated earlier, one of the major constraining factors on effective supervision is the complex trading-, investing- and corporate structure of active international Hedge Funds. Because of these complex structures, both of Hedge Funds and financial intermediaries, most supervisory authorities base their judgment on somewhat incomplete information. The revised Accord will also remedy this problem of asymmetric information because it will be extended on a consolidated basis to holding companies of banking groups in order to ensure that risks within the entire banking group are considered.

Furthermore, various reports suggest improvement of the role of regulators in individual financial intermediaries with significant Hedge Fund business. They thereby confirm the necessity of these changes but assume that this should be done by individual regulators, incurring significant transaction costs and implementation costs, and not by an international organization. An international framework and, thus, Basle II has the great advantage not to require more than one implementation. It is then the responsibility of the participating banks to comply with the framework. Hence, implementation and transactions costs for national regulators can be avoided.

J. Bibliography

Arrow, K.J. (1969): The Organisation of Economic Activity: Issues Pertinent to the Choice of Market versus Non-Market Allocation, In the Analysis and Evaluation of Public Expenditures: The PBB-System, Joint Economic Committee, 91st Cong., 1st sess., Vol.1. Washington, D.C.: Government Printing Office.

Baltensperger, Ernst (1990): Economic Theory of Banking Regulation, Occasional Papers Vol. 2, 1989/90, Center for the Study of the New Institutional Economics, Universität des Saarlands.

Bank for International Settlements (1983): Basle Committee on Banking Regulation and Supervisory Practices, "Principles for the Supervision of Banks' Foreign Establishments" May 1983.

Bank for International Settlements (1989): "Basle Committee on Banking Supervision", July 1989.

Bank for International Settlements (1997): Basle Committee on Banking Supervision (Sep. 1997): Principles for Effective Banking Supervision., The Core Principles Methodology.

Bank for International Settlements (1999a): Basle Committee on Banking Supervision & IOSCO (Feb. 1999): Joint consultative paper on public disclosure of trading and derivatives activities.

Bank for International Settlements (1999b): A New Capital Adequacy Framework - Basel Committee Publications, A consultative paper issued by the Basle Committee on Banking Supervision in Jun 1999.

Bank for International Settlements (1999c): Basle Committee on Banking Supervision (Jan. 1999): Report on banks interactions with HLIs.

Bank for International Settlements (2000): A New Capital Adequacy Framework: Pillar 3 Market Discipline, Basle Committee on Banking Supervision Discussion Paper, Jan. 2000.

Bank for International Settlements (2001a): Basle Committee on Banking Supervision (16 Jan. 2001): New Capital Accord.

Bank for International Settlements (2001b): Basle Committee on Banking Supervision and the International Organization of Securities Commissions: Review of issues relating to Highly Leveraged Institutions (HLIs), March 2001.

Bank for International Settlements (2001c): Multidisciplinary Working Group on Enhanced Disclosure, Final Report to Basle Committee on Banking Supervision, Committee on Global Financial System of the G-10 central banks, International Association of Insurance Supervisors, International Organisation of Securities Commissions, April 26th, 2001.

Bank of New York (2004): Restoring Broken Trust, Study on investor's trust in Hedge Funds (July 2004).

Benninga, Simon; Wiener, Zvi (1998): Dynamic Hedging Strategy, Mathematica in Education and Research, Vol. 7 No.1, 1998.

Berger, Allen N.; Udell, Gegory F. (1995): Did risk-based capital requirements allocate bank credit and cause a "credit crunch" in the United States? Journal of Money, Credit and Banking 26:585-628.

Black, Pam (2004): Going Mainstream, Registered Rep., Mar. 1, 2004.

Board of Governors of the U.S. Federal Reserve System (1st February 1999): Supervisory guidance regarding counter party credit risk management.

Börsen Zeitung (2003): EU Pass für Hedgefonds – Parlament eröffnet Debatte, 08.26.2003.

Börsen Zeitung (2004): EU- Pass für Hedge Fonds, 01.16, 2004.

Börsen Zeitung (2004): Neue Hegefonds-Allianz bildet sich, 01.12.2004.

Bundesaufsichtsamt für das Kreditwesen (1998): Marketing of Foreign Collective Investment Schemes in Germany – Supervisory Aspects, BAKred April 1998.

Coase, Ronald H. (1937): The Nature of the Firm, Economica 4, pp. 386-405.

Commodities and Futures Commission (2004): Proposed Rule - Hedge Fund Regulation under the Adviser Act - Comment Letter to the SEC (October 22, 2004).

Cornford, Andrew (2000): The Basle Committee`s proposals for revised capital standards: Rationale, Design and possible incidence; United Nations Conference on Trade and Development, Geneva; G-24 Discussion Paper No. 3, May 2000.

Counterparty Risk Management Policy Group (1999): Improving Counterparty Risk Management Practices, January 1999.

Crerend, William J. (1998): Fundamentals of Hedge Fund Investing, A Professional Investor's Guide, McGraw-Hill: New York.

Cullen, Iain; Parry, Helen (2001): Hedge Funds: Law and Regulation, Sweet & Maxwell, London.

Deutsche Bundesbank (1999): Hedge-Fonds und ihre Rolle auf den Finanzmärkten; Monthly Report of Deutsche Bundesbank, March 1999, Deutsche Bundesbank: Frankfurt am Main.

Deutsche Bundesbank (1999): Hedge-Fonds und ihre Rolle auf den Finanzmärkten, Monatsbericht / Deutsche Bundesbank, Bd. 51 (1999), 3, S. 31-44, Graph. Darst.

Dewatripont, Mathias; Tirole, Jean (1995): The Prudential Regulation of Banks, New York.

Diamond, Douglas W. (1984): Financial intermediation and delegated monitoring. Review of Economic Studies 51 (3): 393-414.

Dowd, Kevin (1999): Too Big to Fail? Long-Term Capital Management and the Federal Reserve, Cato Institute Briefing Papers, No. 52, September 23, 1999.

Dunbar, Nicholas (2000): Inventing money: the story of Long-Term Capital Management and the legends behind it, Chichester; New York: Wiley.

Edwards, Franklin R. (1999): Hedge funds and the collapse of long-term capital management, in: The journal of economic perspectives: a journal of the American Economic Association, Vol. 13, 2, pp. 189-210.

Eggertsson, Thrain (1990): Economic Behavior and Institutions, Cambridge: Cambridge University Press.

Eichel, Hans (2002): Kontrolle ist besser, FTD Gastkommentar, FTD, 7.02.2002.

European Commission (1993): Capital Requirements Directive / Market Risk Directive. Council Directive 93/6/EEC (Official Journal L 141, 11/06/1993 P. 0001 – 0026) of 15 March 1993 on the capital adequacy of investments firms and credit institutions.

European Commission (2002): Directive 2001/107/EC (Official Journal L 041, 13/02/2002 P. 0020 – 0034) of the European Parliament and of the Council of 21 January 2002 amending Council Directive 85/611/EEC on the coordination of laws, regulations and administrative provisions relating to undertakings for collective investment in transferable securities (UCITS) with a view to regulating management companies and simplified prospectuses.

European Commission (2002): Directive 2001/108/EC (Official Journal L 041, 13/02/2002 P. 0035 – 0042) of the European Parliament and of the Council of 21 January 2002 amending Council Directive 85/611/EEC on the coordination of laws, regulations and administrative provisions relating to undertakings for collective investment in transferable securities (UCITS), with regard to investments of UCITS.

European Commission (2003): European Commission Action Plan for Financial Services, at http://europa.eu.int/comm/internal_market/en/finances/action-plan/index.htm#plans

European Commission (2004): Directive 85/611/EEC on the co-ordination of laws, regulations and administrative provisions relating to undertakings for collective investment in transferable securities (UCITS).

European Commission (2004): Commission Directive 2004/72/EC (Official Journal L 162, 30/04/2004 P. 0070 – 0075) of 29 April 2004 implementing Directive 2003/6/EC of the European Parliament and of the Council as regards accepted market practices, the definition of inside information in relation to derivatives on commodities, the drawing up of lists of insiders, the notification of managers' transactions and the notification of suspicious transactions (Text with EEA relevance)

European Commission (2004): Investment Service Directive. MIFID is due to be implemented by the end of April 2007. Directive 2004/39/EC (Official Journal L 145, 30/04/2004 P. 0001 – 0044) of the European Parliament and of the Council of 21 April 2004 on markets in financial instruments amending Council Directives 85/611/EEC and 93/6/EEC and Directive 2000/12/EC of the European Parliament and of the Council and repealing Council Directive 93/22/EEC.

European Union (2001): EU Press Release IP/01/1728, Financial Services: Commission welcomes adoption of two new Directives on investment funds (UCITS), Brussels, 4th December 2001.

Financial Accounting Standards Board, Financial Accounting Standards, http://www.fasb.org/.

Financial Services Authority (1998): Memorandum to the Treasury Select Committee, 28th of October 1998.

Financial Services Authority (1998): Memorandum to the Treasury Select Committee, 28th of October 1998.

Financial Services Authority (2003a): Discussion Paper 16, "Hedge Funds and the FSA".

Financial Services Authority (2003b): Feedback Statement to DP16, of March 2003.

Financial Services Authority (2003c): Consultation paper "The CIS Sourcebook – A new Approach" of May 2003.

Financial Services Authority (2005): Asset Management Sector Leader Dan Waters, speech "Regulation and the Hedge Fund Industry: An Ongoing Dialogue," Hedge Fund Blueprint Europe Conference, February 8, 2005, Transcript

Financial Stability Forum Working Group of HLIs (2001): "Progress in Implementing the Recommendations of the Working Group on Highly Leveraged Institutions – Note to the FSF by the Chairman of the HLI Working Group", May 2001.

Financial Stability Forum Working Group on HLIs (2000): "Report of the Working Group on Highly Leveraged Institutions", 5. April 2000.

Financial Times UK, Hedge Funds Fall short of German goals, 1/24/05 FTI 26.

Fleming, S. (1999): Disarming bank credit risk, Institutional Investor, August 1999.

Frase, Morton (2001): Hedge Fund Regulation, Cambridge Publishing.

Fung, William; Hsieh, David (2000): Measuring the Market Impact of Hedge Funds, 7 J. of Empirical Fin. 1.

Furubotn E.G.; S. Pejovich (1972): Property rights and Economic Theory: A Survey of Recent Literature, Journal of Economic Literature 10, pp. 1137-1162.

Furubotn, E.G; Richer, Rudolf (1989): The economics and Law of Banking Regulation, Occasional Papers Vol. 2, Universität des Saarlands.

Furubotn, Eiriki G. (1994): "Future Development of the New Institutional Economics: Extension of the Neoclassical Model or New Construct?", Lectiones Jeneses 1:3 –42.

Furubotn, Eiriki G.: Richter, Rudolf (1996): Institutions and Economic Theory – the contribution of the New Institutional Economics, The University of Michigan Press.

Gaurav, Amin S.; Kat, Harry M. (2003): Hedge Fund Performance 1990-2000: Do the "Money Machines" Really Add Value?, 38 Journal of Financial and Quantitative Analysis 2.

Glassman, Cynthia A.; Atkins, Paul S. (2004): Dissent to SEC Proposal to Regulate Hedge Funds, FR Doc. 04-26879, Filed 12-9-04; 8:45am], billing code 9010-01-p, 69 FR 72054-01, 2004 WL 2825810 (F.R.)

Gnutzmann, Steffen; Platzer, Jeannette; Welzel, Robert (2004): Germany Looses its Hedge Fund straightjacket even further – New Rules Look set to Remodel Germany's Investment Landscape for Hedge Funds in Wake of 1 January Implementation, Hedge Funds (Special Report: Germany), April 16, 2004.

Gordon, Jeffrey N. (2003): Corporate Governance and Transnational Integration: The Evolution of German Shareholder Capitalism in the 1990s, Harvard Law & Economics Working Paper Series.

Gottlieb, Jenna (2004): Hedge Fund Deal Raises Product's Bank Profile, American Banker, Oct. 14, 2004.

Grande, John J. (2002): Alternative Investment Strategies Can offer Significant ROI, Ophthalmology Times, May 15, 2002.

Greenspan, Alan (1998): Testimony before the Committee on Banking and Financial Services, U.S. House of Representatives, Private –sector refinancing of the large Hedge Fund, Long-Term Capital Management, Federal Reserve Board, 10.01.1998, pp. 1-8, http://www.bog.frb.fed.us/boarddocs/testimony/19981001.htm.

Greenspan, Alan (2004): Federal Reserve Board Chairman, Testimony before the Senate Banking, Housing and Urban Affairs Committee (July 20, 2004)

Greenspan, Alan (2004): Written response to questions from Chairman Shelby in Connection with Testimony before the Senate Banking, Housing and Urban Affairs Committee, (July 20, 2004).

Gunnarsson, C. (1991): "What is new and what is institutional in the New Institutional Economics: An Essay on Old and New Institutionalism and the Role of the State in Developing countries," Scandinavian Economic History Review, 30 (1), pp. 43-67.

Hacker, Robert; Rotunda, Ronald (1978): SEC Registration of Private Investment Partnerships after Abrahamson v. Fletschner, 78 Colum. L. Rev. 1471, 1477.

Hart, O.D. (1987): Incomplete Contracts, in The New Palgrave: a dictionary of economics, edi. by Eatwell, John; Milgate, Murray; Newman, Peter; London Macmillan; 2, pp. 752-759.

Hazen, Thomas Lee (2002): The Law of Securities Regulation, Hornbook Series, West Group.

Hedge Fund Industry Group (2000): Sound Practices for Hedge Fund Managers, Caxton Corporation, Kingdon Capital Management, Soros Fund Management, Tudor Investment Corporation, February 2000.

Holman Jenkins, Would Hedge Funds even exist without a fatty dollop of moral hazard somewhere along the great protein chain of lending?, WSJ, 15th September 1998.

Holmes, Oliver Wendell (1897): The Path of the Law, 10 Harvard Law Review 457, 469, 474.

International Organisation of Securities Commissions (1998): Objectives and Principles of Securities Regulation, A Report of the International Organisation of Securities Commissions September 1998.

International Organisation of Securities Commissions Technical Committee (1999): Report on Hedge Funds and other Highly Leveraged Institutions, November 1999.

International Swaps and Derivatives Association, Inc. (1998): ISDA Guidelines for Collateral Practitioners, 1998.

International Swaps and Derivatives Association, Inc. (1999): ISDA 1999 Collateral Review, 1999.

Jaeger, Robert A. (2000): Fund of Funds: Risk: Defining it, Measuring it and Managing it, in: Reynolds Parker (2000).

Johnson Brackley, Harriet (2003): New Class of Hedge Funds Reaches Beyond the Wealthy, San Jose Mercury News, Mar. 23, 2003.

Jones, Alfred Winslow (1949): "Fashion of Forecasting", Fortune, March 1949, 88, 186.

Jorion, Philipp (1999): Risk Management Lessons from Long-Term Capital Management, Working Paper UCLA, Irvine California.

Kaal, Wulf A. (2004): Interconnections between the European Investment Services Directive and the Regulatory Situation in the U.S., 24 Journal of Investment & Risk Management Products 4.

Kaal, Wulf A.; Christian Kirchner; Richard W. Painter (2005): Legislatory Competition in EU Corporate Law after Inspire Art: Unbundling Delaware's Product for Europe, 2 European Company and Financial Law Review 1.

Kane, Leslie (2004): Where to Put Your Money: Four Experts Tell Whether You Should put Your Money, Medical Economics, Jan. 9, 2004.

Karacadag, Cem; Taylor, Michael W. (2000): The new capital adequacy framework: Institutional Constraints and Incentive Structures, Sociyr Universitaire Europeenne de Recherches Financieres, Vienna.

Kat, Harry M. (2003): 10 Things That Investors Should Know About Hedge Funds, Institutional Investor (Spring 2003).

Kirchner, Christian (1988): Das Verhältnis der Rechtswissenschaft zur Nationalökonomie. Die neue Institutionenökonomik und die Rechtswissenschaft, Jahrbuch für Politische Ökonomie, Bd. 7, p. 192-208.

Kirchner, Christian (1997a): Wettbewerbspolitik im Spannungsfeld nationaler und internationaler Kartellrechtsordnungen, in: Festschrift für Ingo Schmidt zum 65. Geburtstag, pp. 33-51.

Koendgen (2001): Bankrechtshandbuch, Vol. III, 2nd edition.

Kovas, Ashley (2003): Developments in Hedge Fund Regulation – A UK Perspective, BAI.

Kreps, D. M. (1990): Corporate Culture and Economic Theory, in: James Alt and Kenneth.

Krugman, Paul R. (1999): The return of the depression economics, W.W. Norton & Company, New York, London.

Lang, Norbert (2004): German Hedge Fund Legislation: Modernized but Still Old-Fashioned, 5 Ger. L. Jour. 6.

Leach, James A. (1998): The Failure of Long-Term Capital Management: A Preliminary Assessment," Statement to the House Banking and Financial Services Committee, October 12, 1998, http://www.house.gov/banking/1012981e.htm.

Liang, Bing (2000): Hedge Funds: The Living and the Dead, 35 Journal of Financial and Quantitative Analysis 309-326.

London Metal Exchange's document (1988): `Market Aberrations: The Way Forward', 1988.

Loomis, Carol (1966): "The Nobody Keeps Up With", Fortune, April 1966, pp. 237-247.

Loomis, Carol (1970):"Hard Times Come to the Hedge Funds", Fortune, January 1970, pp. 13-24.

Lowenstein, Roger (2000): When genius failed: the rise and fall of Long-Term Capital Management, New York: Random House, 2000.

Lybecker, Martin E.; Goldfus, Mark B.; Mackey, Mark J. (1980): Investment Company Act Study, 13. Rev. Sec. Reg. 983, Michigan Press.

Managed Account Reports (MAR) /Hedge Funds (2001): Periodical, Managed Accounts Report (MAR).

Managed Account Reports (MAR)/Hedge Funds (2000): Periodical, Managed Accounts Report (MAR).

Mishkin, Frederic S. (2001): Prudential Supervision: what works and what does not, Papers presented at a conference held at Cheeca Lodge, The University of Chicago Press, Chicago.

Nakamura, Leonard I. (1993): Commercial bank information: Implications for the structure of banking, in: Structural change for banking, ed. M. Klausner and L. J. White, 131-160, New York: Irwin.

National Futures Association (2004): Proposed Rule - Hedge Fund Regulation under the Advisers Act - Comment Letter to the SEC (September 14, 2004).

Nazareth, Annette L. (2000): Testimony before the Committee on Agriculture Subcommittee on Risk Management, concerning the Report to Congress on OTC Derivatives, Federal News Service, February 15, 2000.

North, D. C. (1978): Structure and Performance: The task of Economic History, Journal of Economic Literature 16, 963-78.

North, D. C. (1990): Institutions, Institutional Change, and Economic Performance. Cambridge: Cambridge University Press.

North, D.C. (1994): Economic Performance through time, American Economic Review 84, pp.359-368. Alfred Nobel Memorial Price Lecture in Economic Science.

O`Kelley, Charles R.T.; Thompson, Robert B. (1999): Corporations and Other Business Associations, Cases and Materials, Aspen Law & Business, A Division of Aspen Publishers, Inc. Gaithersburg, New York.

Perry, Helen; Grant, Robert (2001): Plumbers, Gurus and Global Markets: The Financial Services Authority and the Regulation of Hedge Funs, in: Cullen/ Parry (2001), pp. 131-132.

Polanyi, M. (1962): Personal Knowledge: Towards a Post-Critical Philosophy, Harper & Row: New York.

Popper, K.R. (1957): The Poverty of Historicism, 2nd. Ed. London: Routledge and Kegan Paul.

Posner, Richard A. (1993): The New Institutional Economics Meets Law and Economics, Journal of Institutional and Theoretical Economics, 149: p. 73-87.

Press, Peter (2001): Hedge Funds in International Markets, Cambridge: Cambridge University Press.

Reynolds Parker, Virginia (2000): Managing Hedge Fund Risk, from the seat of the Practitioner – views from Investors, Counterparties, Hedge Funds and Consultants.

Richter, Rudolf (1989a): Banking Regulation as Seen by the New Institutional Economics, in: The Economics and Law of Banking Regulation, Occasional Papers Vol. 2, Winter 1989/90.

Richter, Rudolf (1989b): The Economic Theory of Banking Regulation – Comment, in: Furubotn, E.G. und Richter, R. (1989), The Economics and Law of Banking Regulation.

Richter, Rudolf; Furubotn, E.G.(1996): Neue Institutionenökonomik: eine Einführung und kritische Würdigung, Tübingen, Mohr.

Rohrer, Julie (1986): The Red-Hot World of Julian Robertson, Institutional Investor, May 1986, pp. 86-92.

Roth, Paul (1995): Chapter 11: Critical Legal and Regulatory Issues, in Lederman, Jess and Robert A. Klein. (ed.), Hedge Funds. New York: Irwin Professional Publishing, p. 145-197.

Schmoller, G. von (1990): Grundriss der Allgemeinen Volkswirtschaftslehre, Munich und Leipzig. Duncker und Humblot.

Schultz, Florian (2001): Investors Should Be Careful About Traps In The Tax Law, Banking and Finance articles in association with Linklaters Oppenhoff & Rädler, Source: Linklaters Oppenhoff & Rädler October 2001.

Securities and Exchange Commission, B.J. Smith No-Action Letter (Dec. 25, 1975).

Securities and Exchange Commission, David Shilling, SEC Staff No-Action Letter (Apr. 3, 1976).

Securities and Exchange Commission, File No. S 7-35-95, www.sec.gov

Securities and Exchange Commission, Hawkeye Bancorporation, SEC Staff No-Action Letter (June 11, 1971).

Securities and Exchange Commission, Implications of the Growth of Hedge Funds, Staff Report to the United States Securities and Exchange Commission, September 2003.

Securities and Exchange Commission, Implications of the Growth of Hedge Funds Staff Report to the United States Securities and Exchange Commission, September 2003.

Securities and Exchange Commission, International Series No. 1047, www.sec.gov

Securities and Exchange Commission, Investment Adviser Act Release No. 2266 (July 20, 2004) [69FR 45171 (July 28, 2004)].

Securities and Exchange Commission, No Action Letter (publ. avail. Feb. 23, 1994).

Securities and Exchange Commission, No-Action Letter – Davenport Management, Inc. (publ. avail. April 13, 1993).

Securities and Exchange Commission, No–Action Letter - Uniao de Bancos de Brasileiros AA, pub. avail. June 6, 1992.

Securities and Exchange Commission, No-Action Letter - Weiss, Peck, & Greer Venture Associates II, LP (1990), pub. avail. Apr. 10, 1990.

Securities and Exchange Commission, Non-Public offering Exemption Sec. Act. Rel. No. 33-4552, 1962 Wl 3573, 1. Fed. Sec. L. Rep. (CCH); 2781 (Nov. 6, 1962).

Securities and Exchange Commission, Registration Under the Adviser Act of Certain Hedge Fund Advisers, Friday December 10, 2004, Final Rule - SEC Release No. IA-2333; File No. S7-3—04, RIN 3235-AJ25.

Securities and Exchange Commission, Release No. 33-7386, www.sec.gov

Securities and Exchange Commission, Release No. 34-38223, www.sec.gov

Securities and Exchange Commission, Release No. FR-48 www.sec.gov

Securities and Exchange Commission, Release No. IA-2333, File No. S7-3-04, RIN 3235-AJ25 – Rules and Regulations Securities and Exchange Commission, 17 C.F. R. Parts 275 and 279 (December 10, 2004)

Securities and Exchange Commission, Release No. IC-22487, www.sec.gov

Securities and Exchange Commission, Ruth Levine, SEC Staff No-Action Letter (Dec. 15, 1976).

Securities and Exchange Commission, S.S. Program Limited, SEC Staff No-Action Letter (Oct. 17, 1974).

Securities and Exchange Commission, Wofsey, Rosen Kweskin & Kuriansky, SEC Staff No-Action letter (Apr. 25, 1974).

Securities Exchange Commission v. PIMCO Advisors Fund Management, LLC, Investment Advisers Act Release No. 2292 (Sept. 13, 2004).

Securities Exchange Commission v. Security Trust Co., N.A., Litigation Release No. 18653 (April 1, 2004).

Securities Exchange Commission, In the Matter of Alliance Capital Management, L.P., Investment Advisers Act Release No. 2205 (Dec. 18, 2003).

Securities Exchange Commission, In the Matter of Banc One Investment Advisors Corporation and Mark A. Beeson, Investment Advisers Act Release No. 2254 (June 29, 2004).

Securities Exchange Commission, In the Matter of James Patrick Connelly, Jr., Investment Advisers Act Release No. 2183 (Oct. 16, 2003).

Securities Exchange Commission, In the Matter of Janus Capital Management, LLC, Investment Advisers Act Release No. 2277 (Aug. 18, 2004).

Securities Exchange Commission, In the Matter of Pilgrim Baxter & Associates, Ltd., Investment Advisers Act Release No. 2251 (June 21, 2004).

Securities Exchange Commission, In the Matter of RS Investment Management, Investment Advisers Act Release No. 2310 (Oct. 6, 2004).

Securities Exchange Commission, In the Matter of Stephen B. Markovitz, Administrative Proceedings Release No. 33-8298 (Oct. 2, 2003).

Securities Exchange Commission, In the Matter of Strong Capital Management, Inc., et al., Investment Advisers Act Release No. 2239 (May 20, 2004).

Securities Industries Association (2003): Report on Management and Professional Earnings in the Securities Industry in 2003.

Shaw Grove, Hanna; Prince, Russ Alan (2003): The Street's Last Lure: Some One Going to Mint Money With the New Hedge Funds For Smaller Investors, Newsweek, May 26, 2003.

Simon, Herbert (1957): Models of Man, John Wiley & Sons: New York.

Simon, Herbert (1972): Theories of Bounded Rationality, in: C. B. McGuire and R. Radner (eds.), Decision and Organization, American Elsevier: New York, pp. 161-176.

Simon, Herbert (1978): Rationality as Process and as Product of Thought, American Economic Review, 68, pp. 1-16.

Steck, A. (2001): Marketing of hedge funds to German investors, Journal of Asset Management, April 2001, vol. 1, no. 4.

Stiglitz, Joseph E.; Weiss, Andrew (1983): Incentive effects of terminations: Applications to credit and labour markets, American Economic Review 73: 912-27.

Strachmann, Daniel A. (2000): Getting started in Hedge Funds, John Wiley & Sons.

Subcommittee on Capital Markets, Securities and Government Sponsored Enterprises, Committee on Banking and Financial Services, Washington, DC, Hearing Thursday, March 16, 2000.

TASS Report (1999): Lipper TASS Database, Lipper Hedgeworld, http://www.hedgeworld.com/database_access.cgi.

Temple, Peter (2001): Hedge Funds - the Courtesans of Capitalism, John Wiley & Sons, Ltd.

The Wall Street Journal (2001): Hong Kong Tries To Repair Links To Hedge Funds, Tuesday, November 6, 2001

Tyle, Craig S. (2004): Letter of General Counsel of the Investment Company Institute, to Jonathan G. Katz, Secretary, U.S. Securities and Exchange Commission, July 2, 2003, available at http://www.ici.org (last visited on Oct. 10, 2004)

U.S. Federal Reserve (1999a): Trading and Capital Markets Activities Manual, March 1999.

U.S. Federal Reserve (1999b): "Supervisory guidance regarding counterparty credit risk management", The Board of Governors of the U.S. Federal Reserve, 1st of February 1999.

U.S. Federal Securities Law Reporter, (CCH), 95, 889.

U.S. House of Representatives (2000): H.R. 2924—The Hedge Fund Disclosure Act.

U.S. House of Representatives, Subcommittee on Capital Markets, Securities and Government Sponsored Enterprises, Committee on Banking and Financial Services (1999): Hearing on "Counterparty Risk Management Policy Group Report", Thursday, June 24th 1999, Washington, D.C.

U.S. President's Working Group on Financial Markets (1999a): Report, Hedge Funds, Leverage, and the Lessons of Long – Term Capital Management, April 1999.

U.S. President's Working Group on Financial Markets (1999b): Over–the-Counter Derivatives.

United States Congress House Committee on Banking and Financial Services Subcommittee on Capital Markets, Securities, and Government Sponsored Enterprises (2000): H.R. 2924, the Hedge Fund Disclosure Act: hearing before the Subcommittee on Capital Markets, Securities, and Government Sponsored Enterprises of the Committee on Banking and Financial Services, U.S. House of Representatives, One Hundred Sixth Congress, second session, Washington: U.S. G.P.O.

United States Congress House Committee on Banking and Financial Services Hedge fund operations (1998): hearing before the Committee on Banking and Financial Services, U.S. House of Representatives, One Hundred Fifth Congress, second session.

United States General Accounting Office (1999): Report to Congressional Requesters, Long-Term Capital Management – Regulators Need to Focus Greater Attention on Systemic Risk, GAO Publication, October 1999.

Van Grover, Robert B. (2001): U.S. Legal and Regulatory Issues Faced by Offshore Funds and their Sponsors, in: Cullen, Ian; Perry, Helen, Hedge Funds – Law and Regulation, Sweet & Maxwell, pp. 37-61.

Volhard, Patricia; Doerre, Christian (2003): Out with the Old: Germany Rings in the New Year With Investment Fund Legislation, Debevoise & Plimpton Publication, December 8, 2003.

Wall Street Journal (2002): SEC Considers Increasing Regulation of Hedge Fund Industry, Thursday 9 May 2002.

Wall Street Journal (2004): Bids and Offers, July 23, 2004, C 4.

Wall Street Journal (2004): C1, December 21, 2004.

Wall Street Journal, Hedge-Matics: How Many Funds Exist?, May 22, 2003, at C5

Williamson, O.E. (1985): The Economic Institutions of Capitalism. New York: Free Press.

Xiong, Wei (2001): Convergence trading with wealth effects – an amplification mechanism in financial markets, Bendheim Center for Finance – Princeton University, March 2001.